1 MONTH OF
FREE
READING

at
www.ForgottenBooks.com

By purchasing this book you are eligible for one month membership to ForgottenBooks.com, giving you unlimited access to our entire collection of over 1,000,000 titles via our web site and mobile apps.

To claim your free month visit:
www.forgottenbooks.com/free927338

ISBN 978-0-260-09176-5
PIBN 10927338

GEM PRONOUNCING DICTIONARY.

AN AUTHORITATIVE HAND-BOOK OF ELEVEN THOUSAND
WORDS IN COMMON USE.

By LILLA M. TENNEY.

NOT FOR DEFINITIONS.

CORRECT SPELLING, CORRECT PRONUNCIATION, WITH
AN EXERCISE IN PRONUNCIATION AND EXTENDED
LIST OF WORDS OFTEN INCORRECTLY
PRONOUNCED.

ALSO MANY VALUABLE TABLES OF WEIGHTS, MEASURES,
AND OTHER USEFUL INFORMATION.

THE BURROWS BROTHERS COMPANY,
NOS. 23, 25, AND 27 EUCLID AVENUE,
CLEVELAND, OHIO.

594370

𝕌niversity 𝕻ress:
JOHN WILSON AND SON, CAMBRIDGE.

PREFACE.

It is the purpose of this work to furnish a convenient and authoritative handbook of words in common use, which are frequently misspelled or mispronounced.

In its compilation the greatest care has been used to make it absolutely reliable. The latest unabridged editions of Webster's, Worcester's, and The Imperial Dictionary have been used; also Stormonth's English Dictionary, Soule and Wheeler's Manual of English Pronunciation and Spelling, Soule and Campbell's Pronouncing Handbook, The Orthoëpist, and incidentally many other works of reference.

The simplest spelling given in either of the Unabridged Dictionaries is the one usually adopted.

The pronunciation which has the greatest weight of authority is given the preference, sometimes to the exclusion of an allowable pronunciation. Two pronunciations are given only when the authorities are about equally divided. By the phonetic method of spelling and the marking of the vowel sounds as explained in the Key, devised expressly for this work, the pronunciation is more simply and accurately given than in other dictionaries.

Many words formed of a root and prefix have been omitted, as the root word, found under its proper letter, is usually sufficient to indicate the correct spelling and pronunciation.

A few simple rules of spelling are given which cover a class of words not inserted.

The practice of reading aloud the exercise in pronunciation at the end of the Dictionary, will be found an excellent ? for those who wish to cultivate correct speaking.

CONTENTS.

	PAGE
Preface	iii
Rules of Orthography	vi
Key to the Pronunciation	vii
Abbreviations used in the Dictionary	viii
Spelling and Pronouncing Dictionary of English Words, including many Foreign Words and Phrases, and Names of Persons and Places	1
Tables of Weights and Measures	103
List of Abbreviations, with Explanations	114
Foreign Words and Phrases, with English Translation	118
Key to Pronunciation of Modern Languages	134
Rules for Spelling	139
Punctuation Marks, and their Origin	140
A Memoir of Adonis and Penelope, an Exercise in Pronunciation	141
List of Words commonly mispronounced	144

RULES OF ORTHOGRAPHY.

1. Verbs ending in ie change the ie into y, on adding ing; as, die, dying.
2. Verbs ending with a single e omit the e when ing is added; as, love, loving. *Exceptions* : dye, hoe, shoe, singe, swinge, tinge.
3. All verbs ending in y, preceded by a consonant, retain the y in adding ing; as, spy, spying; but when ed is added, the y is changed into i; as, spy, spied; and when s is added, y is changed into ie; as, spy, spies.
4. Verbs ending in y preceded by another vowel, on adding ing, ed, or s, do not change y into i; as, delay, delaying, delayed, delays. *Exceptions*: lay, laid; pay, paid; say, said; stay, stayed or staid.
5. Nouns of the singular number ending in ey form their plural by adding s to the singular; as, valley, valleys.
6. Nouns ending in y, preceded by a consonant, form their plural by adding es and changing y into i; as, lady, ladies. This rule includes words ending in quy; as, colloquy, colloquies.
7. Nouns ending in o, preceded by another vowel, form their plural by the addition of s; as, cameo, cameos; but if the final o is preceded by a consonant, the plural is sometimes formed by adding es; as, echo, echoes. [Plurals of this class and others irregularly formed are given in the Dictionary.]
8. Verbs of one syllable, ending with a single consonant, preceded by a single vowel [as plan], and verbs of two or more syllables, ending in the same manner, and having the accent on the last syllable [as regret], double the final consonant of the verb on assuming an additional syllable : as, plan, planned; *regret, regretted*; but if a diphthong precedes the last consonant [as in join], or the accent is not on the last syllable [as in suffer], the consonant is not doubled; as, join, joined; suffer, suffered.

KEY TO THE PRONUNCIATION.

VOWELS.

ā	*long*	āle, fāte, lāce, āid.
a	*short*	at, add, an, have.
â	*long before* r	fâre, beâr, shâre.
ä	*Italian*	ärm, fär, cälm.
à	*intermediate, between* a *and* ä	àsk, fàst, gràss.
ą	*broad*	fąll, tąlk, wąrm.
ē	*long*	mē, fēar, ēve.
e	*short*	met, men, check, sell.
ê	*like* â	thêre, whêre, hêir.
è	*short and obscure*	hèr, fèrn, vèrge.
ī	*long*	īce, pīne, mīle, fīre.
i	*short*	pin, fill, miss.
ō	*long*	ōld, nōte, lōaf, sōre.
o	*short*	odd, not, on.
ōō	*long*	nōōn, fōōd, bōōt.
ŏŏ	*short*	wŏŏl, fŏŏt, wŏŏd.
ū	*long*	tūbe, ūse, sūre.
u	*short*	us, tub, hut.
ū	*French*	ew *as in* few.
oi	*as in*	noise.
ou	"	round.
ow	"	cow.

CONSONANTS.

g	*as in*	get.		z	*as in*	zest.
j	"	jar.		ch	"	chain.
k	"	king.		sh	"	shun.
ṅ	"	*French* ton.		*th*	"	then.
s	"	sun.		th	"	thin.

In the first column, or column of spelling, many times a word is divided by a double space, so that the spelling of two, and sometimes three, words is given in a single line; as, **ar′gument ative**, *argument, argumentative*: **accept′ able ness**, *accept, acceptable, acceptableness*.

In the second column the bracketed word gives the pronunciation of th entire word; as, [ak-sep′ta-bl-nes]; and of the second word; as, [ak-sep′ta a-tiv]; bu It also gives the *vowel* sounds of the *first* word; as, [är-gü-ment′a-tiv]; but ccent of the *first* word is given in the column of spelling, as frequently rs from the accent of the entire word; as, **ar′gument** [är-gü-ment′a-

ABBREVIATIONS

USED IN THE DICTIONARY.

———◆———

a.	*stands for*	. . . .	adjective.
ad.	" "	. . . .	adverb.
conj.	" "	. . . .	conjunction.
Fr.	" "	. . . .	French.
Im.	" "	. . . .	Imperial.
inter.	" "	. . . .	interjection.
It.	" "	. . . .	Italian.
n.	" "	. . . .	noun.
pl.	" "	. . . .	plural.
p.	" "	. . . .	participle.
prep.	" "	. . . .	preposition.
pron.	" "	. . . .	pronoun.
Sp.	" "	. . . .	Spanish.
v.	" "	. . . .	verb.
Web.	" "	. . . .	Webster.
Wor.	" "	. . . .	Worcester.

PRONOUNCING DICTIONARY

OF THE

ENGLISH LANGUAGE.

A.

Abandon [a-ban'dun], n. v.
Abase [a-bās'], v.
Abatis [ab'a-tis, ab-a-tē'], n.
Abatoir [a-bat-wàr'], n.
Ab'ba cy [ab'ba-si], n.
Abbé [ab'bā'], n.
Abbess [ab'bes], n.
Abbreviator [ab-brē'vi-ā-tér], n.
Abdicator [ab'di-kāt-ér], n.
Abdomen [ab-dō'men], n.
Abdominal [ab-dom'in-al], a. n.
Abdominous [ab-dom'in-us], a.
Abduct' or [ab-duk'tér], n.
Aberrance [ab-èr'rans], n.
Aberration [ab-èr-rā'shun], n.
Abeyance [a-bā'ans], n.
Abhor' rence [ab-hor'rens], n.
Ability [a-bil'i-ti], n.
Ab'ject ly [ab'jekt-li], ad.
Abjuration [ab-jū-rā'shun], n.
Ablative [ab'la-tiv], a.
Able [ā'bl] a.
Ablution [ab-lū'shun], n.
Abnegator [ab'nē-gā-tér], n.
Abnormity [ab-nor'mi-ti], n.
Abol'ish er [a-bol'ish-ér], n.
Aboli'tion ist [ab-ō-li'shun-ist], n.
Abominable [a-bom'in-a-bl], a.
Abomination [a-bom-i-nā'shun], n.
Aboriginal [ab-o-rij'in-al], a.
Aborigines [ab-o-rij'in-ēz], n. pl.
Abortion [a-bor'shun], n.
Abrasion [ab-rā'zhun], n.
Abridgment [a-brij'ment], n.
Abrogate [ab'rō-gāt], v.

Abrupt [ab-rupt'], a.
Abscess [ab'ses], n.
Abscond' er [ab-skond'ér], n.
Absence [ab'sens], n.
Ab'sent ee [ab-sen-tē'], n.
Absinthe [ab'santh'], n.
Absolutism [ab'sō-lūt-izm], n.
Absolutory [ab-sol'ū-to-ri], a.
Absorb [ab-sorb'], v.
Absorption [ab-sorp'shun], n.
Abstain' er [ab-stān'ér], n.
Abstemious [ab-stē'mi-us], a.
Abstergent [ab-stérj'ent], a. n.
Abstinence [ab'sti-nens], n.
Abstract [ab-strakt'], v. [ab'st
Abstruse [ab-strōōs'], a.
Absurd' ity [ab-sérd'i-ti], n.
Abundance [a-bun'dans], n.
Abuse [a-būs'], n. [a-būz'], v.
Abut' tal [a-but'al], n. v.
Abysmal [a-biz'mal], a.
Abyss [a-bis'], n.
Abyssinian [ab-is-sin'i-an], n.
Acacia [a-kā'shi-a], n.
Academician [ak-a-dē-mish'an]
Academy [a-kad'ē-mi], n.
Acanthus [a-kan'thus], n.
Acaulescent [a-kal-es'ent], a.
Acaulous [a-kal'us], a.
Accede [ak-sēd'], v.
Accelerator [ak-sel'ér-āt-ér], n.
Accendible [ak-send'i-bl], a.
Accent [ak'sent], n. [ak-sent'
Accentor [ak-sent'ér], n.
Accentuation [ak-sent-ū-ā'shun]

ále, add, beâr, ärm, àsk, fall; mē, met, thère, hèr; pīne, pin; ū
wōōl; ūse, us; ū, Fr.; g, get; j, jar; ñ, Fr. ton; ch, chain; th,

Accept' able ness, Acceptability [ak-sep'ta-bl-nes, ak-sep-ta-bil'i-ti], n.
Acceptably [ak-sep'ta-bli], ad.
Acceptance [ak-sep'tans], n.
Acceptation [ak-sep-tā'shun] n.
Accepter, Acceptor [ak-sept'ér, ak-sept'or], n.
Access' ibility [ak-ses-si-bil'i-ti], n.
Accessible [ak-ses'si-bl], a.
Accessibly [ak-ses'si-bli], ad.
Accessorial [ak-ses-sō'ri-al], a. [a. n.
Accessory [ak'ses-sō-ri, ak-ses'sō-ri],
Accidence [ak'si-dens], n.
Ac'cident al [ak-si-dent'al], a. n.
Accipiter [ak-sip'i-tèr], n.
Accipitres [ak-sip'i-trēz], n. pl.
Acclaim [ak-klām'] n. v.
Acclamatory [ak-klam'a-to-ri], a.
Acclimate [ak-klī'māt], v.
Acclimatize [ak-klī'mat-īz], v.
Acclivity [ak-kliv'i-ti], n.
Acclivous [ak-klīv'us], a.
Accommodate [ak-kom'mō-dāt], a. v.
Accommodator [ak-kom'mō-dāt-ér], n.
Accompanier [ak-kum'pa-ni-ér], n.
Accompaniment [ak-kum'pa-ni-ment], n.
Accompanist [ak-kum'pan-ist], n.
Accomplice [ak-kom'plis], n.
Accom'plish er [ak-kom'plish-ér], n.
Accomplishment [ak-kom'plish-ment], n.
Accomptant [ak-kount'ant], n. The same as *Accountant.*
Accord' ance [ak-kord'ans], n.
Accordion [ak-kord'i-on], n.
Accost [ak-kost'], v.
Accouchement [ak'kōōsh'mäñ'], n.
Accoucheur [ak'kōō'shèr'], n. mas.
Accoucheuse [ak'kōō'shèz'], n. fem.
Account' able [ak-kount'a-bl], a.
Accountably [ak-kount'a-bli], ad.
Accountant [ak-kount'ant], n.
Accou'tre ments [ak-kōō'tér-ments], n. pl.
Accrescence [ak-kres'sens], n.
Accretion [ak-krē'shun], n.
Accretive [ak-krēt'iv], a.
Accrue [ak-krōō'], v.
Accu'mulative ly [ak-kū'mū-lāt-iv-li], ad.
Accumulator [ak-kū'mū-lāt-ér], n.
Accuracy [ak'kū-ra-si], n.
Ac'curate ness [ak'kū-rāt-nes], n.

Accusation [ak-kū-zā'shun], n.
Accusative [ak-kūz'at-iv], a. n.
Accuser [ak-kūz'ér], n.
Accustom [ak-kus'tum], v.
Acephalous [a-sef'al-us], a.
Acerbity [a-sérb'it-i], n.
Acervation [as-ér-vā'shun], n.
Acetal [a-sē'tal], n.
Acetic [a-set'ik], a.
Acetifier [a-set'i-fi-ér], n.
Acetimeter, Acetometer [as-et-im'et-ér, as-et-om'et-ér], n. [a.
Acetose, Acetous [as-et-ōs', a-sē'tus].
Ache [āk], n. v.
Achene, Achenium [a-kēn', a-kē'ni-um], n.
Achievable [a-chēv'a-bl], a.
Achieve' ment [a-chēv'ment], n.
Achillea [a-kil-lē'a], n.
Achirite [ak'i-rit], n.
Achlamydeous [a-kla-mid'ē-us] a.
Achromatism [ak-rō'ma-tizm], n.
Ac'id ify [a-sid'i-fī], v.
Acidimeter [as-id-im'et-ér], n.
Acidity [a-sid'i-ti], n.
Acidulous [a-sid'ū-lus], a.
Acinaceous [as-in-ā'shus], a.
Acinaciform [as-in-as'i-form], a.
Aciniform [a-sin'i-form], a.
Acknowledge [ak-nol'ej], v. [n.
Acknowledgment [ak-nol'-ej-ment],
Acme [ak'me], n.
Acolyte [ak'o-līt], n.
Aconite [ak'on-it], n.
Acorn [ā'korn], n.
Acouchy [a-kōōsh'i], n.
Acoumeter [a-kowm'et-ér], n.
Acoustic [a-kows'tik], a.
Acquaint' ance [ak-kwānt'ans], n.
Acquiescence [ak-kwi-es'ens], n.
Acquirable [ak-kwīr'a-bl], a.
Acquire' ment [ak-kwīr'ment], n.
Acquisition [ak-kwi-zi'shun], n. [n.
Acquis'itive ness [ak-kwiz'it-iv-nes],
Acquit' tal [ak-kwit'al], n.
A'cre age [ā'kér-āj], n.
Acrid [ak'rid], a. n.
Acrimo'nious ness [ak-ri-mō'ni-us-nes], n.
Acrobat [ak'rō-bat], n.
Acrobates [a-krob'at-ēz], n.
Acropolis [a-krop'ō-lis], n.
Across [a-kros'], ad. prep.
Acrostic [a-kros'tik], n.
Actæa [ak-tē'a], n.
Actian [ak'shi-an], a.

ale, add, beår, ärm, åsk, fall ; mě, met, thêre, hèr ; pīne, pin ; õld, odd, nōō

Actinia [ak-tin'i-a], n. Actiniæ [ak-tin'i-ē], pl.
Actinism [ak'tin-izm], n.
Actinograph [ak-tin'ō-graf], n.
Actinometer [ak-tin-om'et-ėr], n.
Actinozoon [ak-tin-ō-zō'on], n. Actinozoa [ak-tin-ō-zō'a], pl.
Action [ak'shun], n.
Activity [ak-tiv'i-ti], n.
Actor [ak'tėr], n.
Actress [ak'tres], n.
Act'ual ity [ak-tū-al'i-ti], n.
Actualize [ak'tū-al-iz], v.
Actually [ak'tū-al-li], ad.
Actuator [ak'tū-āt-ėr], n.
Aculeous [a-kū'lē-us], a.
Aculeus [a-kū'lē-us], n.
Acumen [a-kū'men], n.
Acuminate [a-kū'min-āt], a.
Acute' ness [a-kūt'nes], n.
Adage [ad'āj], n.
Adagio [a-dä'jō], a. ad. n.
Ad'amant ean [ad-a-mant-ē'an], a.
Adamantine [ad-a-mant'in], a.
Adamic [a-dam'ik], a.
Adapt' ability [a-dapt-a-bil'i-ti], n.
Adaptation [ad-ap-tā'shun], n.
Adapter [a-dapt'ėr], n.
Addendum [ad-den'dum], n. Addenda [ad-den'dä], pl.
Addible [ad'i-bl], a.
Addict [ad-dikt'], v.
Addi'tion al [ad-di'shun-al], a. n.
Addle [ad'l], a. n. v.
Address [ad-dres'], n. v.
Adduce [ad-dūs'], v.
Adducible [ad-dūs'i-bl], a.
Adductor [ad-dukt'ėr], n.
Adenose, Adenous [ad'en-ōs, ad'en-us], a.
Adept [a-dept'], a. n.
Adequacy [ad'ē-kwa-si], n.
Ad'equate ly [ad'ē-kwāt-li], ad.
Adhere' nce [ad-hēr'ens], n.
Adhesion [ad-hē'zhun], n.
Adieu [a-dū'], ad. n.
Adipocere, Adipocire [ad'i-pō-sėr], n.
Adipose [ad'i-pōs], a. n.
Adjacency [ad-jā'sen-si], n.
Adja'cent ly [ad-jā'sent-li], ad.
Adjective [ad'jek-tiv], n.
Adjoin [ad-join'], v.
Adjourn' ment [ad-jėrn'ment], n.
Adjudicator [ad-jū'di-kāt-ėr], n.
Ad'junct ive [ad-jungk'tiv], a. n.

Adjuration [ad-jū-rā'shun], n.
Adjure [ad-jūr'], v.
Adjust' er [ad-just'ėr], n.
Ad'jutant cy [ad'jū-tan-si], n.
Administer [ad-min'is-tėr], v. [n.
Administration [ad-min-is-trā'shun],
Administrator [ad-min'is-trāt-ėr], n.
Administratrix [ad-min'is-trāt-riks], n. fem.
Admirable [ad'mi-ra-bl], a.
Admirably [ad'mi-ra-bli], ad.
Ad'miral ty [ad'mi-ral-ti], n.
Admiration [ad-mi-rā'shun], n.
Admire [ad-mir'], v.
Admissible [ad-mis'i-bl], a.
Admissibly [ad-mis'i-bli], ad.
Admission [ad-mi'shun], n.
Admit' tance [ad-mit'ans], n.
Admon'ish er [ad-mon'ish-ėr], n.
Admonition [ad-mō-ni'shun], n.
Admonitor [ad-mon'it-ėr], n.
Adnascent [ad-nas'ent], a.
Adobe [a-dō'be], n.
Adolescence [ad-ō-les'ens], n.
Adonic [a-don'ik], a. n.
Adonis [a-dō'nis], n.
Adopt' er [a-dopt'ėr], n.
Adoption ist [a-dop'shun-ist], n.
Adorable [a-dōr'a-bl], a.
Adorably [a-dōr'a-bli], ad.
Adoration [ad-ōr-ā'shun], n.
Adore [a-dōr'], v.
Adorn' er [a-dorn'ėr], n.
Adroit' ness [a-droit'nes], n.
Adulator [ad'ū-lāt-ėr], n.
Adult' erant [a-dul'tėr-ant], n.
Adulterator [a-dul'tėr-āt-ėr], n.
Adulterer [a-dul'tėr-ėr], n. mas.
Adulteress [a-dul'tėr-es], n. fem.
Adulterine [a-dul'tėr-in], a. n.
Adulterous [a-dul'tėr-us], a.
Adumbrate [ad-um'brāt], v.
Aduncity [ad-un'si-ti], n.
Aduncous [ad-ungk'us], a.
Advance' ment [ad-vans'ment], n.
Advan tage ous [ad-van-tā'jus], a.
Ad'vent itious [ad-ven-tish'us], a.
Adven'tur er [ad-ven'tūr-ėr], n.
Adventuress [ad-ven'tūr-es], n. fem.
Adventurous [ad-ven'tūr-us], a.
Ad'verb ial [ad-vėrb'i-al], a.
Adverbially [ad-vėrb'i-al-li], ad.
Adversary [ad'vėr-sä-ri], a. n.
Ad'verse ly [ad'vėrs-li], ad.
Advert' ence, Advertency [ad-vėrt'en-si], n.

Advertise′ ment [ad-vėr′tiz-ment, ad-ver-tiz′ment], n.
Advice [ad-vis′], n.
Advis′able ness [ad-viz′a-bl-nes], n.
Advisably [ad-viz′a-bli], ad.
Advisedly [ad-viz′ed-li], ad.
Advisory [ad-viz′o-ri], a.
Advocacy [ad′vō-ka-si], n.
Advocate [ad′vō-kāt], n. v.
Advowee [ad-vow-ē′], n.
Advowson [ad-vow′sn], n.
Adynamic, Adynamical [a-di-nam′ik, a-di-nam′ik-al], a.
Adytum [ad′i-tum], n. Adyta [ad′i-ta], pl.
Adze, Adz [adz], n.
Ægis [ē′jis], n.
Æneid [ē′nē-id], n.
Aerate [ā′ėr-āt], v.
Aerator [ā′ėr-āt-ėr], n.
Aerie [ē′rē], n.
Aerial [ā-ē′ri-al], a.
Aerians [ā-ē′ri-ans], n. pl.
Aerification [ā-ėr-i-fi-kā′shun], n.
Aerify [ā′ėr-i-fi], v.
Aerolite, Aerolith [ā′ėr-ō-lit, ā′ėr-ō-lith], n.
Aeromancy [ā-ėr-ō-man′si], n.
Aerometer [ā-ėr-om′et-ėr], n.
Aeronaut [ā′ėr-ō-nąt], n.
Aerophyte [ā′ėr-ō-fit], n.
Aerostat [ā′ėr-ō-stat], n.
Æsculine [es′kū-lin], n.
Æsthetic [es-thet′ik], a. n.
Æstheticism [es-thet′i-sizm], n.
Aetites [ā-e-ti′tēz], n.
Affability [af-fa-bil′i-ti], n.
Affable [af′fa-bl], a.
Affair [af-fār′], n.
Affect′ ation [af-fek-tā′shun], n.
Affec′tion ate [af-fek′shun-āt], a.
Affector, Affecter [af-fekt′ėr], n.
Affiance [af-fi′ans], n. v.
Affidavit [af-fi-dā′vit], n.
Affiliate [af-fil′i-āt], v.
Affinage [af′fin-āj], n.
Affinity [af-fin′i-ti], n.
Affirm′ able [af-fėrm′a-bl], a.
Affirmation [af-fėr-mā′shun], n.
Affirmative [af-fėrm′at-iv], a. n.
Affirmer [af-fėrm′ėr], n.
Affix [af′fiks, n. af-fiks′, v.]
Afflation [af-flā′shun], n.
Afflatus [af-flā′tus], n.
Afflict′ er [af-flikt′ėr], n.
Affliction [af-flik′shun], n.

Affluence [af′flū-ens], n.
Afford [af-fōrd′], v.
Affran′chise ment [af-fran′chiz-ment], n.
Affray [af-frā′], n.
Affright [af-frit′], n. v.
Affront′ ee [af-frunt-ē′], n.
Affusion [af-fū′zhun], n.
Afghan [af′gan], a. n.
Afloat [a-flōt′], ad. a.
Afore′ said [a-fōr′sed], a.
Afoul [a-foul′], a. ad.
Afraid [a-frād′], a.
African [af′rik-an], a. n.
Aft′er math [aft′ėr-math], n.
Afterward, Afterwards [aft′ėr-wėrd, aft′ėr-wėrdz], ad.
Again [a-gen′], ad.
Against [a-genst′], prep.
Agalloch, Agallochum [ag′al-ok, a-gal′lok-um], n.
Agalmatolite [a-gal-mat′ō-lit], n.
Agape [a-gāp′, a-gāp′], ad. a.
Agaphite [ag′a-fit], n.
Agate [ag′āt], n.
Agatize [ag′at-iz], v.
Agave [a-gā′vē], n.
Aged [āj′ed], a.
Agency [ā′jen-si], n.
Agent [ā′jent], n.
Agglomerate [ag-glom′ėr-āt], a. n. v.
Agglutinant [ag-glu′tin-ant], a. n.
Ag′grandize ment [ag′gran-diz-ment, ag-gran′diz-ment], n.
Aggravate [ag′gra-vāt], v.
Aggregate [ag′gre-gāt], a. n. v.
Aggregator [ag′gre-gāt-ėr], n.
Aggress′ or [ag-gres′ėr], n.
Aggrievance [ag-grēv′ans], n.
Aggrieve [ag-grēv′], v.
Aghast [a-gāst′], a.
Agile [aj′il], a.
Agility [a-jil′i-ti], n.
Agio [ā′ji-ō], n.
Agiotage [ā′ji-ot-āj], n.
Agitator [aj′it-āt-ėr], n.
Aglaia [ag-lā′i-a], n.
Agnomen [ag-nō′men], n.
Agnostic [ag-nos′tik], a. n.
Agonize [ag′ō-niz], v.
Agouti [a-gōō′ti], n.
Agra′rian ize [a-grā′ri-an
Agree′able ness [a-grē′a
Agreeably [a-grē′a-bli],
Agreement [a-grē′ment]
Agricolous [a-grik′ō-lus

Air fly [ár

Aisle [il], n.

Aizoon [ā-i-zō'on], v.

Ajar [a-jär'], ad.

Alabaster [al'a-bas-tèr], a. n.

Alacrity [a-lak'ri- n.

A-la-mode [ā'-la'- ad. a. n.

Alarm' ist n.

n.

n.

[al-bū'-

a.

n.

v.

b'a-ran], n.

ed malt liquor

, a. n.

pl.

n.

[pl.

[ant -

Allop

Allop.

Allot'

Allow'

Alloy

All-spi

Allude

Allure'

Allusio1

Alluvial

Ally [al-

Alma M

Almanac

Almandi1

Almighty

Almond [.

Almoner

Almost [a

Alms [amz

Aloe [al'ō],

Alone [a-lō

Aloof [a-lōō

Alpaca [al-

Alpen-horn

Alphabet [

Alphenic [a

Alpine [al'

Already [al

nine [am-a-ranth... ...]
hus [am-a-ranth′us], n.
s [am-a-ril′lis], n.
[am-a-tūr′, am-a-tōōr′], n.
ness [am′at-ıv-nes], n.
ment [a-māz′ment], n.
dor [am-bas′sa-dor], n.
dress [am-bas′sa-dres], n.

is [am′bér-grēs], n.
[am′bi-ent], a.
ty [am-bi-gū′i-ti], n.
ous [am-big′ū-us], a.
n [am-bi′shun], n.
us [am-bi′shus], a.
am′bl], n. v.
ia [am-brō′zhi-a], n.
type [am′brō-tip], n.
nce [am′bū-lans], n.
tor [am′bū-lāt-ér], n.
ade [am-bus-kād′], n. v.
[am′bōōsh], n. v.
ate [a-mēl′yor-āt], v.
ator [a-mēl′yor-āt-ér], n.
ble [a-mē′na-bl], a.
atory [a-mend′a-to-ri], a.
[ā′mınd′], n.
r [a-mend′ér], n.
y [a-men′i-ti], n.
rrhœa [a-mēn-o-rē′a], n.

Amphigene [am′h-jen], n.
Amphiscii [am-fish′i-ī], n. pl.
Amphitheatre [am-fi-thē′a-tė
Amphitrite [am-fi-trī′tė], n.
Ample [am′pl], a.
Amplify [am′pli-fī], v.
Amplitude [am′pli-tūd], n.
Amply [am′pli], ad.
Amputation [am-pū-tā′shun]
Amuse′ ment [a-māz′ment]
Amygdaline [a-mig′da-lin], a
Amylaceous [am-il-ā′shus], a
Amyraldism [am′i-rald-izm]
Amyris [am′i-ris], n.
Anabasis [an-ab′a-sis], n.
Anabole [an-ab′ō-lē], n.
Anachronism [an-ak′ron-izm
Anachronous [an-ak′ron-us]
Anaconda [an-a-kon′da], n.
Anacreontic [a-nak-rē-on′tik
Anæmia [a-nē′mi-a], n.
Anæmic [a-nem′ik], a.
Anæsthetic [an-es-thet′ik], r
Anæsthetize [an-es′the-tīz]
Anaglyph [an′a-glif], n.
Analogist [an-al′o-jist], n.
Analogous [an-al′og-us], a.
Analysis [an-al′i-sis], n.
[an-al′i-sēz], pl.
Analytic, Analytical [an-a

Anchovy [an-chō'vi], n.
Ancient [ān'shent], a. n.
Ancile [an-sī'le], n.
Andalusite [an-da-lū'sīt], n.
Andante [an-dän'tā], a. n.
Andantino [an-dan-tē'no], a.
Andiron [and'ī-érn], n.
Andromache [an-drom'a-ke], n.
Andromeda [an-drom'e-da], n.
Anecdote [an'ek-dōt], n.
Anemometer [an-e-mom'et-ér], n.
Anemone [a-nem'o-ne], n.
Anew [a-nū'], ad.
Angel [ān'jel], n.
Angelus [an'jel-us], n.
Angiosperm [an'ji-ō-sperm], n.
Angle [ang'gl], n. v.
Anglican [ang'glik-an], n.
Anglicize [ang'gli-sīz], v.
Angrily [ang'gri-li], ad.
Angry [ang'gri], a.
Anguineal [an-gwin'e-al], a.
Anguish [ang'gwish], n. v.
Angular ity [ang-gū-lar'i-ti], n.
Aniline [an'i-lin], n.   [n.
Animadvert' er [an-i-mad-vèrt'èr],
An'imal cule [an-i-mal'kūl], n.
Animate [an'i-māt], a. v.
Animosity [an-i-mos'i-ti], n.
Anise-seed [an'is-sēd], n.
Ankle [ang'kl], n.
Annalist [an'nal-ist], n.
Anneal [an-nēl'], v.
Annex' ation [an-neks-ā'shun], n.
Annihila'tion ist [an-ni-hil-ā'shun-
   ist], n
Annihilator [an-nī'hil-āt-èr], n.
Anniversary [an-ni-vèrs'a-ri], a. n.
Annotator [an'nō-tāt-èr], n.
Annotinous [an-not'in-us], a.   [n.
Announce' ment [an-nouns'ment],
Annoy' ance [an-noi'ans], n.
An'nual ist [an'nū-al-ist], n.
Annually [an'nū-al-li], ad.
Annuity [an-nū'i-ti], n.
Annul [an-nul'], v.

Anonaceæ [an-o-nā'sē-ē], n. pl.
Anonymous [a-non'im-us], a.
Another [an-u'/r'èr], a.
Anserine [an'sèr-in], a.
An'swer able [an'sèr-a-bl], a.
Ant [ant], n.   An insect.
Antagonist [an-tag'ō-nist], a. n.
Antagonize [an-tag'ō-nīz], v.
Antalgic [an-tal'jik], n.
Antarctic [ant-ärk'tik], a.
Antecedent [an-tē-sē'dent], a. n.
Antecessor [an-tē-ses'ér], n.
Antediluvian [an-tē-di-lū'vi-an], a. n.
Antelope [an'tē-lōp], n.
Antenna [an-ten'na], n.   Antennæ
   [an-ten'nē], pl.
Antepenult [an-te-pe-nult'], n.
Ante'rior ity [an-tē-ri-or'i-ti], n.
Anthelion [ant-hē'li-on], n.   Anthe-
   lia [ant-hē'li-a], pl.
Anthem [an'them], n.
Anthesis [an-thē'sis], n.
Anthine [an'thin], a.
Anthracite [an'thra-sīt], n.
Anthracitic [an-thra-sit'ik], a.   [n.
Anthropologist [an-thrō-pol'o-jist],
Anthropophagite [an-thrō-pof'a-jīt],
   n.   Anthropophagi [an-thrō-pof'-
   a-jī], n. pl.
Anticipate [an-tis'i-pāt], v.
Anticipator [an-tis'i-pāt-èr], n.
Antidotal [an'ti-dōt-al], a.
Antidote [an'ti-dōt], n.
Antimonious [an-ti-mō'ni-us], a.
Antimony [an'ti-mo-ni], n.
Antinomian [an-ti-nō'mi-an], a. n. [n.
Antinomy [an'ti-nō-mi, an-tin'o-mi],
Antiphon [an'ti-fon], n.
Antipode [an'ti-pōd], n.   Antipodes
   [an-tip'o-dēz], pl.
Antiquarian [an-ti-kwā'ri-an], n.
Antique [an-tēk'], a. n.
Antiquity [an-tik'wi-ti], n.
Antiseptic [an-ti-sep'tik], a. n.
Antithesis [an-tith'e-sis], n.   Antith-
   eses [an-tith'e-sēz], pl.

Apathetic [ap-a-thet'ik], a.
Apellous [a-pel'lus], a.
Apennine [ap'en-nin], a.
Aperient [a-pe'ri-ent], n.
Aperture [ap'ér-tûr], n.
Apex [a'pex], n.
Aphelion [a-fe'li-on], n. Aphelia [a-fe'li-a], pl.
Aphis [a'fis], n. Aphides [af'i-dez].
Aphorism [af'or-izm], n.
Aphrodite [af-ro-di'te], n.
Apiarist [a'pi-a-rist], n.
Apiary [a'pi-a-ri], n.
Apocalypse [a-pok'a-lips], n.
Apocrypha [a-pok'ri-fa], n.
Apodosis [a-pod'o-sis], n.
Apogee [ap'o-je], n.
Apollinaris [a-pol-li-na'ris], a.
Apollo Belvedere [a-pol'o-bel've-dér], n.
Apollyon [a-pol'li-on], n.
Apologetic al [a-pol-o-jet'ik-al], a.
Apologize [a-pol'o-jiz], v.
Apologue [ap'o-log], n.
Apology [a-pol'o-jic], n.
Apophyge [a-pof'i-lit, ap-o-fil'lit], Apophyllite [a-pof'i-sis], n. Apophyses [a-pof'i-sez], pl.
Apophysis [a-pof'i-sis], n.
Apoplectic al [ap-o-plek'tik-al], a.
Apoplexy [ap'o-plek-si], n.
Apostasy [a-pos'ta-si], n.
Apostatize [a-pos'ta-tiz], v.
Apostle [a-pos'l], n.
Apostolic al [a-pos-tol'ik-al], a.
Apostrophe [a-pos'tro-fe], n.
Apostrophic [ap-os-trof'ik], a.
Apothecary [a-poth'e-ka-ri], n.
Apothecium [ap-o-the'si-um], n. Apothecia [ap-o-the'si-a], pl.
Apothegm [ap'o-them], n.
Apotheosis [ap-o-the'o-sis], n.
Apothesis [a-poth'e-sis], n.
Appalachian [ap-pa-la'ki-an], a.
Appall [ap-pal'], n. v.
Apparatus [ap-pa-ra'tus], n. sing. and pl.
Apparel [ap-par'el], n. v.
Apparent [ap-pâr'ent], a.
Apparition [ap-pa-rish'un], n.
Appeal [ap-pel'], n. v.
Appear [ap-pér'], v.
Appearance [ap-pér'ans], n.
Appease [ap-pez'], v.
Appellant [ap-pel'ant], a. n.
Appellation [ap-pel-a'shun], n.
Appellee [ap-pel-le'], n.
Appellor [ap-pel'or], n.

Append' age [ap-pend'aj], n.
Appendant [ap-pend'ant], a. n.
Appendix [ap-pen'diks], n. Appendixes [ap-pen'diks-ez], pl.
Appertain [ap-pér-tan'], v.
Appetite [ap'pe-tit], n.
Appetize [ap'pe-tiz], v.
Applause [ap-plaz'], n.
Apple [ap'pl], n. v.
Appliance [ap-pli'ans], n.
Applicable [ap'pli-ka-bl], a.
Applicably [ap'pli-ka-bli], ad.
Application [ap'pli-ka'shun], n.
Appoggiatura [ap-poj-a-too'ra], n.
Appoint' ee [ap-point-e'], n. er [ap-pór'shun-ér], n.
Apportion [ap-pór'shun], v.
Apposite [ap'po-zit], a.
Appraisal [ap-praz'al], n.
Appraise' ment [ap-praz'ment], n.
Appreciable [ap-pre'shi-a-bl], a.
Appreciably [ap-pre'shi-a'bli], ad.
Appreciation [ap-pre-shi-a'shun], n.
Apprehensible [ap-pre-hen'si-bl], a.
Apprehensive [ap-pren'tis], n. v.
Apprentice [a-priz'], v. To inform.
Apprise [ap-priz'], n. v. To appraise.
Apprize [ap-proch'], n. v.
Approach [ap-pro-ba'shun], n.
Approbation [ap'pro-ba-tiv], a.
Approbative [ap-pro'pri-at], a. v. [n.
Appropriate [ap-pro'pri-a'shun],
Appropriation [ap-pro'pri-at-ér], n.
Appropriator [ap-proov'al], n.
Approval [ap-proov'ment], n.
Approve' ment [ap-prok'si-mat], a. v.
Approximate [ap-pér'ten-ans], n.
Appurtenance [a'pri-kot], n.
Apricot [a'purn, a'prun], n.
Apron [ap'ro'po'], ad. a.
Apropos [aps], n.
Apse [ap'ti-tud], n.
Aptitude [ap-i-ret'ik], a.
Apyretic [ap'i-rus], a.
Apyrous [a-kwa'ri-um], n.
Aquarium [a-kwat'ik], a. n.
Aquatic [ak'we-dukt], n.
Aqueduct [a'kwe-us], a.
Aqueous [ak'wi-la], n.
Aquila [ak'wi-lin, ak'wi-lin]
Aquiline [ar'ab-esk], a. n
Arab esque [a-ra'bi-an], a.
Arabian [ar'ab-ik], a.
Arabic [ar'a-bl], a.
Arable [a-ra'shus]
Araceous [ar'a-kis]
Arachis [a-rak'ni-d]
Arachnida [a-rak'ni-d]

Araignée [a'rän'yä'], n.
Arainæ [a-rä-ĭ'nē], n. pl.
Arbiter [är'bit-ẽr], n. v.
Arbitrament [är-bit'ra-ment], n.
Arbitration [är-bi-trä'shun], n.
Arbitrator [är'bi-trät-ẽr], n.
Arboreous [är-bō'rē-us], a.
Arborescence [är-bor-es'ens], n.
Arboretum [är-bo-rē'tum], n.
Arbor-vitæ [är'bor-vī'tē], n.
Arbutus [är-bū'tus, är'bū-tus], n.
Arcade [är-kād'], n.
Arcanum [är-kän'um], n. Arcana [är-kän'a], pl.
Archæology [är-kē-ol'o-ji], n.
Archaism [är'kā-izm], n.
Archangel [ärk-än'jel], n.
Archelogy [är-kel'o-ji], n.
Archetypal [är'kē-tĭp-al], a.
Archiater [är-kĭ'a-tẽr], n.
Archidiaconal [är-ki-di-ak'on-al], a.
Archimedean [är-ki-mē-dē'an], a.
Archipelago [är-ki-pel'a-gō], n.
Architecture [är'ki-tek-tūr], n.
Architrave är'ki-träv], n.
Archive [är'kīv], n.
Arctic [ärk'tik], a.
Arcturus [ärk-tū'rus], n.
Ardeidæ [är-dē'i-dē], n. pl.
Ardor [är'dẽr], n.
Arduous [är'dū-us], a.
Are [är], v.
Area [ā'rē-a], n. A definite space.
Areca [a-rē'ka], n.
Arena [a-rē'na], n.
Arenaceous [ar-ē-nā'shus], a.
Areola [a-rē'ō-la], n. Areolæ [a-rē'ō-lē], n. pl.
Areometer [ā-re-om'et-ẽr], n.
Areopagus [ar-ē-op'a-gus], n.
Argand [är'gand], n.
Argemone [är-je-mō'nē], n.
Argent [är'jent], a. n.
Argentine [är'jen-tīn], a. n.
Ar'gil laceous [är-jil-lā'shus], a.
Argillous [är-jil'lus], a.
Argive [är'jiv], a. n.
Argonaut [är'gō-nat], n. [a.
Ar'gument ative [är-gū-ment'a-tiv],
Argue [är'gū], v.
Aria [ä'ri-a], n. A song.
Ariadne [ā-ri-ad'ne], n.
A'rian ism [ā'ri-an-izm], n.
Arid [ar'id], a.
Aridity [a-rid'i-ti], n.
Aries [ā'ri-ēz], n.

Aright [a-rīt'], ad.
Arion [a-rī'on], n.
Arioso [ä-rē-ō'sō], a.
Arise [a-rīz'], v.
Aristocracy [ar-is-tok'ra-si], n.
Aristocrat [a-ris'to-krat, ar'is-to-krat], n.
Arithmetic [ar-ith'met-ik], n.
Arithmetical [ar-ith-met'ik-al], a.
Arithmetician [a-rith-me-ti'shan], n.
Ark [ärk], n. A chest, a vessel.
Arkansas [är'kan-saw], n.
Arm ada [är-mä'da], n.
Armadillo [är-ma-dil'lō], n.
Armament [är'na-ment], n.
Armature [är'ma-tūr], n.
Armenian [är-mē'ni-an], n.
Armful [ärm'fool], n.
Armillary [är'mil-la-ri], a.
Arminian [är-min'i-an], a. n.
Armistice [är'mis-tis], n.
Ar'mor er [är'mẽr-ẽr], n.
Armorial [är-mō'ri-al], a.
Arnica [är'ni-ka], n.
Aroma [a-rō'ma], n.
Aromatic [ar-ō-mat'ik], a. n.
Arpeggio [är-ped'jē-ō], n.
Arquebuse [är'kwē-bus], n.
Arquebusier [är-kwē-bus-ẽr'], n.
Arraign [a-rän'], n. v.
Arrange' ment [a-ränj'ment], n.
Arrant [ar'ant], a.
Arras [ar'as], n. v.
Array' er [a-rā'ẽr], n.
Arrear' age [a-rēr'äj], n.
Arrest [a-rest'], n.
Arrival [a-rī'val], n.
Arrogance [ar'rō-gans], n.
Arrogate [ar'ro-gāt], v.
Arrow [ar'ō], n. v.
Arsenal [är'se-nal], n.
Arsenic [är'sen-ik], a. n.
Arsenious [är-sē'ni-us], a.
Arson [är'son], n.
Artemisia [är-tē-mis'i-a], n.
Arterial [är-tē'ri-al], a.
Arteriotomy [är-tē-ri-ot'o-mi], n.
Artesian [är-tē'zhan], a.
Artful [ärt'fool], a.
Arthritis [är-thrī'tis], n.
Artichoke [är'ti-chōk], n.
Article [är'ti-kl], n. v.
Articulata [är-tik-ū-lä'ta], n. pl.
Articulation [är-tik-ū-lā'shun], n.
Articulator [är-tik-ū-lät'ẽr], n.
Artificer [är-tif'is-ẽr], n.

Apathetic [ap-a-thet'ik], a.
Apellous [a-pel'us], a.
Apennine [ap'en-nin], a.
Aperient [a-pē'ri-ent], n.
Aperture [ap'ér-tūr], n.
Apex [ā'pex], n.
Aphelion [a-fē'li-on], n. Aphelia [a-fē'li-a], pl. [pl.
Aphis [ā'fis], n. Aphides [af'i-dēz],
Aphorism [af'or-izm], n.
Aphrodite [af-ro-di'te], n.
Apiarist [ā'pi-a-rist], n.
Apiary [ā'pi-a-ri], n.
Apocalypse [a-pok'a-lips], n.
Apocrypha [a-pok'ri-fa], n.
Apodosis [a-pod'o-sis], n.
Apogee [ap'o-jē], n.
Apollinaris [a-pol-li-nā'ris], a.
Apollo Belvedere [a-pol'lō-bel've-dēr], n.
Apollyon [a-pol'li-on], n.
Apologet'ic al [a-pol-o-jet'ik-al], a.
Apologize [a-pol'o-jīz], v.
Apologue [ap'o-log], n.
Apophyge [a-pof'i-je], n. [n.
Apophyllite [a-pof'i-lit, ap-o-fil'lit].
Apophysis [a-pof'i-sis], n. Apophyses [a-pof'i-sēz], pl.
Apoplec'tic al [ap-o-plek'tik-al], a.
Apoplexy [ap'o-plek-si], n.
Apostasy [a-pos'ta-si], n.
Apostatize [a-pos'ta-tīz], v.
Apostle [a-pos'l], n.
Apostol'ic al [ap-os-tol'ik-al], a.
Apostrophe [a-pos'tro-fe], n.
Apostrophic [ap-os-trof'ik], a.
Apothecary [a-poth'e-ka-ri], n.
Apothecium [ap-o-thē'si-um], n. Apothecia [ap-o-thē'si-a], pl.
Apothegm [ap'o-them], n.
Apotheosis [ap-o-thē'o-sis], n.
Apothesis [a-poth'e-sis], n.
Appalachian [ap-pa-lā'ki-an], a.
Appall [ap-pal'], n. v.
Apparatus [ap-pa-rā'tus], n. sing. and pl.
Apparel [ap-par'el], n. v.
Apparent [ap-pâr'ent], a.
Apparition [ap-pa-rish'un], n.
Appeal [ap-pēl'], n. v.
Appear' ance [ap-pēr'ans], n.
Appease [ap-pēz'], v.
Appellant [ap-pel'ant], a. n.
Appellation [ap-pel-ā'shun], n.
Appellee [ap-pel-lē'], n.
Appellor [ap-pel'ar], n.

Append' age [ap-pend'āj], n.
Appendant [ap-pend'ant], a. n.
Appendix [ap-pen'diks], n. Appendixes [ap-pen'diks-ez], pl.
Appertain [ap-pér-tān'], v.
Appetite [ap'pe-tīt], n.
Appetize [ap'pē-tīz], v.
Applause [ap-plaz'], n.
Apple [ap'pl], n. v.
Appliance [ap-pli'ans], n.
Applicable [ap'pli-ka-bl], a.
Applicably [ap'pli-ka-bli], ad.
Application [ap-pli-kā'shun], n.
Appoggiatura [ap-poj-a-tōō'ra], n.
Appoint' ee [ap-point-ē'], n.
Appor'tion er [ap-pôr'shun-ér], n.
Apposite [ap'pō-zit], a.
Appraisal [ap-prāz'al], n.
Appraise' ment [ap-prāz'ment], n.
Appreciable [ap-prē'shi-a-bl], a.
Appreciably [ap-prē'shi-a-bli], ad.
Appreciation [ap-prē-shi-ā'shun], n.
Apprehensible [ap-prē-hen'si-bl], a.
Apprentice [ap-pren'tis], n. v.
Apprise [ap-prīz'], v. To inform.
Apprize [ap-prīz'], v. To appraise.
Approach [ap-prōch'], n. v.
Approbation [ap-prō-bā'shun], n.
Approbative [ap'prō-bā-tiv], a.
Appropriate [ap-prō'pri-āt], a. v. [n.
Appropriation [ap-prō-pri-ā'shun].
Appropriator [ap-prō'pri-āt-ér], n.
Approval [ap-prōōv'al], n.
Approve' ment [ap-prōōv'ment], n.
Approximate [ap-prok's-i-māt], a. v.
Appurtenance [ap-pér'ten-ans], n.
Apricot [ā'pri-kot], n.
Apron [ā'purn, ā'prun], n.
Apropos [ap'rō-pō'], ad. a.
Apse [aps], n.
Aptitude [ap'ti-tūd], n.
Apyretic [ap-i-ret'ik], a.
Apyrous [ap'i-rus], a.
Aquarium [a-kwā'ri-um], n.
Aquatic [a-kwat'ik], a. n.
Aqueduct [ak'wē-dukt], n.
Aqueous [ā'kwe-us], a.
Aquila [ak'wi-la], n.
Aquiline [ak'wi-lin, ak'wi-lin]
Ar'ab esque [ar'ab-esk].
Arabian [a-rā'bi-an], a.
Arabic [ar'ab-ik], a.
Arable [ar'a-bl], a.
Araceous [a-rā'shus].
Arachis [ar'a-kis], n.
Arachnida [a-rak'ni-

ale, add, bear, ärm, ask, fall; mē, met, thêre, hèr; pīne, pin;

—————— —   —

Ar——— -   ·itos
Ar—— -
Ar—— -
Ar——————
Ar————.
Ar————.
Ar——— .
Ar———en.en
Ar———·—
Ar———·—
Ar———
Ar———
Ar———

  .

Ar——— .—
Ar—————
Ar———·—
Ar———— —
Ar————·—
Ar———·
Ar————— ·—
Ar——————
Ar———·—
Ar————·—
Ar————·—
Ar—— .
Ar—.
Ar————
Ar————
Ar—·—
Ar——.
Ar
Area
Area
Area
Area——. —   ·it.
Area——
                                                                            !·L
Area————
Ar———— —
Argu——
Argen———
Argen.
Argen———
Arg——— ·
Arg—— ·—
Arg—·—
Arg—·—
Ar——— ·—
Ar——— ·—
Ar——.

Artifi'cial ity [är-ti-fish-al'i-ti], n.
Artillerist [är-til'lér-ist], n.
Artizan [är'ti-zan], n.
Artist [ärt'ist], n.
Artiste [är'tēst'], n.
Artless [ärt'les], a.
Arum [ā'rum], n.
Arundelian [ar-un-dē'li-an], a.
Arvicola [är-vik'ō-la], n.
Aryan [är'yan, ä'ri-an], a.
Asafetida [as-a-fet'e-da], n.
Asbestos [as-bes'tos], n.
Ascension [as-sen'shun], n.   [ing.
Ascent [as-sent'], n. The act of ris-
Ascertain [as-sér-tān'], v.
Ascetic [as-set'ik], a. n.
Asclepias [as-klē'pi-as], n.
Ascription [as-krip'shun], n.
Ashamed [a-shamd'], a. p.
Asiatic [ā-she-at'ic], a.
Asinine [as'i-nin], a.
Asitia [a-sī'ti-a], n.
Askance [a-skans'], ad.
Askew [a-skū'], ad.
Asparagus [as-par'a-gus], n.
Aspen [asp'en], a. n.
Asperity [as-per'i-ti], n.
Aspersion [as-pèr'shun], n.
Asphalt' um [as-falt'um], n.
Aspirant [as-pir'ant], n.
Aspirate [as'pi-rāt], a. n. v.
Aspirator [as'pi-rāt-ér], n.
Assai [as-sä'ē], a. A musical term.
Assai [as-sī'], n. A South American
   beverage.
Assail' ant [as-sāl'ant], a. n.
Assailer [as-sāl'ér], n.
Assassin ator [as-sas'sin-āt-ér], n.
Assault [as-salt'], n. v.
Assay' er [as-sā'ér], n.
Assemblage [as-sem'blāj], n.
Assembly [as-sem'bli], n.
Assent [as-sent'], n. v. To concur.
Assert' ion [as-sér'shun], n.
Assess' or [as-ses'ér], n.
Assets [as'sets], n.
Asseverate [as-sev'ér-āt], v.
Assiduity [as-si-dū'i-ti], n.
Assiduous [as-sid'ū-us], a.
Assignation [as-sig-nā'shun], n.
Assign [as-sīn'], v.
Assignee [as-sin-ē'], n.
Assignor [as-sin-or'], n.
Assimilate [as-sim'il-āt], v. To make
   alike; to incorporate.   [feign.
Assimulate [as-sim'ū-lāt], v.   To

Assist' ance [as-sist'ans], n.
Associate [as-sō'shi-āt], v. a.
Association [as-sō-she-ā'sh]
Associator [as-sō'shi-āt-ér], n.
Assonance [as'sō-nans], n.
Assort' ment [as-sort'men], n.
Assuage [as-swāj'], v.
Assumption [as-sum'shun], n.
Assurance [a-shoor'ans], n.
Assure [a-shoor'], v.
Asterisk [as'tér-isk], n.
Asteroid [as'tér-oid], a. n.
Asthma [ast'ma], n.
Astonish [as-ton'ish], v.
Astound [as-tound'], v.
Astringency [as-trin'jen-si], n.
Astrography [as-trog'ra-fi], n.
Astrologer [as-trol'o-jér], n.
Astronomer [as-tron'o-mér], n.
Astronomic [as-tro-nom'ik], a.
Astute' ness [as-tūt'nes], n.
Asunder [a-sun'dér], ad.
Asylum [a-sī'lum], n.
Ate [āt], v. From eat.   [ven
Ate [ā'tē], n. The goddess of
Atelier [at'e-ā'], n.
Atheist [ā'thē-ist], a. n.
Atheneum [ath-e-nē'um], n.
Athlete [ath'lēt], n.
Athleticism [ath-let'i-sizm], n.
Athwart [a-thwart'], ad. prep.
Atlantic [at-lan'tik], a. n.
Atlas [at'las], n.
Atmospheric [at-mos-fer'ik], a.
At'om ist [at'om-ist], n.
Atone' ment [a-tōn'ment], n.   [
Atrium [ā'tri-um], n. Atria [ā'tri-
Atrocious [a-trō'shus], ad.
Atrocity [a-tros'i-ti], n.
Atrophy [at'ro-fi], n.
Attache [ä'tä'shä'], n.
Attach' ment [at-tach'ment], n.
Attack' able [at-tak'a-bl], a.
Attain' ment [at-tān'ment], n.
Attempt [at-temt'], n. v.
Attend' ance [at-tend'ans], n.
Attention [at-ten'shun], n.
Attenuate [at-ten'ū-āt], a. v.
Attest' er [at-test'ér], n.
At'tic ism [at'ti-sizm], n.
Attire [at-tir'], n. v.
Attitude [at'ti-tūd], n.
Attitudinize [at-ti-tūd'in-iz], v.
Attorney [at-tér'ni], n.
Attract' ion [at-trak'shun], n.
Attractor [at-trakt'ér], n.

Attribute [at-trib′ūt], v. [at′tri-būt], n.
Attrition [at-trish′un], n.
Auburn [a′bèrn], a.
Auchenia [a-kē′ni-a], n.
Auc′tion eer [ak-shun-ĕr′], n. v.
Audacious [a-dā′shus], a.
Audacity [a-das′i-ti], n.
Audible [a′di-bl], a.
Audience [a′di-ens], n.
Au′dit or [a′dit-ĕr], n.
Auditory [a′di-to-ri], a. n.   [elist.
Auerbach [ow′er-bäk]. German nov-
Augean [a-jē′an], a.   [boring.
Auger [a′gĕr], n. An instrument for
Aught [at], n. Anything. [Incor-
rectly written ought.]
Augment [ag-ment′], v. [ag′ment], n.
Augmenter [ag-ment′ĕr], n.
Au′gur y [a′gĕr-i], n. A foretelling.
August [a-gust′], a. [a′gust], n.
Augustine [a′gus-tīn]. The author.
[a-gus-tēn′]. The town.
Auk [ak], n.   [father or mother.
Aunt [änt], n. The sister of one's
Aura [a′ra], n.
Aurated [a′rāt-ed], a.
Aureate [a′rē-āt], a.
Aurelia [a-rē′li-a], n.   [n.
Aureola, Aureole [a-rē′ō-la, a′rē-ōl],
Auricula [a-rik′ū-la], n.
Aurist [a′rist], n.   [n.
Aurora Borealis [a-rō′ra-bō-re-ā′lis],
Auscultator [as′kul-tāt-ĕr], n.
Auspice [a′spis], n.
Auspicious [a-spi′shus], a.
Austere [a-stēr′], a.
Austerity [a-ster′i-ti], n.
Authen′tic ity [a-then-tis′i-ti], n.
Au′thor ity [a-thor′i-ti], n.
Authorize [a-thor-īz′], v.
Autocracy [a-tok′ra-si], n.
Autocrat [a′tō-krat], n.

Auto de fe [au′tō-dā-fā′], n. **Autos de fe**, pl.
Autograph [a′tō-graf], a. n.
Autography [a-tog′ra-fi], n.
Automaton [a-tom′a-ton], n.
Autopsy [a′top-si], n.
Autotype [a′tō-tīp], n.
Autumn [a′tum], n
Autumnal [a-tum′nal], a. n.
Auxiliary [ag-zil′ya-ri], a. n.
Avail′ able [a-vāl′a-bl], a.
Avalanche [av′a-lansh], n.
Avaricious [av-a-ri′shus], a.
Avatar [av-a-tär′], n.
Avaunt [a-vant′], inter.
Avenger [a-venj′ĕr], n.
Aventine [av′en-tīn], n.
Avenue [av′e-nū], n.
Average [av′ĕr-āj], a. n. v.
Averse [a-vèrs′], a.
Avert′ er [a-vèrt′ĕr], n.
Aviary [ā′vi-a-ri], n.
Avidity [a-vid′i-ti], n.
Avis [ā′vis], n. **Aves** [ā′vēs], pl.
Avocation [av-ō-kā′shun], n.
Avoid′ ance [a-void′ans], n.
Avoirdupois [av-ĕr-dū-pois′], n.
Avon [ā′von]. River and town.
Awe some [a′sum], a.
Aw′ful ly [a′fŏŏl-li], ad.
Awkward [ak′wĕrd], a.
Awl [al], n. A pointed instrument.
Awning [an′ing], n.
Awry [a-rī′], a. ad.
Ax′il lary [aks′il-la-ri], a.
Axiom [aks′i-om], n.
Axis [aks′is], n. **Axes** [aks′ēz], pl.
Axle [aks′l], n.
Ay, Aye [ī], n. An affirmative.
Aye [ā], ad. Always ; forever.
Azoic [a-zō′ik], a.
Azote [az′-ōt, a-zōt′], n.
Azure [ā′zhur, azh′ur], a. n. v.

B.

Babble [bab′bl], n. v.
Baboon [ba-bŏŏn′], n.
Ba′by ish [bā′bi-ish], a.
Baccalaureate [bak-ka-la′rē-āt], a.n.
Baccate [bak′kāt], a.
Bacchanal [bak′a-nal], a. n.
Bacchanalian [bak-a-nā′li-an], n.
Bacchant [ba-kant′], n.

Bacchante [ba-kan′te], n. fem.
Bacchus [bak′us], n.
Bacciferous [bak-sif′ĕr-us], a.
Bach [bäk]. The musical composer.
Bachelor [bach′el-ĕr], n.
Backgammon [bak-gam′mon], n.
Back′ ward ness [bak′wĕrd-nes], n.
Bacon [bā′kn], n.

wŏŏl ; ūse, us ; ū, Fr. ; g, get ; j, jar ; ñ, Fr. ton ; ch, chain ; *th*, then ; th

wings , to feed

Baize [bāz], n.
Bak'er y [bāk'er-i], n.
Balance [bal'ans], n. v.
Balbuties [bal-bū'ti-ēz], n.
Balcony [bal'kō-ni], n.
Baldachin, Baldachino [bal'da-kin, bal-da-kē'no], n.
Balderdash [bal'dér-dash], n.
Baldness [bald'nes], n.
Bale [bāl], n. A bundle.
Bale'ful ly [bāl'fōl-ly], ad.
Balk y [bak'i], a.
Ballad [bal'lad], n.
Ballast [bal'last], n. v.
Ballet [bal'lā'], n. v.
Balloon [bal-lōon'], n.
Ballot [bal'lot], n. v.
Balmoral [bal-mor'al], n.
Balm y [bäm'i], a.
Balsam [bal'sam], n. v.
Baltic [bal'tik], a.
Baluster [bal'us-tér], n.
Balustrade [bal-us-trād'], n.
Balzac [bal'zak]. French novelist.
Bamboo' zle [bam-bōo'zl], v.
Banana [ba-nā'na, ba-nä'na], n.
Band age [band'āj], n. v.
Bandana [ban-dan'a], n.
Bandeau [ban'dō], n. Bandeaux [ban'dōz], pl.
Bandit [ban'dit], n. Bandits, Banditti [ban-dit'ti], pl.
Bandoline [ban'do-lin], n. v.
Bane ful [bān'fōl], a.
Bangle [ban'gl], n.
Banian, Banyan [ban'yan], a. n.
Ban'ish ment [ban'ish-ment], n.
Banjo [ban'jō], n.

Bar...
Barcarolle [bar-ka...]
Bare [bâr], a. v. Naked.
Barege [ba-rāzh'], n.
Bargain [bar'gn], n. v.
Barilla [ba-ril'la], n.
Baritone [bar'i-tōn], a. n.
Barley [bar'li], n.
Barn acle [bar'na-kl], n.
Barometer [ba-rom'et-er], n.
Ba'ron ess [bar'on-es], n. fem
Baronial [ba-rō'ni-al], a.
Barouche [ba-rōosh'], n.
Barrack [bar'ak], n.
Barranca [bar-ran'ka], n.
Barrel [bar'el], n.
Bar'ren ness [bar'en-nes], n.
Barricade [ba-ri-kād'], n. v.
Barrier [bar'i-ér], n.
Barrister [bar'is-tér], n.
Barrow [bar'ō], n.
Bar'ter er [bar'tér-ér], n.
Baryta [ba-ri'ta], n.
Barytes [ba-ri'tēz], n.
Basalt' ine [ba-salt'in], a.
Bascinet [bas'i-net], n.
Base ment [bās'ment], n.
Bash'ful ness [bash'fōl-nes], n.
Bashi-bazouk [bash-ē ba-zōok]
Basil [baz'il], n. v.
Basilica [ba-zil'ik-a], n.
Basilisk [baz'il-isk], n.
Basin [bā'sn], n.
Basis [bās'is], n. Bases [
Bask et [bas'ket], n.
Basque [bask], n.
Bas-relief, Basso-rilievo [bäs'so-rē-lē-ā-vō], n.

Bass-relief [bas-rē-lēf'], n.
Bass [bas], n. A tree; a fish.
Bass [bås], a. n. A musical term.
Bassoon' ist [bas-sōōn'ist], n.
Bastard [bas'tèrd], a. n.
Bastile [bas-tēl'], n.
Bastinado [bas-ti-nā'dō], n. v.
Basting [bāst'ing], n.
Bastion [bast'yun], n.
Batatus [ba-tā'tus], n.
Batavian [ba-tā'vi-an], a. n.
Batch elor [bach'el-ėr], n.
Bate [bāt], v. To abate; to leave
   out. [pl.
Bateau [bä-tō'], n. Bateaux [bä-tōz'],
Bath [bāth], n.
Bathe [bāth], v.
Bathos [bā'thos], n.
Bathybius [ba-thib'i-us], n.
Baton [bat'on, bi'ton'], n.
Batrachia [ba-trā'ki-a], n. pl.
Battalion [ba-tal'yun], n.
Bat'ter y [bat'tėr-i], n.
Bat'tle ment [bat'l-ment], n.
Battue [bat'tōō], n.
Bauble [ba̤'bl], n.
Bawd iness [ba̤'di-nes], n.
Bay adere [bä-ya-dēr'], n.
Bayonet [bā'on-et], n. v.
Bayou [bi'ōō], n.
Bazar [ba-zär'], n.
Bdellium [del'yum], n.
Beach [bēch], a. n. **The shore.**
Beacon [bē'kn], n. v.
Bead le [bē'dl], n.
Beagle [bē'gl], n.
Beak er [bēk'ėr], n.
Beam [bēm], n. v.
Bean [bēn], n.
Bear [bâr], n. An animal. v. To
   uphold; to carry; to suffer.
Beard less [bērd'les], a.
Beast liness [bēst'li-nes], n.
Beat [bēt], n. A stroke. v. **To strike;**
   to conquer.
Beatitude [bē-at'i-tūd], n.
Beatrice Cenci [bā-ā-trē'chā chen'-
   chē], n.
Beau [bō], n. Beaux [bōz], pl.
Beauteous [bū'tē-us], a.
Beautiful [bū'ti-fōōl], a.
Beaver [bē'vėr], a. n.
Because [be-ca̤z'], con.
Beckon [bek'n], n. v.
Bedehouse [bēd'hous], n.
Bede'vil ment [bē-de'vil-ment], n.

Bedizen [bē-dīz'n], v.
Bed'lam ite [bed'lam-it], n.
Bedouin [bed'ōō-in], n.
Bed stead [bed'sted], n.
Bee [bē], n. An insect.
Beech [bēch], n. A tree.
Beef [bēf], a. n.
Beelzebub [bē-el'zē-bub], n.
Been [bin], p.
Beer [bēr], n. A beverage.
Bees-wax [bēs'waks], n.
Beet [bēt], n. A vegetable. [poser.
Beethoven [bā'tō-fen]. Musical com-
Beetle [bē'tl], n. v.
Beetling [bēt'ling], a.
Beeves [bēvs], n. pl.
Beg gar [beg'gėr], n. v.
Begin' ner [bē-gin'ėr], n.
Begonia [bē-gō'ni-a], n.
Beguile' r [bē-gil'ėr], n.
Behavior [bē-hāv'yėr], n.
Behemoth [bē'hē-moth], n.
Behind [bē-hind'], ad. prep.
Behold' er [bē-hōld'ėr], n.
Behoove [bē-hōōv'], a. v.
Belch [belsh], n. v. [n.
Beldam, Beldame [bel'dam, bel'dām],
Beleaguer [bē-lėg'ėr], v.
Belfry [bel'fri], n.
Belial [bē'li-al], n.
Belief [bē-lēf'], n.
Believe [bē-lēv'], v.
Bell adonna [bel-la-don'na], n.
Belle [bel], n. A young lady.
Bellicose [bel'li-kōs], a.
Belligerent [bel-lij'ėr-ent], a. n.
Bellow [bel'lō], n. v.
Bellows [bel'lus], n. [p.
Beloved [bē-luv'ed], a. [bē-luvd'],
Belvedere [bel-ve-dēr'], n.
Bench [bensh], n. v.
Beneath [bē-nēth'], ad. prep.
Ben'edict ion [ben-e-dik'shun], n.
Benefaction [ben-e-fak'shun], n.
Benefactor [ben-e-fak'tėr], n.
Benefactress [ben-e-fak'tres], n.
Beneficence [be-nef'i-sens], n.
Beneficial [ben-e-fi'shal], a.
Beneficiary [ben-e-fi'shi-a-ri], a. n.
Benefit [ben'e-fit], n. v.
Benevolence [be-nev'o-lens], n.
Benignant [bē-nig'nant], a.
Benignity [bē-nig'ni-ti], n.
Benign' ly [be-nin'ly], ad.
Benison [ben'i-zn], n.
Benzine [ben'zin], n.

nzoin [ben-zō'in], n.
ranger [bā'roñ'zhā']. French poet.
equeath [bē-kwerh'], v.
ereave' ment [bē-rēv'ment], n.
ergamot [bèr'ga-mot], n.
Berlin [bèr'lin], a. n.
Berlioz [ber'le'ō']. Musical composer.
Bernouse [bèr-nōōs'], n.
Berry [be'ri], n. A fruit.
Berth [bèrth], n. A place in a ship or car to sleep.
Ber'yl ine [ber'il-lin], a.
Beseech [bē-sēch'], v.
Beset' ment [bē-set'ment], n.
Besiege [bē-sēj'], v.
Besom [bē'zum], n.
Besot' ted [bē-sot'ed], a. p.
Best ial [best'yal], a.
Bestiality [best-ye-al'i-ti], n.
Bestow' al [bē-stō'al], n.
Betray' er [bē-trā'ėr], n.
Betroth' al [bē-troth'al], n.
Betrothment [bē-troth'ment], n.
Between [bē-twēn'], n. prep.
Betwixt [bē-twikst'], prep.
Bevel [bev'el], a. n. v.
Beverage [bev'ėr-āj], n.
Beware [bē-wâr'], v. [n.
Bewil'der ment [bē-wil'dėr-ment],
Bewitch' ery [bē-wich'ėr-i], n.
Bey [bā], n. A Turkish governor.
Beyond [bē-yond'], ad. prep.
Bezique [be-zēk'], n.
Bi'as ed [bi'asd], p.
Bible [bi'bl], n.
Biblicist [bib'li-sist], n.
Bibliographer [bib-li-og'ra-fėr], n.
Bibulous [bib'ū-lus], a.
Bick'er er [bik'ėr-ėr], n.
Bicycle [bi'si-kl], n.
Bicyclist [bi'si-klist], n.
Biennial [bi-en'ni-al], n.
Bier [bēr], n. A carriage or frame for conveying the dead.
Big amous [big'a-mus], a.
Biggin [big'in], n.
Big'ot ry [big'ot-ri], n.
Bilboes [bil'bōz], n. pl.
Bilboquet [bil-bō-kā'], n.
Bilge [bilj], n. v.
Biliary [bil'ya-ri], a.
Bilious [bil'yus], a.
Billet-doux [bil'le-dōō'], n.
Billiards [bil'yėrdz], n.
Billow [bil'lō], n. v.
Bingen [bing'en]. A town.

Binnacle [bin'a-kl], n.
Binomial [bi-nō'mi-al], a. n.
Biogenesis [bi-ō-jen'e-sis], n.
Biographer [bi-og'ra-fėr], n.
Biographical [bi-ō-graf'ik-al], a.
Biped [bi'ped], n.
Birch [bėrch], a. n.
Bird [bėrd], n.
Birth [bėrth], n. A coming into life
Biscuit [bis'ket], n.
Bish'op ric [bish'up-rik], n. [man
Bismarck [bis'märk]. Prussian states
Bismuth [biz'muth], n.
Bison [bi'son], n.
Bistoury [bis'tōō-ri], n.
Bitch [bich], n.
Bittern [bit'tėrn], n.
Bitumen [bi-tū'men], n.
Bituminous [bi-tū'min-us], a.
Bivouac [biv'wak], n. v.
Bizarre [bi-zär'], a. [author
Bjornson [be-yorn'son]. Norwegian
Black amoor [blak'a-mōōr], n.
Blackguard [blag'gärd], a. n.
Blackmail [blak'māl], n.
Bladder [blad'ėr], n.
Blade [blād], n. v.
Blain [blān], n.
Blamable [blām'a-bl], a.
Blame less [blām'les], a.
Blanch [blansh], n. v.
Blanc-mange [blä-monj'], n.
Bland ishment [blan'dish-ment],
Blanket [blan'ket], n. v.
Blarney [blär'ni], n. v.
Blasé [blä'zā'], a.
Blaspheme [blas-fēm'], v.
Blasphemous [blas'fēm-us], a.
Blatant [blā'tant], a.
Blather-skite [blath'ėr-skit], n
Blaze [blāz], n. v.
Blazon [blā'zn], n. v.
Bleach'er y [blēch'ėr-i], n.
Bleak ness [blēk'nes], n.
Blear [blēr], n. v.
Bleat er [blēt'ėr], n.
Bleed [blēd], v.
Blemish [blem'ish], n.
Blessed [bles'ed], a.
Blight [blit], n. v.
Blind ness [blind'ne
Bliss ful [blis'fool]
Blithe some [blith'
Bloat [blōt], v.
Block ade [blok-ā
Blond [blond], a.

Blonde [blond], n.
Blood ily [blud'i-li], ad.
Bloom er [bloom'er], n.
Blossom [blos'som], n. v.
Blotch [bloch], n. v. [workmen.
Blouse [blouz], n. A frock worn by
Blowze [blouz], n. A ruddy, fat-faced
wench.
Blowzy [blouz'i], a.
Blubber [blub'er], n. v. [marshal.
Blucher [bloo'ker]. Prussian field-
Bludgeon [bluj'on], n.
Blue [blu], a, n. v. A color.
Blumenthal [bloo'men-täl]. Musical
composer.
Blun'der buss [blun'der-bus], n.
Blus'ter er [blus'ter-er], n. [n.
Boa-constrictor [bo'a-con-strict'er.]
Board er [bord'er], n.
Boast ful [bost'fool], a.
Boatswain [bot'swän], n.
Bobbin [bob'in], n.
Bobolink [bob'o-link], n
Boccaccio [bo-kä'chö, bok-kät'chö].
Italian novelist.
Bode ful [böd'fool], a.
Bodice [bod'is], n.
Bodily [bo'di-li], a.
Bodkin [bod'kin], n.
Body [bo'di], n.
Bœotian [be-ö'shan], a. n.
Boggle [bog'gl], n. v.
Bohea [bo-he'], n.
Boil er [boil'er], n.
Boisterous [bois'ter-us], a.
Bolero [bo-lä'rö], n.
Boletus [bo-le'tus], n.
Boleyn, Anne [an bool'in], n.
Bolingbroke [bol'ing-brook]. English
statesman.
Bollard [bol'lard], n. [n.
Bologna-sausage [bo-lön'ya-sạ'sä]),
Bolognese [bō-lön-yēz'], a.
Bolster [böl'ster], n. v.
Bomb [bum], n. v.
Bombard [bum-bärd'], v.
Bombardier [bum-bärd-er'], n.
Bombast [bum'bast], a. n.
Bombazine [bum-ba-zēn'], n.
Bombic [bom'bik], a.
Bombyx [bom'biks], n.
Bonanza [bo-nan'za], n.
Bond age [bond'äj], n.
Bon-mot [boñ'-mö'], n.
Bonnet [bon'net], n. v.
Bon-ton [boñ'-ton'], n.

Booby [boo'bi], a. n.
Boomerang [boom'e-rang], n.
Boorish [boor'ish], a
Boot ee [boot-ē'], n.
Bootes [bo-ö'tēz], n.
Booth [booth], n.
Borachio [bo-rat'chö], n.
Boracite [bö'ras-it], n.
Boraginaceæ [bo-raj-i-nä'sē-ē], n. pl.
Borax [bö'raks], n.
Bor'der er [bor'der-er], n.
Boreas [bö'rē-as], n.
Borecole [bor'köl], n.
Borghese [bar-gä'zä], n. Princess.
Borough [bur'ö], n.
Bor'row er [bor'rö-er], n.
Bosom [boo'um], n. v.
Bosporus, Bosphorus [bos'pö-rus,
bos'fö-rus], n.
Botanist [bot'an-ist], n.
Botch er [boch'er], n.
Bother [both'er], n. v.
Botrychium [bo-trik'i-um], n.
Botryolite [bot'ri-o-lit], n.
Bottle [bot'l], n. v.
Bottom [bot'om], a. n. v.
Bouche [boosh], n. v. [and actor.
Boucicault [boo-se-kö']. Dramatist
Boudoir [boo'dwạr], n.
Bough [bow], n.
Bought [bat]. p. from buy.
Bougie [boo'zhē'], n.
Bouillon [bool'yon'], n. Soup.
Boulanger [boo'lon'zhä']. French
general.
Boulder [böl'der], n.
Boulevard [bool'e-vär'], n.
Boulogne [boo'lön']. French town.
Bounce [bouns], ad. n. v.
Bound ary [bound'a-ri], n.
Bounteous [boun'tē-us], a.
Bountiful [boun'ti-fool], a.
Bouquet [boo'kä', boo-kä'], n.
Bour'bon ist [boor'bon-ist], n.
Bourgeois [bur-jois'], n. A kind of
type.
Bourgeois [boorzh'wạ'], n. A citizen.
Bourgeoisie [boorzh'wạ'zē'], n. The
middle classes of a country.
Bourn [börn], n.
Bourse [boors], n.
Bovine [bö'vin], a.
Bowel [bow'el], n. v.
Bow'ie-knife [bö'i-nif'], n.
Bowl der [böl'der], n.
Bowling-alley [böl'ing-al'i], n.

Bowsprit [bō'sprit], n.
Brace let [brās'let], n.
Brachial [brak'yal, brä'ki-al], a.
Brachygraphy [bra-kig'ra ō], n.
Brachypterous [bra-kip'tér-us], a.
Bracket [brak'et], n.
Brag gadocio [brag-a-dō'shi-ō], n.
Braggart [brag'ärt], a. n.
Braid [brād], n. v.
Brain [brān], n. v.
Braize [brāze], n. v.
Brake [brāk], n. A fern; an appa-
  ratus for checking the motion of a
  wheel.
Bramble [bram'bl], n.
Bramin [brä'min], n.
Branch [bransh], n. v.
Branchiæ [brang'ki-ē], n. pl. [pl.
Branchiopoda [brang-ki-op'o-da], n.
Brand ied [bran'did], a. Mingled
  with brandy.
Brazier [brä'zhér], n.
Bravado [bra-vä'dō], a. n.
Bravo [brä'vō], inter. n. Bravoes
  [brä'vōz], n. pl.
Bravura [brä-vōō'ra], a. n.
Brawl er [brạl'ér], n.
Brawn y [brạn'i], a.
Brazil' ian [bra-zil'yan], a. n.
Breach [brēch], n. v. A break.
Bread [bred], n. Food made of grain.
Breadth [bredth], n. [rend.
Break [brāk], n. A rupture. v. To
Breakfast [brek'fast], n. v.
Breast plate [brest'plāt], n.
Breath [breth], n.
Breathe [brēth], v.
Breccia [bret'cha], n.
Brecciated [brek'shi-āt-ed], a.
Breech [brēch], n. v. The hinder
  part of anything, especially the part
  of the cannon, or other fire-arm, be-
  hind the bottom of the bore; the
  lower part of the body behind.
Breeches [brich'ez], n. pl.
Breed [brēd], n. v.
Breeze [brēz], n. v.
Brethren [breth'ren], n. pl.
Breton [bret'on], a. n.
Brevet [bre-vet'], a. n. v.
Breviary [brēv'ya-re], n.
Brevier [bre-vēr'], n.
Brevity [bre'vi-ti], n.
Brew er y [brōō'ér-i], a.
Bribe ry [brīb'ér-i], n.
Brick-kiln [brik'kil], n.

Bridal [brid'al], a.
Bridegroom [brid'grōōm], n.
Bridemaid, Bridesmaid
  [bridz'mād], n.
Bridge [brij], n. v.
Bridle [brī'dl], n. v.
Brief ly [brēf'li], ad.
Brier [brī'ér], n.
Brigade [bri-gād'], n. v.
Brigadier [brig-a-dēr'], n.
Brig'and age [brig'and-āj], n.
Brigantine [brig-an-tīn'], n. A
  of small brig.
Bright en [brīt'n], v.
Brillante [bril-än'te]. (Mus.) N
  a gay and live y manner.
Brilliancy [bril'yan-si], n.
Brilliant [bril'yant], a. n.
Brim stone [brim'stōn], a. n.
Briny [brīn'i], a.
Brisk et [bris'ket], n.
Bristle [bris'l], n. v.
Britannia [bri-tan'i-a], n.
Britannic [bri-tan'ik], a.
Briton [brit'on], n.
Brittle [brit'l], a.
Britzska [brits'ka], n.
Broach [brōch], n. A tool; a pec
  tion on the head of a young sta
  candle rod. v. To tap; to n
  public; to cause to begin.
Broad cast [brad'kast], a. ad. n
Brocade [brō-kād'], n.
Brocatel [brō'ka-tel], n.
Broccoli [brok'o-li], n.
Brochure [brō-shōōr'], n.
Brogan [brō'gan], n.
Brogue [brōg], n.
Bro'ker age [brō'kér-āj], n.
Bromide [brō'mid], n.
Bromine [brō'min], n.
Bronchial [brong'ki-al], a.
Bronchitis [brong-ki'tis], n.
Bronte, Charlotte [bron'te].
Bronze [bronz, brōnz], n. v.
Brooch [brōch], n. An ornamer
Brothel [broth'el], n.
Brother [bruth'ér], n.
Brougham [brōō'am], n.
Brown ie [broun'i], n.
Browse [brouz], n. v.
Bruin [brōō'in], n.
Bruise [brōōz], n. v.
Bruit [brōōt], n. v. A report.
Brunette [brōō-net'], n.
Brusk, Brusque [brusk], a.

Bru'tal ism [broot'al-ism], n.
Brute [broot], a. n. A beast. [n.
Bryony, Bryonia [bri'ō-ni, bri-ō'ni-a],
Bubble [bub'l], n. v.
Bu'bo ninæ [bū-bō-nī'nē], n.
Bubonocele [bū-bon'ō-sēl], n.
Buccaneer [buk-a-nér'], n.
Buck et [buk'et], n.
Buckle [buk'l], n. v.
Bucolic [bū-kol'ik], a. n.
Buddha [bood'da], n.
Buddhist [bood'dist], n.
Budget [buj'et], n.
Buffalo [buf'fa-lō], n.
Buffet [buf'fet], n. v.
Buffoon [buf-foon'], a. n.
Bugaboo [bug'a-boo], n.
Buggy [bug'gi], n.
Bugle [bū'gl], a. n.
Build er [bild'ér], n. [a.
Bulbous, Bulbose [bul'bus, bul'bōs],
Bulgarian [bul-gā'ri-an], n.
Bulk iness [bulk'i-nes], n. [v.
Bul'let in [bool'e-tēn, bool'e-tin], n.
Bullion [bool'yon], n. Uncoined gold
  or silver.
Bullock [bool'ok], n. v.
Bulrush [bool'rush], n.
Bulwark [bool'wérk], n. v.

Bumble-bee [bum'bl-bē], n.
Bunch [bunsh], n. v.
Bundle [bun'dl], n. v.
Bunion, Bunyon [bun'yun], n.
Buoy ancy [bwoi'an-si], n.
Bur'den some [bér'dn-sum], a.
Bureau [bū-rō'], n.
Burgher [bérg'ér], n.
Burg'lar y [bérg'la-ri], n.
Burgundy [bér'gun-di], n.
Burial [be'ri-al], n.
Burlesque [bér-lesk'], a. n. v.
Bur'nish er [bér'nish-ér], n.
Burnoose [bér-noos], n.
Burr ow [bur'ō], n. v.
Bury [be'ri], v. To cover with
  earth.
Bush el [boosh'el], n.
Busily [bi'zi-li], ad.
Business [biz'nes], a. n.
Buskin [bus'kin], n.
Bustle [bus'l], n. v.
Butcher [booch'ér], n. v.
But'ter ine [but'ér-in], n.
Button [but'n], n. v.
Buttress [but'res], n. v.
Buzz ard [buz'érd], a. n.
Byzantine [biz'an-tin], n. [biz'an-
  tin, biz-an'tin, biz-an'tīn], a.

C.

Cabal [ka-bal'], n. v. An intrigue.
Cabala [kab'a-lä], n.
Cabalist [kab'al-ist], n.
Cabaret [kab'a-rä], n.
Cabbage [kab'bäj], n. v.
Cab'in et [kab'in-et], n.
Cable [kā'bl], n. v. A large, strong
  rope or chain.
Caboose [ka-boos'], n.
Cabriolet [kab'ri'ō'lā'], n.
Cacao [ka-kā'ō], n.
Cachalot [kash'a-lot], n.
Cache [kash], n.
Cachet [kash'ā'], n.
Cacoexy [ka-kek'si], n.
Cachinnation [kak-in-nā'shun], n.
Cacholong [kash'ō-long], n. [chief.
Cacique [ka-sēk'], n. An Indian
Cackle [kak'l], n. v.
Cacoethes [kak-ō-ē'thēz], n.
Cacophony [ka-kof'ō-ni], n. [pl.
Cactus [kak'tus], n. Cactuses, Cacti,

Cadaverous [ka-dav'ér-us], a.
Caddis [kad'is], n.
Cadence [kā'dens], n. v.
Cadet [ka-det'], n.
Cadi [kā'di], n.
Caducous [ka-dū'kus], a. [poet
Cædmon [kod'mun], n. Anglo-Saxon
Cæsura [sē-zū'ra], n.
Café [kaf'ā'], n.
Caffeine [kaf-fē'in], n.
Caffre [kaf'ér], n.
Cahier [kā'e'yā'], n.
Cahoot [ka-hoot'], n.
Caic, Caique [kä-ēk'], n. A skiff
  used in the Bosporus.
Cairn [kārn], n.
Cairo [kī'rō], Egypt ; [kā'rō], U. S.
Caisson [kā-soon'], n.
Caitiff [kā'tif], a. n.
Cajole [ka-jōl'], v.
Calaboose [kal-a-boos'], n.
Calamitous [ka-lam'i-tus], a.

Calamus [kal'a-mus], n.
Calash [ka-lash'], n.
Calcareous [kal-kā'rē-us], a.
Calceolaria [kal-sē-ō-lā'ri-a], n.
Calcimine [kal'si-min], n. v.
Calcinable [kal-sī'na-bl], a.
Calcine [kal-sīn'], v.
Calcium [kal'si-um], n.
Calculator [kal'kū-lā-tér], n.
Calculus [kal'kū-lus], n. Calculi [kal'kū-lī], pl.
Caldron [kal'dron], n.
Calendar [kal'en-dér], n. An almanac; a list. v. To register.
Calender [kal'en-dér], n. A hot press for cloth. v. To press in a calender.
Calescence [ka-les'ens], n.
Calf [käf], n. Calves [kävz], pl.
Caliber [kal'i-bér], n.
Calico [kal'i-kō], n. Calicoes, pl.
Calif [kā'lif], n.
Caligraphy [ka-lig'ra-fi], n.
Calisthenics [kal-is-then'iks], n.
Calk er [kak'ér], n.
Calla [kal'la], n.
Calliope [kal-lī'o-pe], n.
Callous [kal'lus], a.
Callus [kal'lus], n.
Calm ness [käm'nes], n.
Calomel [kal'o-mel], n.
Calophyllum [kal-ō-fil'um], n.
Caloric [ka-lor'ik], a. n.
Calorimeter [kal-o-rim'e-tér], n.
Calorimotor [ka-lor-i-mō'tér], n.
Calorist [kal'or-ist], n.
Calotte [ka-lot'], n.
Calumet [kal'ū-met], n.
Calumniator [ka-lum-ni-ā'tér], n.
Calumnious [ka-lum'ni-us], a.
Calumny [kal'um-ni], n.
Calve [käv], v.
Cal'vin ist [kal'vin-ist], n.
Calypso [ka-lip'sō], n.
Calyx [kā'liks], n. Calyxes, pl.
Cambric [kām'brik], n.
Camellia [ka-mel'i-a], n.
Cam'el opard [ka-mel'o-pärd], n.
Cameo [kam'e-ō], n.
Camera [kam'ér-a], n.
Campaign' er [kam-pān'ér], n.
Campanile [kam-pa-nē'lā], n. Campanili [kam-pa-nē'lē], pl.
Campanula [kam-pan'ū-la], n. [n. pl.
Campanulaceæ [kam-pan-ū-lā'sē-ē],
Camphine [kam'fen], n.
Camphor [kam'fér], n.

Camphoric [kam-for'ik], a.
Canaanite [kā'nan-īt], n.
Canaille [ka-nāl'], n.
Canal [ka-nal'], n.
Canard [ka-när'], n.
Can'cel lation [kan-sel-lā'shun]
Can'cer ous [kan'sér-us], a.
Candelabrum [kan-de-lā'brum Candelā'bra, pl.
Candescence [kan-des'ens], n.
Can'did ate [kan'di-dāt], n.
Can'dle mas [kan'dl-mas], n.
Candor [kan'dér], n.
Can'dy tuft [kan'di-tuft], n.
Canescent [ka-nes'ent], a.
Canine [ka-nīn'], a.
Canister [kan'is-tér], n.
Can'ker ous [kang'kér-us], a.
Cannibal [kan'ni-bal], a. n.
Can'non eer [kan-nun-ēr'], n.
Canoe [ka-nōō'], n.
Can'on icity [kan-on-is'i-ti], n
Canopus [ka-nō'pus], n.
Canorous [ka-nō'rus], a.
Cantaloupe [kan'ta-lōōp], n.
Cantankerous [kan-tang'kér-
Cantata [kan-tä'tä], n.
Canteen [kan-tēn'], n.
Cantharis [kan'tha-ris], n. Car des [kan-thar'i-dēz], pl.
Canticle [kan'ti-kl], n.
Canton [kan'ton], n.
Canvas [kan'vas], a. n. Cloth
Canvass [kan'vas], n. v. To ine; to solicit votes.
Canvasser [kan'vas-ér], n.
Canyon [kan'yon], n.
Canzone [kan-tsō'nā], n.
Caoutchouc [kōō'chōōk], n.
Capability [kā-pa-bil'i-ti], n.
Capable [kā'pa-bl], a.
Capacious [ka-pā'shus], a.
Capacity [ka-pas'i-ti], n.
Cap-a-pie [kap'a'pē'], ad.
Caparison [ka-par'i-son], n. v.
Capias [kā'pi-as], n.
Capillaire [ka-pil-lär'], n.
Capillary [kap'il-la-ri], a. n.
Capital [kap'i-tal], a. Chief upper part of a pillar; or city; a large letter.
Capitol [kap'i-tol], n. A p for the use of a leg
Capitoline [kap'i-tō
Capitulator [ka-pit
Capon [kā'pn], n. v

Capote [ka-pōt'], n.
Capriccio [ka-prē'chō], n.
Capriccioso [ka-prē-chē-ō'zō], a.
Caprice [ka-prēs'], n.
Capricious [ka-pri'shus], a.
Capsicine [kap'si-sin], n.
Capsize [kap-sīz'], n. v.
Capsule [kap'sūl], n.
Captain [kap'tin], n.
Captious [kap'shus], a.
Captivity [kap-tiv'i-ti], n.
Captor [kap'tėr], n.
Capture [kap'tūr, kapt'yōōr, kapt'-yėr], n. v.
Capuchin [kap-ū-shēn'], n.
Capybara [ka-pi-bā'ra], n.
Caracci [kär-rät'chē], n.
Caracole [kar'a-kōl], n. v.
Caramel [kar'a-mel], n.   [grains.
Carat [kar'at], n.   A weight of four
Caravan' sary [kar-a-van'sa-ri], n.
Carbine [kär'bin], n.
Car'bon aceous [kär-bo-nā'shus], a.
Carbuncle [kär'bungk-kl], n.
Car'buret ted [kär'bū-ret-ed], a.
Carcajou [kär'ka-jōō], n.
Carcass [kär'kas], n.   [a.
Carcino'ma tous [kär-si-nom'a-tus],
Cardamom [kär'da-mum], n.
Cardiac [kär'di-ak], a. n
Cardinal [kär'di-nal], a. n.
Career [ka-rēr'], n. v.
Care'ful ness [kār'fōōl-nes], n.
Caress [ka-res'], n. v.   thus [ˆ]
Caret [kā'ret], n.   A mark made
Caribbean [kar-ib-bē'an], a.
Cariboo, Caribou [kar'i-bōō], n.
Caricature [kar-i-ka-tūr'], n.
Caricous [kar'i-kus], a.
Caries [kā'ri-ēz], n.
Cariole [kar'i-ōl], n.
Carmine [kär'min], n.
Carnal [kär'nal], a.
Carnation [kär-nā'shun], n.
Carnivorous [kär-niv'ō-rus], a.
Carol [kar'ol], n. v.
Carotid [ka-rot'id], a. n.
Carousal [ka-row'zal], n.
Carouse [ka-rowz'], n. v.   [the wrist.
Carpal [kär'pal], a.   Pertaining to
Carpel [kär'pel], n.   Botanical term.
Carriage [kar'rij], n.
Carrier [kar'ri-ėr], n.
Carrion [kar'ri-on], a. n.
Carrot [kar'rot], n.   A vegetable.
Carte-blanche [kärt'blänsh'], n.

Carte-de-visite [kärt'de-vī'zēt'], n.
Carthaginian [kär-tha-jin'i-an], n.
Cartilage [kär'ti-läj], n.
Cartilaginous [kär-ti-laj'i-nus], a.
Cartouch [kär-tōōsh'], n.
Cartridge [kär'trij], n.
Caryatides [kar-i-at'i-dēz], n. pl.
Cascade [kas-kād'], n. v.
Case ment [kāz'ment], n.
Caseous [kā'sē-us], a.
Cashew [ka-shōō'], n.
Cash ier [kash-ēr'], n. v.
Cask et [kas'ket], n.
Cassia [kash'i-a], n.
Cassimere [kas'si-mėr], n.   [cards.
Cassino [kas-sē'nō], n.   A game of
Cassiopea [kas-si-ō-pē'a], n.
Cassock [kas'sok], n.
Cassowary [kas'sō-wa-ri], n.
Cast anet [kas'ta-net], n.
Caste [kast], n.   An order or class.
Caster [kas'tėr], n.   A cruet; a small wheel.
Castigator [kas'ti-ga-tėr], n.
Castle [kas'l], n. v.
Castor [kas'tėr], n.   The generic name of the beaver; a cruet.
Cas'ual ty [kazh'ū-al-ti], n.
Cas'uist ry [kaz'ū-ist-ri], n.
Cataclysm [kat'a-klizm], n.
Catacomb [kat'a-kōm], n.
Catafalque [kat'a-falk], n.
Cataleptic [kat-a-lep'tik], a.
Catalogue [kat'a-log], n. v.
Catalysis [ka-tal'i-sis], n.
Catamaran [kat-a-ma-ran'], n.
Catamount [kat'a-mount], n.
Cataract [kat'a-rakt], n.
Catarrh' al [ka-tär'al], n.
Catastrophe [ka-tas'trō-fe], n.
Catastrophic [ka-tas-trof'ik], a.
Catawba [ka-tȧ'ba], n.   [n.
Catch up, Catsup [kach'up, kat'sup],
Catechise [kat'ē-kīz], v.
Cat'echu men [kat-ē-kū'men], n.
Categorical [kat-ē-gor'ik-al], a. n.
Category [kat'ē-gor-i], n.
Ca'ter er [kā'tėr-ėr], n.
Caterpillar [kat'ėr-pil-lėr], n.
Caterwaul [kat'ėr-wȧl], v.
Cathartic [ka-thär'tik], a. n.
Cathedral [ka-thē'dral], a. n.
Catheter [kath'e-tėr], n.
Cath'olic ism [ka-thol'i-sizm], n.
Catholicity [kath-o-lis'i-ti], n.
Cattle [kat'l], n. pl.

tail.
to a
ink.
one.
ame-

Centenary [sen′te-na-ri], a. n.
Centennial [sen-ten′ni-al], a. n.
Center, Centre [sen′tėr], n. v.
Centimeter [sen-tim′e-tėr], n.
Cen′tral ize [sen′tral-īz], v.
Centrifugal [sen-trif′ū-gal], a.
Centripetal [sen-trip′e-tal], a.
Centurion [sen-tū′ri-on], n.
Century [sen′tū-ri], n.
Cephalic [sē-fal′ik], a. n.
Cephalous [sef′a-lus], a.
Ceraceous [sē-rā′shus], a.
Ceramic [se-ram′ik, ke-ram′ik], a
Cerate [sē′rāt], n.
Cerberus [sėr′bėr-us], n.
Cereal [sē′rē-al], a. n. A grain.
Cerebellum [ser-ē-bel′lum], n. Ce
bel′lā, pl.
Cerebral [ser′ē-bral], a. n.
Cerebrum [ser′ē-brum], n.
Cerement [sēr′ment], n.

also

Ceremonial [ser-ē-mō′ni-al], a. n.
Ceremonious [ser-ē-mō′ni-us], a.
Ceres [sē′rēz], n.
Cer′tain ty [sėr′tin-ti], n.
Certificate [sėr-tif′i-kāt], n. v.
Certiorari [sėr-shi-ō-rā′ri], n.
Certitude [sėr′ti-tūd], n.
Cerulean [sē-rōō′lē-an], a.

sur-

Cerumen [se-rōō′men], n.
Ceruminous [se-rōō′mi-nus], a.
Ceruse [sē′rōōs], n. v. [novel
Cervantes [sėr-van′tez]. Span
Cervical [sėr′vi-kal], a.
Cessation [ses-sā′shun], n.
Cessavit [ses-sā′vit], n.
Cession [sesh′un], n. A surrend
the act of ceding.

r a

Cessionary [sesh′un-a-ri], a.
Cesspool [ses′pōōl], n.
Cetacea [sē-tā′shē-a], n. pl.
Chafe r [chāf′ėr], n. One who chaf
a yellow beetle.

v.

Chaff er [chaf′ėr], n. v. To barga
to buy.
Chafing-dish [chāf′ing-dish], n.

ich

Chagrin [sha-grēn′, sha-grin′],
Chain [chān], n. v.

e of

Chair [châr], n. v.
Chaise [shāz], n.
Chalcedony [kal-sed′ō-ni],
Chalcography [kal-kog′ra
Chaldron [kal′drun], n.
Chalet [shā′lā′], n.
Chalice [chal′is], n.

.

Chalk y [chạk′i], a.

Challenge [chal'lenj], n. v.
Chalybeate [ka-lib'e-āt], a. n.
Cham'ber lain [chām'bér-lin], n.
Chameleon [ka-mē'lē-on], n.
Chamois [sham'mi, sha-moi'], n.
Chamomile [kam'ó-mil], n. [wine.
Champagne [sham-pān'], n. A light
Champaign [sham-pān'], a. n. A flat,
open country.
Champion [cham'pi-on], a. n. v.
Chan'cel lor [chan'sel-ér], n.
Chancery [chan'se-ri], n.
Chancrous [shangk'rus], a.
Chandelier [shan-de-lēr'], n.
Change able [chānj'a-bl], a.
Changeful [chānj'fool], a.
Channel [chan'nel], n. v.
Chan'son nette [shän-son-net'], n.
Chant [chänt], n. v.
Chanticleer [chan'ti-klēr], n.
Chaos [kā'os], n.
Chaotic [kā-ot'ik], a.
Chaparral [chap-ar-al'], n.
Chapeau [sha'pō'], n. Chapeaux
[sha'pōz'], pl.
Chapel [chap'el], n.
Chaperon [shap'ér-ōn], n. v.
Chaplain [chap'lin], n.
Chaplet [chap'let], n.
Chapter [chap'tér], n. [a. n.
Char'acter istic [kar-ak-tér-ist'ik],
Charade [sha-rād'], n.
Char coal [chär'kōl], n.
Charge able [chärj'a-bl], a. [n. pl.
Chargé d'affaires [shär'zhä'dat'fär'],
Chariness [chär'i-nes], n.
Char'iot eer [char-i-o-tér'], n.
Charitable [char'it-a-bl], a.
Charivari [shä'rē'vä'rē'], n.
Charlatan [shär'la-tan], n. [peror.
Charlemagne [shar-le-mān'] Em-
Charlotte-russe [shär'lot-roos], n.
Charm er [chärm'ér], n.
Charnel [chär'nel], n.
Charon [kā'ron], n. [ing wounds.
Charpie [shär'pē], n. Lint for dress-
Charter er [chär'tér-ér], n.
Chary [chā'ri], a.
Charybdis [ka-rib'dis], n.
Chase [chās], n. v.
Chasm [kazm], n.
Chasseur [shas'sér], n.
Chasteness [chāst'nes], n.
Chastisement [chas'tiz-ment], n.
Chastity [chas'ti-ti], n.
Chasuble [chaz'ū-bl], n.

Chateau [sha'tō'], n. Chateaux [sha
tōz'], pl.
Chatelaine [shat'e-lān], n.
Chattel [chat'tel], n.
Chat'ter er [chat'tér-ér], n.
Cheap en [chēp'n], v.
Cheat er [chēt'ér], n.
Check mate [chek'māt], n. v.
Cheek [chēk], n. v.
Cheep [chēp], n. v. To chirp.
Cheer ful [chēr'fool], a.
Cheerily [chēr'i-li], ad.
Cheese monger [chēz'mung-gér], n.
Chef [shef], n. [d'œuvre, pl.
Chef-d'œuvre [shā'dōö'vr'], n. Chefs-
Chemical [kem'ik-al], a. n.
Chemise [she-mēz'], n.
Chemisette [shem-i-zet'], n.
Chem'ist ry [kem'ist-ri], n.
Chenille [she-nēl'], n.
Cheops [kē'ops], n.
Cher'ish er [cher'ish-ér], n.
Chersonese [ker'sō-nēz], n.
Cherub [cher'ub], n.
Cherubic [che-roob'ik], a.
Cherubini [kā-roo-bē'nē], Italian
musical composer.
Chest nut [ches'nut], a. n.
Chevalier [shev-a-lēr'], n.
Chevet [she'vā'], n.
Cheviot [chev'i-ot, chē'vi-ot], a. n.
Chew [chōō], n. v.
Chiaroscuro, Chiaro-oscuro [ki-ä'rō-
skōō'rō, ki-ä'rō-os-kōō'rō], n.
Chibouk [chi-book'], n.
Chicanery [shi-kān'ér-i], n.
Chick en [chik'en], n.
Chicory [chik'o-ri], n.
Chief tain [chēf'tin], n.
Chiffonnier [shif-fon-ér'], n. A kind
of cabinet. See "List of Words
commonly mispronounced."
Chignon [shē'nyōn'], n.
Chilblain [chil'blān], n.
Child ish [child'ish], a.
Chill iness [chil'i-nes], n.
Chimera [ki-mē'ra], a.
Chimney [chim'ni], n.
Chimpanzee [chim-pan'zē], n.
Chinchilla [chin-chil'la], n.
Chinese [chi-nēz'], n. pl.
Chintz [chints], n.
Chlococca [ki-ō-kok'ka], n.
Chirographer [ki-rog'raf-ér], n.
Chiromancy [ki'ro-man-si], n.
Chiropodist [ki-rop'od-ist], n.

Claque ur [klăk′ĕr], n.
Clare-obscure [klăr′ob-skūr], n.
Claret [klar′et], n.
Clarify [klar′i-fī], v.
Clarinet [klar′i-net], n.
Clarion [klar′i-on], a. n.
Classic [klas′ik], a. n.
Classification [klas-i-fi-kā′shun], n.
Classifier [klas′i-fi-ĕr], n.
Clat′ter er [klat′ĕr-ĕr], n.
Clause [kląz], n.
Clavate [klā′vāt], a.
Clavichord [klav′i-kord], n.
Clavicle [klav′i-kl], n.
Clavier [klä′ve′ā′, klā′vi-ĕr], n.
Clay ey [klā′i], a.
Cliёan liness [klen′li-nes], n.
Clear ance [klĕr′aus], n.
Cleave [klĕv], v.
Clematis [klem′a-tis], n.
Clemency [klem′en-si], n.
Cleopatra [kle-o-pā′tra], n.
Clepsydra [klep′si-dra], n.
Cler′gy man [klĕr′ji-man], n.
Clerk [klĕrk], n.
Clev′er ness [klev′ĕr-nes], n.
Clew. Clue [klū], n. v.
Client [klī′ent], n.
Cliff [klif], n.
Climacteric [klī-mak-ter′ik, klī-mak′-ter-ik], a. n.
Climate [klī′māt], n.
Climb [klīm], v. To ascend.
Clime [klīm], n. Climate.
Clinch [klinsh], v.
Clin′ic al [klin′ik-al], a.
Clio [klī′ō], n.
Clique [klēk], n.
Cloak [klōk], n. v.
Cloister [klois′tĕr], n. v.
Close [klōz], n. v. The end. [klōs], a. n. An enclosed place; a passage.
Clothes [klō⁄hz], n. pl.
Clothier [klō⁄h′yĕr], n.
Cloud y [kloud′i], a.
Clough [kluf], n.
Clown ish [kloun′ish], a.
Clutch [kluch], n. v.
Clyster [klis′tĕr], n.
Coach [kōch], n.
Coadjutant [kō-ad′ju-tant], a. n.
Coadjutor [kō-ad-jūt′ĕr], n.
Coagulator [kō-ag′ō-lā-tĕr], n.
Coal [kōl], n.
Coalescence [kō-a-les′ens], n.
Coalition [kō-a-li′shun], n.

Coarse ness [kōrs′nes], n.
Coast er [kōst′ĕr], n.
Coax er [kōks′ĕr], n.
Cobalt [kō′bąlt], n.
Cobbler [kob′lĕr], n.
Cocaine [kō′ka-in], n.
Coccyx [kok′siks], n.
Cochineal [koch′i-nēl], n.
Cock atrice [kok′a-tris], n.
Cockle [kok′l], n.
Cockney [kok′ni], a. n.
Cockswain [kok′swān], n.
Cocoa-nut [kō′kō-nut], n.
Cocoon [kō-kōon′], n.
Codeine [kō-dē′in], n.
Codicil [kod′i-sil], n.
Codify [kod′i-fi], v.
Coercion [kō-ĕr′shun], n.
Cœur de Lion [kĕr′de′le′on′].
Coffee [kof′i], n.
Coffin [kof′in], n. v.
Cogency [kō′jen-si], n.
Cogitate [ko′ji-tāt], v.
Cognac [kōn′yak], n.
Cognizance [kog′ni-zans, kon′i-za
Cognomen [kog-nō′men], n.
Cohesion [kō-hē′zhun], n.
Cohort [kō′hort], n.
Coif fure [koif′fŭr], n.
Coin age [koin′āj], n.
Coincidence [kō-in′si-dens], n.
Coix [kō′iks], n.
Colander, Cullender [kul′an-dĕr],
Colchicum [kol′ki-kum], n.
Coleoptera [kol-ē-op′tĕr-a], n. pl.
Coleridge [kōl′rij]. English poet.
Col′ic ky [kol′ik-i], a. [r
Coligny [ko′lēn′ye′]. French ad
Coliseum, Colosseum [kol-i-sē′um],
Collaborator [kol-lab′ō-rā-tĕr], n.
Collapse [kol-laps′], n. v.
Collar [kol′ĕr], n. v.
Collateral [kol-lat′ĕr-al], a. n.
Collation [kol-lā′shun], n.
Colleague [kol′ēg], n.
Collect [kol′ekt], n. [kol-lekt′],
Collection [kol-lek′shun], n.
Collector [kol-lekt′ĕr], n.
College [kol′ej], n.
Collegiate [kol-lē′ji-āt], a.
Collenchyma [kol-en′ki-ma], n.
Col′lier y [kol′yĕr-i], n.
Collimator [kol-im′ā-tĕr], n.
Collision [kol-li′zhun], n.
Collodion [kol-lō′dion], n.
Colloquial [kol-lō′kwi-al], a.

Colloquy [kol'lŏ-kwi], n.
Collusion [kol-lū'zhun], n.
Colocynth [kol'ŏ-sinth], n.
Cologne [kŏ-lōn'], n.
Colonel [kẽr'nel], n.
Colonial [ko-lō'ni-al], a.
Colonnade [kol-on-nād'], n.
Color [kul'ẽr], n. v.
Colossal [ko-los'sal], a.
Colporter [kol'pŏr-tẽr], n.
Columbarium [kol-um-bā'ri-um], n.
   Columbaria, pl.
Columbine [kol'um-bīn], n.
Column [kol'um], n.
Comatose [kŏ'ma-tōs], a.
Comb [kōm], n. v.
Com'bat ant [kum'ba-tant, kom'ba-tant], a. n.
Com'bative ness [kum'ba-tiv-nes, kom'ba-tiv-nes], n.
Combination [kom-bi-nā'shun], n.
Combustible [kom-bust'i-bl], a. n.
Combustion [kom-bust'yun], n.
Comedian [ko-mē'di-an], n.
Comeliness [kum'li-nes], n.
Comely [kum'li], a. ad.
Comet [kom'et], n.
Comfit [kum'fit], n.
Com'fort er [kum'fẽrt-ẽr], n.
Com'ical ity [kom-ik-al'i-ti], n.
Comity [kom'i-ti], n
Command' ant [kom-man-dänt'], n.
Commander [kom-mànd'ẽr], n.
Commemoration [kom-mem-o-rā'-
   shun l, n. [n.
   *** [kom-mem'or-āt-ẽr],
     ··'ment l.

Communicant [kom-mū'ni-kant], n.
Communicator [kom-mū'ni-kā-tẽr],
Communion [kom-mūn'yun], n. [n.
Communist [kom'mūn-ist], n.
Commutator [kom'mū-tā-tẽr], n.
Compact [kom-pakt'], a. v. [kom'-
   pakt], n.
Companion [kom-pan'yun], n.
Company [kum'pa-ni], n.
Comparable [kom'pa-ra-bl], a.
Comparative [kom-par'a-tiv], a.
Compare [kom-pár'], v.
Comparison [kom-par'i-sun], n.
Compass [kum'pas], n. v. [a. v.
Compas'sion ate [kom-pa'shun-āt],
Compatible [kom-pat'i-bl], a.
Compatriot [kom-pā'tri-ot], a. n.
Compeer [kom-pēr'], n. v.
Compel' ler [kom-pel'ẽr], n.
Com'pend ious [kom-pen'di-us], a.
Compendium [kom-pen'di-um], n.
Compensator [kom'pen-sā-tẽr], n.
Competence, Competency [kom'pē-
   tens, kom'pē-ten-si], n.
Competitor [kom-pet'i-tẽr], n.
Compilation [kom-pi-lā'shun], n.
Complacence, Complacency [kom-
   plā'sens, kom-plā'sen-si], n.
Complain' er [kom-plān'ẽr], n.
Complaisance [kom-pla-zance', kom-
   pla-zance], n.
Completion [kom-plē'shun], n.
Com'plex ity [kom-pleks'i-ti], n.
Compliance [kom-pli'ans], n.
Complication [kom-pli-kā'shun], n.
Complicity [kom-plis'i-ti], n.
Com'pliment ary [kom-pli-men'ta-

lit [kom'pro-mit], v.
ller [kon-trōl'ēr], n.
don [kom-pul'shun], n.
ction [kom-pungk'shun], n.
ation [kom-pū-tā'shun], n.
ator [kom-pū-tā'tèr], n.
e [kom'rād, kum'rād], n.
ore [kon a-mō're], It.
' ment [kon-sēl'ment], n.
 [kon-sēl'], v.
[kon-sēt'], n. v.
able [kon-sēv'a-bl], a.
e [kon-sēv'], v.
rate [kon-sen'trāt], v.
rator [kon'sen-trā-tèr], n.
ion [kon-sep'shun], n.
[kon-sèrn'], n. v.
[kon'sèrt], n. [kon-sèrt'], v.
na [kon-sèr-tē'na], n.
 [kon-sèr'tō], n.
on [kon-se'shun], n.
ongk], n.
kong'ka], n.
l al [kong-koi'dal], a.
e [kon'sàr'], n.
or [kon-sil'i-ā-tèr], n.
kon-sis'], a.
[kon-klūd'], v.
n [kon-klū'zhun], n.
ion [kon-kok'shun], n.
ant [kon-kom'i-tant], a. n.
kong'kèrd], n. Town. [kon-
 Harmony.
nce [kon-kard'ans], n.
n [kon-krē'shun], n.
ige [kon-kū'bi-nāj], n.
 [kong'kū-bin], n.
ence [kon-kū'bi-sens], n
ence [kon-kur'ens], n.
n [kon-ku'shun], n. [n.
ation [kon-dem-nā'shun],
r [kon-dem'èr], n.
ion [kon-den-sā'shun], n.
[kon-dens'], v.
d [kon-dē-send'], v.
sion [kon-dē-sen'shun], n.
con-dīn'], a.
[kon'di-ment], n.
[kon-di'shun], n. v
 [kon-dōl'ens], n.
m'dèr], n.
[kon-dū'siv], a. [v.
 on'dukt], n. [kon-dukt'],
[kon-duk'tèr], n.
n'dit, kon'dit], n.
or [kon-fab'ū-lā-tèr], n.

Confec'tion er [kon-fek'shun-èr], n.
Confederacy [kon-fed'èr-a-si], n. [n.
Confederation [kon-fed-èr-ā'shun],
Confer' ee [kon-fèr-ē'], n.
Conference [kon'fèr-ens], n.
Confess' ion al [kon-fe'shun-al], a. n.
Confessor [kon-fes'èr], n.
Confidant [kon'fi-dant'], n.
Confidence [kon'fi-dens], n.
Confidential [kon-fi-den'shal], a.
Confine [kon'fīn], a. n. [kon-fīn'], v.
Confirm' ation [kon-fèrm-ā'shun], n.
Confiscator [kon'fis-kā-tèr], n.
Conflagration [kon-fla-grā'shun], n.
Confluence [kon'flū-ens], n.
Conform' er [kon-form'èr], n.
Conformity [kon-form'i-ti], n.
Confrere [kòn'frār], n.
Confusion [kon-fū'zhun], n.
Conge [kon'jē], n.
Congeal [kon-jēl'], v. [a.
Congenial [kon-jēn'yal, kon-jēn'i-al],
Congeniality [kon-jēn-yal'i-ti, kon-
 jēn-i-al'i-ti], n.
Congest' ion [kon-jest'yun], n. [v.
Conglomerate [kon-glom'èr-āt], a. n.
Congratulator [kon-grat'ū-lā-tèr], n.
Congrega'tion al ist [kong-grē-gā'-
 shun-al-ist], n.
Con'gress ional [kon-gre'shun-al], a.
Congruity [kon-grōō'i-ti], n.
Congruous [kong'grōō-us], a.
Con'ic al [kon'ik-al], a.
Conicity [kō-nis'i-ti], n.
Coniferæ [kō-nif'èr-ē], n. pl.
Coniferous [kō-nif'èr-us], a.
Conjecture [kon-jek'tūr, kon-jekt'-
 yoor, kon-jekt'yèr], n. v.
Conjure [kun'jèr], v. To bewitch.
 [kon-jūr'], v. To adjure.
Conjugal [kon'ju-gal], a.
Conjurer [kun'jèr-èr], n. A juggler.
Conjuror [kon-jū'rar], n. (Law.) One
 bound by oath with others.
Connect' ion, Connexion [kon-nek'-
 shun], n.
Connector [kon-nek'tèr], n.
Connivance [kon-nīv'ans], n. [n.
Connoisseur [kon'is'sūr', kon'is'sèr'],
Connubial [kon-nū'bi-al], a.
Conoid [kōn'oid], a. n.
Con'quer or [kong'kèr-èr], n.
Conquest [kong'kwest], n.
Consanguinity [kon-sang-gwin'i-ti],
Conscience [kon'shens], n.
Conscientious [kon-shi-en'shus], a.

Conscionable [kon'shun-a-bl], a.
Conscious [kon'shus], a.
Con'script ion [kon-skrip'shun], n.
Consecrator [kon'sĕ-krā-tĕr], n.
Consecutive [kon-sek'ŭ-tiv], a. n.
Consent' er [kon-sent'ĕr], n.
Consequence [kon'sĕ-kwens], n.
Consequential [kon-sĕ-kwen'shal], a.
Conservator [kon'sĕr-vā-tĕr], n.
Conservatory [kon-sĕrv'a-tor-i], n.
Consid'er ation [kon-sid-ĕr-ā'shun],
Consign' ee [kon-sin-ĕ'], n.   [n.
Consignor [kon-sin'ĕr], n.
Consist' ory [kon'sis-tor-i, kon-sis'-
   tor-i], n.
Consolable [kon-sōl'a-bl], a.
Consolatory [kon-sol'a-tor-i], a.
Console [kon'sōl], n. A projecting
   ornament. [kon-sōl'], v.
Consolidate [kon-sol'id-āt], a. v.
Consols [kon'solz], n. pl.
Consomme [kon'som'mā'], n.
Consonant [kon'sŏ-nant], a. n.
Consort [kon'sort], n. [kon-sort'], v.
Conspicuous [kon-spik'ŭ-us], a.
Conspiracy [kon-spir'a-si], n.
Conspirator [kon-spir'āt-ĕr], n.
Con'stable ry [kun'sta-bl-ri], n.
Constancy [kon'stan-si], n. [peror.
Constantine [kon'stan-tin]. The Em-
Constellation [kon-stel-lā'shun], n.
Consternation [kon-stĕr-nā'shun], n.
Constipation [kon-sti-pā'shun], n.
Constituency [kon-stit'ŭ-en-si], n.
Constitution [kon-sti-tū'shun], n.
Constrict' er [kon-strikt'ĕr], n.
Construct' ion [kon-struk'shun], n.
Construe [kon'strōō], v.
Consuetude [kon'swē-tūd], n.
Consul [kon'sul], n.
Consume' r [kon-sūm'ĕr], n.
Consummate [kon-sum'āt], a. v.
Consumption [kon-sum'shun], n.
Contagion [kon-tā'jun], n.
Contagious [kon-tā'jus], a.
Contain [kon-tān'], v.
Contaminate [kon-tam'in-āt], v.
Contemn' er [kon-tem'ĕr], n.   [n.
Contemplation [kon-tem-plā'shun].
Contemplative [kon-tem'plā-tiv], a.n.
Contemplator [kon-tem'plāt-ĕr], n.
Contemporaneity [kon-tem-pō-rā-
   nē'i-ti], n.
Contemporaneous [kon-tem-pō-rā'-
   nē-us], a.
Contempt' ible [kon-tem'ti-bl], a.

Contemptuous [kon-temt'ū-us], a.
Content' ion [kon-ten'shun], n.
Contentious [kon-ten'shus], a.   [pl.
Contents [kon-tents', kon'tents], n.
Contest [kon'test], n. [kon-test'], v.
Contiguity [kon-ti-gū'i-ti], n.
Contiguous [kon-tig'ū-us], a.
Continence, Continency [kon'ti-
   nens, kon'ti-nen-si], n.
Con'tinent al [kon-ti-nent'al], a. n.
Continual [kon-tin'ū-al], a.
Continuance [kon-tin'ū-ans], n.
Continuator [kon-tin'ū-āt-ĕr], n.
Continue [kon-tin'ū], v.
Continuity [kon-ti-nū'i-ti], n.
Continuous [kon-tin'ū-us], a.
Contor'tion ist [kon-tor'shun-ist], n.
Contour [kon-tōōr'], n. v.
Contraband [kon'tra-band], a. n. [v.
Contract [kon'trakt], n. [kon-trakt'],
Contractor [kon-trakt'ĕr], n.
Contradict' er [kon-tra-dikt'ĕr], n.
Contralto [kon-tral'tō], a. n.
Contrariety [kon-tra-ri'e-ti], n.   [v.
Contrast [kon'trast], n. [kon-trast'],
Contravene [kon-tra-vēn'], v.
Contributor [kon-trib'āt-ĕr], n.
Contrition [kon-tri'shun], n.
Contrivance [kon-triv'ans], n.
Control' lable [kon-trōl'a-bl], a.
Controller [kon-trōl'ĕr], n.
Con'trovert er [kon-trō-vĕrt'ĕr], n.
Contumacious [kon-tū-mā'shus], a.
Contumelious [kon-tū-mē'li-us], a.
Contumely [kon'tu-me-li, kon'tu-mē-
   li], n.
Contusion [kon-tū'zhun], n.
Conundrum [ko-nun'drum], n.
Convalescence [kon-va-les'ens], n.
Convene [kon-vēn'], v.
Convenience, Conveniency [kon-
   vēn'yens, kon-vēn'yen-si], n.
Con'vent icle [kon-ven'ti-kl]
Convention [kon-ven'shun].
Conventual [kon-ven'tū-al]
Conversant [kon'vĕrs-ant]
Conversa'tion al ist [kon-vĕrs-ā'-
   shun-al-ist], n.
Conversazione [kon-vĕr-sat-si-ō'-
   n. Conversazioni [kon-vĕr-sat-si-
   ō'nē], pl.
Converse [kon'vĕrs].
Conversely [kon-vĕrs'li]
Conversion [kon-vĕr'shun]
Convert [kon'vĕrt]
Converter [kon-vĕrt'ĕr]

vertible [kon-vèrt'i-bl], a.
a'vex ity [kon-veks'i-ti], n.
nveyance [kon-vā'ans], n.
nvey' er [kon-vā'èr], n.
nvict [kon'vikt], n. [kon-vikt'], v.
nviction [kon-vik'shun], n.
onvincible [kon-vins'i-bl], a.
onviv'ial ist [kon-vi'vi-al-ist], n.
onvocation [kon-vō-kā'shun], n.
onvolvulus [kon-volv'ū-lus], n.
onvoy [kon'voi], n. [kon-voi'], v.
onvulse [kon-vuls'], v.
Cony [kō'ni, kun'i], n.
Conyza [kō-ni'za], n.
Cook y [kook'i], n.
Cool ly [kōōl'li], ad.
Cooly [kōōl'i], n.
Coop er [kōōp'ér], n.
Copaiba [kō-pā'ba], n.
Copernican [kō-pér'ni-kan], a.
Copious [kō'pi-us], a.
Cop'per as [kop'pér-as], n.
Copse [kops], n. v.
Copula [kop'ū-la], n. Copulæ [kop'-ū-lē], pl.
Cop'y ist [ko'pi-ist], n.
Coquet [kō-ket'], v.
Coquetry [kō-ket'ri], n.
Coquette [kō-ket'], n.
Cor'al line [kor'al-in], a. n.
Corbeil [kor'bel], n.
Cord [kard], n. A string; a quantity of wood. v.
Cordial [kard'yal, kar'di-al], a. n.
Cordiality [kard-yal'i-ti, kar-di-al'i-ti], n.
Cordillera [kar-dil-lē'ra; Sp. pro. kar-dēl-yā'ra], n. A mountain range.
Corduroy [kar'dū-roi], n.
Coriaceous [kō-re-ā'shus], a.
Cormorant [kar'mō-rant], a. n.
Cornea [kar'nē-a], n.
Corneous [kar'nē-us], a.
Cornet [kar'net], n.
Cornice [kar'nis], n. [nucopiæ, pl.
Cornucopia [kar-nū-kō'pi-a], n. Cor-
Corolla [ko-rol'la], n.
Corollaceous [ko-rol-lā'shus], a.
Coronal [ko-rō'nal, kor'o-nal], a. n.
Coronation [ko-rō-nā'shun], n.
Coroner [ko'rō-nèr], n.
Coronet [ko'rō-net], n.
Corot [ko'rō] French painter.
Corporal [kar'po-ral], a. n.
Corporate [kar'po-rāt], a.
Corporeal [kar-pō'rē-al], a.

Corps [kōr], n. A body of troops.
Corps d'armée [kōr dar'mā'], Fr.
Corps diplomatique [kōr dē'plu'mā'těk'], Fr.
Corpse [karps], n. The dead body of a human being.
Corpulent [kar'pū-lent], a.
Corpuscle [kar'pus-l], n.
Corral [kor'ral], n. [kor-rāl'], v
Correct' or [kor-rekt'ér], n.
Correlation [kor-re-lā'shun], n.
Correlative [kor-rel'a-tiv], n. [n.
Correspondence [kor-re-spond'ens],
Corridor [kor'ri-dōr], n. [n.
Corroboration [kor-rob-ō-rā'shun],
Corrode [kor-rōd'], v.
Corrosion [kor-rō'zhun], n.
Corrugator [kor'rū-gāt-ér], n.
Corrupt' er [kor-rupt'ér], n.
Corruptible [kor-rupt'i-bl], n.
Corsair [kar'sàr], n.
Corset [kar'set], n.
Cortége [kar'tāzh'], n.
Cortical [kar'ti-al], a.
Coruscation [ko-rus-kā'shun], n.
Corvette [kar-vet'], n.
Corymb [kor'imb], n.
Coryza [ko-ri'za], n.
Cosey [kō'zi], a. n.
Cosmogonist [koz-mog'on-ist], n.
Cosmopolitan, Cosmopolite [koz-mo-pol'i-tan, koz-mop'o-lit], a. n.
Cost al [kost'al], a.
Cos'tive ness [kos'tiv-nes], n.
Costume [kos'tūm], n.
Cote [kōt], n. A cot.
Coterie [kō'tè'rē'], n.
Cotillon [ko-til'yun], n.
Cottage [kot'āj], n.
Cotton [kot'tn], a. n. v.
Cotyledon [kot-il-ē'don], n.
Couch ant [kouch'ant], a.
Couchée [kōō'shā'], n.
Cougar [kōō'gar], n.
Cough [kof], n. v.
Coulter [kōl'tèr], n.
Coun'cil lor [koun'sil-or], n. The member of a council.
Coun'sel lor [koun'sel-or], n. A person who gives counsel.
Countenance [koun'ten-ans], n.
Count'er feiter [koun'tèr-fit-èt], n.
Counterpane [koun'tèr-pān], n.
Coup d'état [kōō dā'tä'] Fr.
Coupé [kōō'pā'], n. A carriage
Couple [kup'pl], n. v.

Coupon [kōō'pon], n.
Cour'age ous [ku-rā'jus], a.
Courbet [kōōr'bā']. French painter.
Courier [kōō'ri-ėr], n. A messenger ; a traveling servant.
Course [kōrs], n. v.
Court [kōrt], n. v.
Courteous [kėr'te-us, kōrt'yus], a.
Courtesan [kėr-ti'zan], n.
Courtesy [kėrt'si], n. A depression of the body.
Courtier [kōrt'yėr], n.
Cousin [kuz'n], n.
Covenant [kuv'en-ant], n. v.
Cov'er let [kuv'ėr-let], n.
Cov'et ous [kuv'et-us], a.
Covey [kuv'e], n.
Cow'ard ice [kow'ėrd-is], n.
Cowl [kowl], n.
Coxcomb [koks'kōm], n.
Crab bed [krab'ed], a.
Crack le [krak'l], v.
Cradle [krā'dl], n. v.
Craft iness [kraf'ti-nes], n
Cranberry [kran'ber-ri], n.
Craniology [krā-ni-ol'o-ji], n.
Craunch [krånch], v.
Cream [krēm], n.
Crease [krēs], n. v.
Creation [kre-ā'shun], n.
Creator [krē-āt'ėr], n.
Creature [krē'tūr, krēt'yōōr, krēt'-yėr], n.
Credential [krē-den'shal], n.
Credibility [kred-i-bil'i-ti], n.
Credit [kred'it], n. v. [n. Fr.
Credit Mobilier [krā'dē'mō'bē'lyā'].
Creditor [kred'it-ėr], n.
Credulous [kred'ū-lus], a.
Creek [krēk], n. v.
Cremation [kre-mā'shun], n.
Crematorium [krem-a-tō'ri-um], n.
Crematory [krem'a-tō-ri], a.
Crenellate [kren'el-lāt], v.
Creole [krē'ōl], n.
Creosote [krē'ō-sōt], n.
Crescendo [kre-shen'dō], n.
Crescent [kres'ent], a. n.
Cretonne [kre-ton'], n.
Crevasse [kre-vas'], n.
Crevice [kre'vis], n. v.
Crew el [krōō'el], n. A kind of yarn.
Crib bage [krib'āj], n.
Crick'et er [krik'et-ėr], n.
Crimea [kri-mē'a], n.
Criminal [krim'in-al], a. n.

Crimson [krim'z
Crinite [krin'it],
Crinkle [kring'k
Cripple [krip'pl
Crisis [krī'sis], n
Criterion [krī-tē pl.
Crit'ic al [krī'ti
Criticise [krī'ti-s
Critique [krī-tēl
Croak er [krōk
Crochet [krō'shi
Crocodile [krō'k
Croquet [krō-kā
Croquette [krō-l meat ball.
Crosier [krō'zhē
Crotchet [kroch
Crouch [krouch
Croup ier [krōō
Crowd [kroud].
Crown [kroun].
Crucial [krōō'sh
Crucible [krōō's
Cruciferæ [krōō
Cru'cifix ion [k
Cruel [krōō'el],
Cruise [krōōz],
Crumble [krum
Crusade' r [krō
Crustacea [krus
Crustaceous [kr
Crutch [kruch].
Crypt [kript], n
Crys'tal line [k
Crystallize [kri-
Cubeb [kū'beb].
Cubit [kū'bit], n
Cuckold [kuk'ol
Cuckoo [kōō'kō
Cucumber [kū'k
Cudbear [kud'b
Cuddle [kud'dl].
Cudgel [kuj'el].
Cue [kū], n.
Cui'rass' ier [k
Cuisine [kwē'zē
Cul-de-sac [kōōl
Culinary [kū'lin
Culmination [ki
Cultivator [kul'
Culture [kul'tū yėr], n. v.
Cumbrous [kum
Cumulative [k
Cunning [kun'

Cu'pid ity [kū-pid'ĭ-ti], n.
Cupola [kū'po-la], n.
Curaçoa [kōō-ra-sō'], n.
Curassow [kū-ras'sō], n.
Curate [kū'rāt], n.
Curator [kū-rāt'ēr], n
Curdle [kérd'l], v.
Curfew [kér'fū], n.
Curiosity [kū-ri-os'ĭ-ti], n.
Curious [kū'ri-us], a.
Curlew [kér'lū], n.
Curmudgeon [kér-muj'on], n.
Currant [ku'rant], n. A fruit.
Currency [ku'ren-si], n.
Current [ku'rent], a. n. A stream.
Curricle [ku'ri-kl], n.
Curriculum [ku-rik'ū-lum], Curric-
ula, pl. [es leather.
Currier [ku'ri-ēr], n. One who dress-
Cursed [kérs'ed], a. [kérst], p.
Cursory [kér'so-ri], a.
Curtail' er [kér-tāl'ēr], n.
Curtain [kér'tin], n. v.
Curvature [kérv'a-tūr], n.

Cushion [kōōsh'un], n. v.
Custard [kus'térd], n.
Custodian [kus-tō'di-an], n.
Cus'tom er [kus'tum-ēr], n.
Cutaneous [kū-tā'nē-us], a.
Cuticle [kū'ti-kl], n.
Cutlery [kut'le-ri], n.
Cyanic [si-an'ik], a.
Cycle [si'kl], n. v.
Cyclamen [sik'la-men], n.
Cyclone [si'klōn], n.
Cyclopean [si-klō-pē'an], a.
Cygnet [sig'net], n. A young swan.
Cylinder [si'lin-dér], n.
Cylindric [si-lin'drik], a.
Cymbal [sim'bal], n.
Cynic [sin'ik], a. n. [n.
Cynosure [si'no-shōōr, sin'o-shōōr],
Cypress [si'pres], n.
Cyprian [si'pri-an], a. n.
Cyst [sist], n.
Czar ina [zä-rē'na], n.
Czarowitz [zär'ō-vits], n.
Czerny [cher'nē]. Musical composer.

D.

Dabble [dab'bl], v.
Dace [dās], n.
Dactyl [dak'til], n.
Dado [dā'do, dä'do], n.
Daffodil [daf'fō-dil], n.
Dagger [dag'ér], n.
Daguerreotype [da-ger'ō-tip], n. v.
Dahabieh [da-ha-bē'ä], n.
Dahlia [dä'li-a, dā'li-a], n.
Daily [dā'li], a. ad. n.
Daintily [dān'ti-li], ad.
Dairy [dā'ri], a. n.
Dais [dā'is], n.
Daisy [dā'zi], n.
Dalliance [dal'li-ans], n.
Dam'age able [dam'āj-a-bl], a.
Dam'ask een [dam'ask-ēn], v.
Damn able [dam'na-bl], a.
Damnation [dam-nā'shun], n.
Damsel [dam'zel], n.
Damson [dam'zn], n
Dance [dans], n. v.
Dandelion [dan'di-li-un], n.
Dandruff [dan'druf], n
Dan'ger ous [dān'jér-us], a.
Danish [dān'ish], a. n.
Daphne [daf'nē], n. A shrub.

Daphnia [daf'ni-a], n. The water flea.
Dark some [därk'sum], a.
Darwinian [där-win'i-an], a. n.
Dastard [das'térd], a. n v.
Dasypus [da'si-pus], n
Data [dā'ta], n. pl.
Daub er [dab'ér], n.
Daughter [da'tér], n.
Daunt less [dänt'les], a.
Dauphin [da'fin], n. mas.
Dauphine [da'fēn], n. fem.
Davit [dā'vit], n.
Dawdle [da'dl], n. v.
Dawn [dan], n. v.
Day break [dā'brāk], n
Dazzle [daz'zl], n. v.
Deacon ess [dē'kon-es], n.
Dead en [ded'n], v.
Deaf [def], a.
Deal er [dēl'ér], n.
Dean ery [dēn'é-ri], n.
Dear [dēr], a. ad. n. A darling.
Dearth [dérth], n.
Death [deth], n.
Debacle [dē-bä'kl], n.
Debark' ation [dē-bärk-ā'shun], n.
Debase' r [dē-bās'ér], n.

Debatable [dĕ-bāt'a-bl], a.
Debauchee [deb-o-shē'], n.
Debauch' er [de-bach'ér], n.
Debeige [de-bāzh'], n.
Debilitate [dĕ-bil'i-tāt], v.
Debonair [de-bo-nār'], a.
Debouch [de-bōōsh'], v.
Debris [dā'brē'], n.
Debt or [det'ér], n.
Début [dā'bū'], n. [The Fr. û has no
  equivalent in English. The sound
  is made by pronouncing ē with the
  teeth closed, and the lips curved as
  in giving the sound of o in move.]
Débutant [dā'bū'tän'], n. mas.
Débutante [dā'bū'tänt'], n. fem.
Decade [dek'ad], n.
Decadence [de-kā'dens], n.
Decagon [de'ka-gon], n.
Decalogue [de'ka-log], n.
Decant' er [dĕ-kant'ér], n.
Decease [dĕ-sēs'], n. v.
Deceit' ful [dĕ-sēt'fŏol], a.
Deceivable [dĕ-sēv'a-bl], a.
Deceive [dĕ-sēv'], v.
December [dĕ-sem'bér], n.
Decemvirate [dĕ-sem'vér-āt], n.
Decency [dē'sen-si], n.
Decennial [dĕ-sen'ni-al], a.
De'cent ly [dē'sent-li], ad.
Deception [dĕ-sep'shun], n.
Decide [dĕ-sīd'], v.
Deciduous [de-sid'ū-us], a.
Decimal [de'si-mal], a. n.
Decimator [de'si-māt-ér], n.
Decision [dĕ-sĭ'zhun], n.
Deci'sive ness [dĕ-sī'siv-nes], n.
Declaim' er [dĕ-klām'ér], n.
Declamation [de-kla-mā'shun], n.
Declaration [de-kla-rā'shun], n.
Declare [dĕ-klār'], v.
Declension [dĕ-klen'shun], n.
Declination [de-klin-ā'shun], n.
Declinator [de'klin-āt-ér], n.
Declivity [dĕ-kli'vi-ti], n.
Declivous, Declivitous [dĕ-kli'vus,
  dĕ-kli'vit-us], a.
Decoct' ion [dĕ-kok'shun], n.
Décolleté [dā'kol'le'tā'], a.
Decorative [dek'o-ra-tiv], a.
Decorator [de'ku-rāt-ér], n.
Decorous [de-kō'rus, dek'o-rus], a.
Decorum [de-kō'rum], n.
Decoy [de-koi'], n. v.
Decrease [de-krēs'], n. v.
Decree [de-krē'], n. v.

Decrement [dek're-ment], n.
Decrep'it ude [dĕ-krep'it-ūd]
Decrial [de-krī'al], n.
Decumbiture [de-kum'bi-tūr]
Dedecorous [de-dek'o-rus], a.
Dedication [de-di-kā'shun], n.
Ded'icator y [de'di-kāt-ér-ri]
Deducible [de-dūs'i-bl], a.
Deduct' ion [de-duk'shun], n.
Deep en [dēp'n], v.
Deer [dēr], n. sing. and pl.
Deface' ment [de-fās'ment], n
Defalcate [de-fal'kāt], v.
Defalcation [de-fal-kā'shun], s
Defalcator [de'fal-kāt-ér], n.
Defamation [de-fa-mā'shun], r
Defame' r [de-fām'ér], a.
Default' er [de-falt'ér], n.
Defeasance [de-fēz'ans], n.
Defeat [de-fēt'], n. v.
Defecate [de'fe-kāt], a. v.
Defecator [de'fē-kāt-ér], n.
Defection [de-fek'shun], n.
Defend' ant [de-fend'ant], a.
Defender [de-fend'ér], n.
Defensive [de-fens'iv], a. n.
Defer' ence [de'fér-ens], n.
Deferential [de-fér-en'shal], a
Defiance [de-fī'ans], n.
Deficiency [de-fī'shen-si], n.
Deficit [def'i-sit], n.
Defile [de-fīl'], n.
Definable [de-fīn'a-bl], a.
Definition [de-fi-ni'shun], n.
Deflagrator [de-fla-grā'tér], n
Deflect' or [de-flekt'ér], n.
Deflour' er [de-flour'ér], n.
Deform' ity [de-form'i-ti], n.
Defraud' er [de-frad'er], n.
Defunct [de-fungkt'], a.
Degeneracy [de-jen'ér-a-si]
Deglutition [deg-lu-tish'un],
Degradation [de-gra-dā'shun
Degree [de-grē'], n.
Dehiscence [de-his'ens], n.
Deification [dĕ-if-ik-ā'shun],
Deify [dē'i-fī], v.
Deign [dān], v.
Deity [dē'i-ti], n.
Deject' ion [de-jek'shun], n
Delaine [de-lān'], n.
Delaroche [de'lā'rosh']. Fren
Delectable [de-lekt'a-bl], a.
Delegate [de'lē-gāt], n. v.
Deleterious [del-e-tē'ri-us]
Delian [dē'li-an], a.

Deliberator [de-lib'é-rãt-ér], n.
Delicacy [de'li-ka-s], n.
Delicious [de-li'shus] a.
Delight' ful [de-lit'fool], a.
Delineator [de-lin'é-ãt-ér], n.
Delinquency [de-ling'kwen-s], n.
Deliquescence [de-li-kwes'ens], n.
Deliquium [de-li'kwi-um], n.
Delirious [de-lir'i-us], a.
Deliv'er er [de-liv'ér-ér], n.
Deltoid [del'toid], a. n.
Deluge [del'üj], n. v.
Delusion [de-lu'zhun], n.
Demagogism [dem'a-gog-izm], n.
Demagogue [dem'a-gog], n.
Demand' er [de-mãnd'ér], n.
Demarcation [dē-märk-ã'shun], n.
Demean' or [de-mēn'ér], n.
Dementia [de-men'shi-a], n.
Demesne, Demain [de-mēn', de-mãn'], n. [Oxford.
Demi [dē-mī'], n. A half fellow at
Demijohn [de'mi-jon], n.
Demise [de-miz'], n. v.
Demiurgic [de-mi-ér'jik], a.
Democracy [de-mok'ra-si], n.
Demoiselle [dä'mwä'zel'], n.
Demolition [dem-o-lish'un], n.
Dē'mon iacal [dem-ō-ni'ak-al], a.
Demonstrable [de-mon'stra-bl], a.
Demonstrate [de-mon'strãt], v.
Demure [de-mūr'], a.
Demurrage [de-mur'äj], n.
Demur' rer [de-mér'ér], n.
Denizen [de'ni-zen], n.
Denominator [de-nom'in-ãt-ér], n.
Dénouement [dã'nōō'mon'], n.
Denounce [de-nouns'], v.
Density [dens'i-ti], n.
Dental [den'tal], a. n.
Dentifrice [den'ti-fris], n.
Dentine [den'tin], n.
Den'tist ry [den'tist-ry], n.
Denudation [den-ö-dä'shun], n.
Denunciator [de-nun'shi-ãt-ér], n.
Deodorizer [de-ō'dér-iz-ér], n.
Depart' ure [de-pärt'ūr, de-pärt'-yér], n.
Depend' ence [de-pend'ens], n.
Depict' ure [de-pik'tūr, de-pikt'yōōr, de-pikt'yér], v.
Depilatory [de-pil'a-to-ri], n.
Depletion [de-plē'shun], n.
Deplorable [de-plör'a-bl], a.
Deponent [de-pōn'ent], n. [trustee.
Depos'it ary [de-poz'it-a-ri], n. A

Deposition [dep-o-z sh'un], n.
Depositor [de-poz'it-ér], n.
Depository [de-poz'it-o-ri], n. A place where anything is lodged for safe keeping.
Depot [de-pō', dē'pō], n.
Depravity [de-prav'i-ti], n.
Deprecator [de'prē-kãt-ér], n.
Depredator [de'prē-dãt-ér], n.
Depress' or [de-pres'ér], n.
Deprivation [dep-ri-vã'shun], n.
Depth [depth], n.
Deputation [de-pū-tã'shun], n.
Deraign' ment [de-rãn'ment], n. A law term.
Derail [de-rãl'], v.
Derange' ment [de-rãnj'ment], n. Disorder of the intellect.
Derelict [der'e-likt], a. n.
Derision [de-ri'zhun], n.
Derisive [de-ri'siv], a.
Derivable [de-riv'a-bl], a.
Derivative [de-riv'a-tiv], a. n.
Dernier [därn'yã'], a.
Derogation [de-rō-gã'shun], n.
Derogatory [de-rog'a-to-ri], a.
Derrick [de'rik], n. [opher.
Descartes [dä'kärt']. French philos-
Descend' ant [de-send'ant], n.
Descendent [de-send'ent], a.
Descendible [de-send'i-bl], a.
Descension [de-sen'shun], n.
Describable [de-skrib'a-bl], a.
Description [de-skrip'shun], n.
Desecrate [de'sē-krãt], v.
Desert [dez'ért], a. Waste. n. A wil-derness.
Desert [de-zért'], n. That which is deserved. v. To forsake.
Deserter [de-zért'ér], n.
Desiccate [de-sik'ãt], v.
Desideratum [de-sid-ér-ã'tum], n. Desiderata, pl.
Designator [de'sig-nã-tér], n.
Design' er [de-sin'ér], n.
Desirable [de-zir'a-bl], a. n.
Desirous [de-zir'us], a.
Desist [de-sist'], v.
Desolate [de'sō-lãt], a. v.
Despair' er [de-spãr'ér], n.
Despatch' er, Dispatcher [de-spach'-ér, dis-pach'er], n.
Desperado [des-pē-rä'dō], n.
Desperation [des-pē-rã'shun], n.
Despicable [des'pi-ka-bl], a.
Despite' ful [de-spīt'fool], a.

Despond' er [de-spond'ėr], n.
Des'pot ism [des'pot-izm], n.
Dessert [dez-zėrt'], n. A service of fruit, pastry, etc., at the close of a meal.
Destination [des-tin-ā'shun], n.
Destitution [des-ti-tū'shun], n.
Destroy' er [de-stroi'ėr], n.
Destruction [de-struk'shun], n.
Desuetude [des'we-tūd], n.
Desultory [des'ul-to-ri], a.
Detach' ment [de-tach'ment], n.
Detail' er [de-tāl'ėr], n.
Detain' er [de-tān'ėr], n.
Detect or [de-tekt'ėr], n.
Detention [de-ten'shun], n.
Deterge' nt [de-tėrj'ent], a. n.
Deteriorate [de-tē'ri-ō-rāt], v.
Determinable [de-tėr'min-a-bl], a.
Deter'mine r [de-tėr'min-ėr], n.
Detest' ation [de-test-ā'shun], n.
Detonator [de'tō-nāt-ėr], n.
Detonize [de'tō-nīz], v.
Détour [dā'tōōr], n.
Detract' or [de-trakt'ėr], n.
Detriment [det'ri-ment], n. v.
Detritus [de-trīt'us], n.
De trop [de'trō], Fr.
Deuce [dūs], n.
Devastate [de'vas-tāt, dev'as-tāt], v.
Devastation [de-vas-tā'shun], n.
Devel'op er [de-vel'up-ėr], n.
Deviation [dē-vi-ā'shun], n.
Device [de-vis'], n.
Dev'il ish [de'vil-ish], a.
Devious [dē'vi-us], a.
Devisee [de-vi-zē'], n.
Deviser [de-vīz'ėr], n. A contriver.
Devisor [de-vīz'ėr], n. **One who gives** by will.
Devoir [de-vwar'], n.
Devotee [de-vō-tē'], n.
Devotion [de-vō'shun], n.
Devour' er [de-vour'ėr], n.
Devout [de-vout'], a.
Dew y [dū'i], a.
Dexterous [deks'tėr-us], a.
Dextrine [deks'trin], n.
Dhow [dow], n.
Diabetes [dī-a-bē'tēz], n. sing. and pl.
Diablery [de-ab'bl-re], n.
Diabol'ic al [dī-a-bol'ik-al], a.
Diaconal [dī-ak'on-al], a.
Diacope [dī-a'ko-pē], n.
Diadem [dī'a-dem], n. v.
Diagnosis [dī-ag-nō'sis], n.

Diagonous [dī-ag'on-us],
Diagram [dī'a-gram], n.
Diagraph [dī'a-graf], n.
Di'al ect [dī'a-lekt], n.
Dialogue [dī'a-log], n.
Dialysis [dī-a'li-sis], n. I
Diameter [di-am'et-ėr], n
Diamond [dī'a-mund], a.
Diana [dī-an'a, dī-ā'na], i
Diapason [dī-a-pā'zon], n
Diaper [dī'a-pėr], n. v.
Diaphanous [dī-af'an-us]
Diaphoretic [dī-a-fo-ret'i
Diaphragm [dī'a-fram], i
Diaphysis [dī-af'i-sis], n.
Diarrhea [dī-a-rē'a], n.
Diarrhetic [dī-a-ret'ik], a
Diary [dī'a-ri], n.
Diastole [dī-as'tō-lē], n.
Diatribe [dī'a-trib], n.
Dice [dis], n. v.
Dichotomous [dī-kot'om-
Dicky [dik'i], n.
Diclinous [dik'li-nus], a.
Dictator [dik-tā'tėr], n.
Dictatorial [dik-ta-tō'ri-a
Dic'tion ar v [dik'shun-a
Dictyogen [dik'ti-o-jen],
Didactic [di-dak'tik], a. i
Didactyl [di-dak'til], a. n
Didymous [di'di-mus], a.
Lie [lī], v. To cease to l
Dieresis [dī-er'e-sis], n.
Di'et etics [di-et-et'iks],
Dif'fer ence [dif'fėr-ens]
Dif'ferent ia [dif-fėr-en's
Dif'ficult y [dif'fi-kul-ti],
Diffidence [dif'fi-dens], n.
Diffluence [dif'flōō-ens], i
Diffuse [dif-fūs'], a. [dif-
Diffuseness [dif-fūs'nes],
Diffusible [dif-fūz'i-bl], a
Diffusive [dif-fū'siv], a.
Digest [di'jest], n. [di]
Digestion [di-jest'yun], n.
Digitalis [di-jit-ā'lis], n
Dignitary [dig'ni-ta-ri]
Digress' ion [di-gre'sh
Dike [dīk], n. v.
Dilapidator [di-la'pi-
Dilation [di-lā'shun],
Dilatoriness [di'la-to
Dilemma [di-lem'ma
Dilettante [di-le-ta
tanti [di-le-tan'ī
Diligence [di'li-jei

ăle, add, beăr, ärm, ăsk, fặll ; mē, met, thêre, hėr ; pine.

..igence [dĕ'lĕ'zhäns'], n. A stage-
coach.

..ilution [di-lū'shun], n.

Dimension [di-men'shun], n.

Dimin'ish er [di-min'ish-ér], n.

Diminution [di-min-ū'shun], n.

Dimple [dim'pl], n. v.

Dimyaria [di-mi-ā'ri-a], n

Dinginess [din'ji-nes], n.

Dinner [din'nèr], n.

Diocesan [dī-os'e-san], a. n.

Diorama [dī-o-rā'ma], n   [n.

Diphtheria [dip-thē'ri-a, dif-thē'ri-a],

Diphtheritic [dip-thē-rit'ik], a.

Diphthong [dip'thong, dif'thong], n.

Diplo'ma cy [di-plŏ'ma-si], n.

Diplomate [dip'lŏ-mat], n.

Diplomatist [di-plŏ'ma-tist], n.

Dipper [dip'ér], n.

Dipsomania [dip-sŏ-mā'ni-a], n.

Dipyre [di-pīr'], n.

Dipyrenous [di-pī-rē'nus], a.

Direct' or [di-rekt'ér], n.

Directrix [di-rekt'riks], n. fem.

Dire ful [dīr'fōol], a.

Dirge [dérj], n.

Dirk [dérk], n.

Dirt iness [dèrt'i-nes], n.

Disaster [diz-as'ter], n.

Disburse' r [dis-bèrs'ér], n.

Discard [dis-kärd'], n. v.

Discern' er [diz-zèrn'ér], n.

Discernible [diz-zèrn'i-bl], a.

Disciple [dis-sī'pl], n. v.   [n.

Disciplinarian [dis-si-plin-ā'ri-an], a.

Discipline [dis'si-plin], n. v.

Disclosure [dis-klŏ'zhur], n.

Discom'fit ure [dis-kum'fit-ūr], n.

Disconsolate [dis-kon'sŏ-lāt], a.

Dis'cord ance [dis-kard'ans], n. [v.

Discount [dis'kount], n. [dis-kount'],

Discourage [dis-ku'rāj], v.

Discourse [dis-kōrs'], n. v.

Discoursive [dis-kōrs'iv], a.

Discov'er er [dis-kuv'ér-ér], n.

Discreet [dis-krēt'], a. Prudent.

Discrepance, Discrepancy [dis'kre-
pans, dis'kre-pan-si], n.   [tinct.

Discrete [dis'krēt], a. Separate; dis-

Discretion [dis-kre'shun], n.

Discriminator [dis-krim'in-āt-ér], n.

Discursion [dis-kér'shun], n.

Discuss' ion [dis-ku'shun], n.

Disdain' ful [diz-dān'fōol], a.

Disease [diz-ēz'], n. v.

Disgrace' ful [dis-grās'fōol], a.

Disguise [dis-gīz'], n. v.

Dishabille [dis-a-bil'], n.

Dishearten [dis-härt'n], v.

Dishevelled [di-shev'ld], a.

Dismal [diz'mal], a.

Dismiss' al [dis-mis'al], n.

Disparage [dis-pa'rāj], v.

Disparity [dis-pa'ri-ti], n.

Dispel' ler [dis-pel'ér], n.

Dispensable [dis-pens'a-bl], a.

Dispensary [dis-pens'a-ri], n.

Dispersion [dis-pér'shun], n.

Displace ment [dis-plās'ment], n.

Disposable [dis-pŏz'a-bl], a.

Disposition [dis-pŏ-zi'shun], n.

Disputable [dis'pu-ta-bl], a.

Disputant [dis'pu-tant], n.

Disquisition [dis-kwi-zi'shun], n.

Disraeli [diz-rā'el-e]. English states
man.

Disrupt' ion [dis-rup'shun], n.

Dissect' or [dis-sekt'ér], n.

Dissemble [dis-sem'bl], v.

Disseminator [dis-se'min-āt-ér], n.

Dissension [dis-sen'shun], n.

Dissent' er [dis-sent'ér], n.

Dissidence [dis'si-dens], n.

Dissipation [dis-si-pā'shun], n.

Dissociate [dis-sŏ'she-āt], v.

Dissolute [dis'sŏ-lūt], a.

Dissolve [diz-zolv'], v.

Dissonance [dis'sŏ-nans], n.

Dissuade [dis-swād'], v.

Dissyllabic [dis-sil-lab'ik], a.

Distaff [dis'taf], n.

Distance [dis'tans], n. v.

Distich [dis'tik], n.

Distil' lation [dis-til-ā'shun], n.

Distinct' ion [dis-tingk'shun], n.

Distinguish [dis-ting'gwish], v.

Distort' ion [dis-tor'shun], n

Distract' er [dis-trakt'ér], n.

Distractible [dis-trakt'i-bl], a.

Distrait [dis'trā'], a. Absent-minded

Distraught [dis-trat'], a. Distracted.

Distress' ful [dis-tres'fōol], a.

Distribute [dis-tri'būt], v.

Distribution [dis-tri-bū'shun], n.

District [dis'trikt], n. v.

Disturb' ance [dis-tèrb'ans], n.

Disturber [dis-tèrb'ér], n.

Ditch er [dich'ér], n.

Dithyrambic [di-thi-ramb'ik], a.

Ditto [dit'ō], ad. n.

Diurnal [di-èrn'al], a. n.

Divan [di-van'], n.

wōol s ūse, us ; û, Fr. ; g, get ; j, jar ; h, Fr. ton : ch, chain ; ch, then ; th.

3

Dost [dust], v. trom *do.*
Dotage [dōt′āj], n.
Double [du′bl], a. ad. n. v.   [Fr.
Double-entendre [dōō′bl′oñ′toñ′dr′].
n. **Doubt ful** [dout′fōōl], a.
Douceur [dōō′sēr], n.
Douche [dōōsh]. n.
Doucine [dōō-sēn′]. n.
Dough [dō], n.
Doughty [dow′ti], a.
Douse [dous], v.
Dove-cot [duv′kot], n.
Dowager [dow′a-jēr], n.
Dow′dy ish [dow′di-ish], a.
Down [down], ad. n. prep. v.
Doxology [doks-ol′o-ji], n.
Dozen [du′zn], a.
Doziness [dōz′i-nes], n.
Drab ble [drab′bl], v.
Drag gle [drag′gl], v.
Dragoman [dra′gō-man], n.
Dragoon [dra-gōōn′], n.
Drain able [drān′a-bl], a.
Drama [drä′ma, drä′ma,] n.
Dramatis personæ [dra′ma-tis pēr-
sō′nē], n. pl.

ı [drungk'en-nes], n.	Dupe [dūp], n. v.
, n.	Duplicature [dū'pli-kā-tūr], n.
, n.	Duplicity [dū-p'si-ti], n.
'al-izm], n. The divid-	Durability [dūr-a-bil'i-ti], n.
	Durable [dūr'a-bl], a.
l'e-ti], n.	Duramen [dū-rā'men], n.
i-us], a.	Durance [dūr'ans], n.
'bit-a-bl], a.	Duration [dūr-ā'shun], n.
, a.	Duress [dūr'es], n.
], n.	Dusk iness [dusk'i-nes], n.
'es], n.	Duteous [dū'tē-us], a.
'til], a.	Dutiable [dū'ti-a-bl], a.
un], a. n.	Dutiful [dū'ti-fōd], a.
'el-ist], n. One who	Duumvir [dū-um'vĕr], n.
le combat.	Dwarf ish [dwarf'ish], a.
ı'na], n.	Dwindle [dwin'dl], n. v.
	Dye ing [dī'ing], p. To color.
ul-ka-mā'ra], n.	Dying [dī'ing], a. n. Death.
t], a.	Dynamics [di-nam'iks], n.
-si-a'na], n.	Dynamite [dī'nam-īt], n. [Web. alone
'si-mèr], n.	gives di'nam-īt.]
'ĕrd], a. n.	Dynamo [din'a-mō, dī'na-mō], n.
d.	Dynasty [din'as-ti, dī'nas-ti], n.
i']. French novelist.	Dysentery [dis'en-te-ri], n.
a. n.	Dyspepsy, Dyspepsia [dis'pep
um-found'], v.	dis-pep'si-a], n.
ınp'ish], a.	Dyspeptic [dis-pep'tik], a.
('jun], n. v.	Dysthymic [dis-thim'ik], a.
ʂon-gē'yä], n.	Dysury [dis'ū-ri], n.
10-ō-de'si-mal], a. n.	Dzeren [zē'ren], n.

E.

'on.	Ecarte [ā'kār'tā'], n.
a.	Ecbole [ek'bō-lē], n.
	Eccentric [ek-sen'trik], a.
'dum], n.	Eccentricity [ek-sen-tris'i-ti], n
i-nes], n.	Eccle'siast ic [ek-klē-zi-as'tik] a. n.
ı. ad.	Ecdysis [ek'di-sis], n.
-st], a. n.	Echeneis [ek-e-nē'is], n.
[ĕrth'quäk], n	Echo [e'kō], n. v.
əol], a.	Echometer [e-kom'et-ér], n.
	Eclaircissement [ā'klār'sis'män'], n.
], ad.	Eclat [ā'klā'], n.
r], n.	Eclectic [ek-lek'tik] a. n.
-bl], a. n.	Eclecticism [ek-lek'ti-sizm], n
ıe [ō de kō'lōn'], n.	Eclipse [e-klips'], n. v.
de vĕ], n.	Ecliptic [e-klip'tik], n.
ı. pl.	Eclogue [ek'log], n.
[thor.	Economical [ek-ō-nom'i-kal, ō-kon-
'bers] German au-	om'ik-al], a.
'on-iz], v.	Economy [e-kon'o-mi], n.
'e-ti], n.	Ecstasy [ek'sta-si], n.
ml'yent], a.	Ecstatic [ek-stat'ik], a.
ul-li'shun], n.	

ú, Fr. ; g, get ; j, jar ; n. Fr. ton ; ch, chain ; th, then ; th,

-di'shun], n.
l'it-or], n.
[ed-i-tō'ri-al], a. n.
ı [ed-ū-kā'shun], n.
[ed'ū-kāt-ér], n.
[e-dūs'i-bl], a.
n [e-duk'shun], n.
tor [e-duk'ʌō-rāt-ér], n.
A contraction for *Ever*.
i], a. Serving to inspire fear.
[ér'i-nes], n.
ble [ef-fās'a-bl], a
r [ef-fekt'ér], n
cy [ef-fem'in-a-ṣi], n.
ence [ef-fèr-ves'ens], n.
ible [ef-fèr-ves'i-bl], a.
f-fēt'], a.
us [ef-fi-kā'shus], a.
[ef'fi-ka-si], n.
y [ef-fi'shen-si], n.
[ef-fij'i-ēz], n.
f'fi-ji], n.   [pl.
m [ef-flū'vi-um], n. **Effluvia,**
ef'fōrt], n.
ıry [ef-frun'te-ri], n.
ıce [ef-fulj'ens], n.
ı [ef-fū'zhun], n.
ı [ef-fū'siv], a.
ē-jē'an], ı. n.
___ A flood : a flower.

Eleampane [   ]
Elect' ion [e-lek'shun], n.
Elector [e-lekt'ér], n.
Elec'tric al [ē-lek'trik-al], a.
Electrician [ē-lek-tri'shan], n.
Electricity [ē-lek-tris'i-ti], n.
Electrizer [e-lek'triz-ér], n.
Electrode [e-lek'trōd], n.
Electrolysis [ē-lek-trol'i-sis], n.
Eleemosynary [el-ē-mos'i-na-ri], a
Elegance [el'e-gans], n.
Elegiac [el-e-jī'ak, el-ē'ji-ak], a. n
El'ement al [el-e-ment'al], a.
El'ephant ine [el-e-fant'in],
Elevator [el-e-vāt'ér], n.
Eleventh [e-lev'nth], a. n.
Elf ish [elf'ish], a.
Elgin [el'gin], a. n.
Ella, Essays of [ē'li-a].
Eligibility [el-i-ji-bil'i-ti], n.
Eligible [el'i-ji-bl], a.
Eliminate [e-lim'in-āt], v.
Eliquation [e-li-kwā'shun], n.
Elision [e-lizh'un], n.
Élite [ā'lēt'], n.
Elixir [e-liks'ér], n.
Elizabethan [e-liz'a-beth-an], a.
Elk [elk], n. The moose-deer.
Elke [elk], n. A bird ; a kind of
Ellagic [el-laj'ik], a. Noting an

n [e-mā-shi-ā'shun], n.	**Encore** [äṅ'kōr'], ad. v.
n [em-a-nā'shun], n.	**Encounter** [en-koun'tèr], n. v.
tor [e-man'si-pāt-ér], n.	**Encroach' er** [en-krōch'èr], n.
tor [e-mas'kū-lāt-ér], n.	**Encumbrance** [en-kum'brans], n.
er [em-bäm'ér], n.	**Encyclopedia** [en-si-klo-pē'di-a], n.
a [em-ba'ras], v.	**Encyclopedic** [en-si-klo-pēd'ik], a.
[em'bas-si], n.	**Encyclopedist** [en-si-klo-pēd'ist], n.
h er [em-bel'lish-ér], n.	**Encysted** [en-sist'ed], a. p.
[em-bez'zl], v.	**Endeav'or er** [en-dev'èr-ér], n.
n er [em-blā'zn-ér], n.	**Endless** [end'les], a.
t'ic al [em-blem-at'ik-al], a.	**Endocyst** [en'dō-sist], n.
ticize [em-blem-at'i-siz], v.	**Endorhiza** [en-do-rī'zä], n.
r [em-bo'di-ér], n.	**Endorse** [en-dors'], n. v.
int [äṅ'boṅ'pwän'], n.	**Endow' er** [en-dow'ér], n.
ure [äṅ'bōō'shōōr'], n.	**Endurable** [en-dūr'a-bl], a.
[em-brās'], n. v.	**Enema** [en'ē-ma], n.
ire [em-brā'zhūr], n.	**Enemy** [en'e-mi], n.
io [em-brō'lyō], n.	**Energetic** [en-ér-jet'ik], a.
der er [em-broi'dér-ér], n.	**Energize** [en'ér-jiz], v.
[em'bri-ō], n.	**Enervate** [e-nérv'āt], a. v.
ator [e'mend-āt-ér], n.	**Enervation** [e-nérv-ā'shun], n.
l [e'me-rald], a. n.	**En famille** [äṅ fā'mēl'], Fr.
ace, Emergency [e-mèr'jens,	**Enfeoff** [en-fef'], v.
'en-si], n.	**En'gine er** [en-jin-ér'], n. v.
us [e-mer'it-us], a. n.	**Enginery** [en'jin-ri], n.
on [e-mèr'shun], n. The act of	**English** [ing'glish], a. n.
ring; opposed to *Immersion.*	**Engross' er** [en-grōs'ér], n.
on [e-mik'shun], n.	**Enhance** [en-hans'], v.
nt [em'i-grant], a. n.	**Enigma** [e-nig'ma], n.
ice [em'in-ens], n.	**Enigmat'ic al** [e-nig-mat'ik-al], a.
l'mir], n.	**Ennui** [äṅ'nwē'], n.
ry [em'is-sa-ri], a. n.	**Enormity** [e-nor'mi-ti], n.
on [e-mit'shun], n.	**Enormous** [e-nor'mus], a.
nt [e-mol'yent], a. n.	**Enough** [e-nuf'], a. ad. inter. n.
ment [e-mol'ū-ment], n.	**Enrich' er** [en-rich'ér], n.
on [e-mō'shun], n. v.	**Enroll' er** [en-rōl'ér], n.
i [em-pāl'], v.	**Enrolment** [en-rōl'ment], n.
or [em'pér-ér], n.	**En route** [äṅ rōōt'].
sis [em'fa-sis], n.	**Ensconce** [en-skons'], v.
size [em'fa-siz], v.	**Ensemble** [äṅ'säm'bl'], ad. n.
ysis [em'fü-sis], n.	**En'sign cy** [en'sin-si], n.
c [em-pi'rik], a. n.	**Ensilage** [en'sil-āj], n.
cism [em-pir'ri-sizm], n.	**Entablature** [en-tab'la-tūr], n.
yee [em-ploi'ē], n.	**Entail' er** [en-tāl'ér], n.
ium [em-pō'ri-um], n.	**En'ter prise** [en'tér-priz], n.
ss [em'pres], n	**Entertain' er** [en-tér-tān'ér], n.
ness [en'ti-nes], n.	**Enthrall** [en-thral'], v.
ma [em-pi-ē'ma], n.	**Enthralment** [en-thral'ment], n.
ean [em-pi-rē'an], n.	**Enthrone' ment** [en-thrōn'ment], n
tor [em'ū-lāt-ér], n.	**Enthusiasm** [en-thū'zi-azm], n.
us [em'ū-lus], a.	**Enthymeme** [en'thi-mēm], n.
on [e-mul'shun], n.	**Entice' ment** [en-tis'ment], n.
or [en-akt'ér], n.	**Entire' ty** [en-tir'ti], n.
l ler [en-am'el-ér], n.	**Entomologist** [en-to-mol'o-jist], n.
r [en-am'ér], v.	**Entozoon** [en-to-zō'on], n. **Ento**
e [äṅ'sänt'], a. n.	[en-to-zō'a], pl.

Entrails [en'trālz], n. pl.
Entrance [en'trans], n. [en-trans'],v.
Entrancement [en-trans'ment], n.
Entreat' y [en-trēt'i], n.
Entrée [än'trā'], n.
Entremets [än'tre'mā'], n.
Entresol [än'tre'sol'], n.
Entrochite [en'trok-īt], n.
Enucleate [e-nū'klī-āt], v.
Enumerator [e-nū'mer-āt-ēr], n.
Enunciator [e-nun'shi-āt-ēr], n.
Envelop [en-vel'up], v.
Envelope [en've-lōp, än've-lōp], n.
Enviable [en'vi-a-bl], a.
Envious [en'vi-us], a.
Environ [en-vī'ron], v.
Envoy [en'voi], n.
Eocene [ē'ō-sēn], a. n.
Eolian [e-o'li-an], a.
Epaulet [ep'a-let], n.
Epergne [e-pērn'], n.
Ephemeral [e-fe'me-ral], a. n.
Epicene [ep'i-sēn], a.
Ep'icure an [ep-i-kū-rē'an], a. n.
Epidemic [e-pi-dem'ik], a. n.
Epidermis [e-pi-dērm'is], n. [n.
Ep'igram matist [e-pi-gram'mat-ist],
Epigraph [e'pi-graf], n.
Epilepsy [e'pi-lep-si], n.
Epileptic [e-pi-lep'tik], a. n.
Epilogue [e'pi-log], n.
Epiphany [e-pif'a-ni], n.
Epiphragm [e'pi-fram], n.
Epiphyte [e'pi-fīt], n.
Episcopalian [e-pis-ko-pā'li-an], a. n.
Episode [e'pi-sōd], n.
Epistle [e-pis'l], n.
Epistolary [e-pis'to-la-ri], a.
Epitaph [e'pi-taf], n. v.
Epithelium [e-pi-thē'li-um], n.
Epithet [e'pi-thet], n.
Epitome [e-pit'o-mi], n.
Epitomize [e-pit'o-mīz], v.
Epizootic [ep-i-zō-ot'ik], a.
Epizooty [e-pi-zō'o-ti], n.
Epoch [ep'ok], n.
Epode [ep'ōd], n.
Equability [ē-kwa-bil'i-ti], n.
Equable [ē'kwa-bl], a.
E'qual ity [ē-kwol'i-ti], n.
Equalize [ē'kwal-īz], v.
Equanimity [ē-kwa-nim'i-ti], n.
Equation [e-kwā'shun], n.
Equator [e-kwā'tēr], n.
Equatorial [ē-kwa-tō'ri-al], a. n.
Equerry [e'kwe-ri], n.

Equestrian [e-kwes'tri-an], a. n.
Equilibrium [ē-kwi-li'bri-um], n.
Equinoctial [ē-kwi-nok'shal], a. n.
Equinox [ē'kwi-noks], n.
Equip' age [e'kwi-pāj], n.
Equipoise [ē'kwi-poiz], n.
Equitable [e'kwit-a-bl], a.
Equity [e'kwi-ti], n.
Equivalent [e-kwiv'a-lent], a. n.
Equivocal [e-kwiv'ō-kal], a.
Equivocator [e-kwiv'ō-kāt-ēr], n.
Equus [ē'kwus], n.
Eradicate [e-rad'i-kāt], v.
Erasable [e-rās'a-bl], a.
Erasure [e-rā'zhūr], n.
Ere [âr], ad. prep.
Erebus [e're-bus], n.
Erect' er [e-rekt'ēr], n.
Erectile [e-rekt'il], a.
Ermine [ēr'min], n.
Err [ēr], v.
Errand [er'rand], n.
Er'rant ry [er'rant-ri], n.
Erratic [er-rat'ik], a.
Errhine [er'rin], a. n.
Erroneous [er-rō'nē-us], a.
Error [er'rēr], n. v.
Erudite [er'ōō-dīt], a.
Erudition [er-ōō-di'shun], n.
Erupt' ion [e-rup'shun], n.
Erysipelas [e-ri-si'pe-las], n.
Escalade [es-ka-lād'], n. v.
Escallop [es-kol'lop], n.
Escapade [es-ka-pād'], n.
Escape' ment [es-kāp'ment], n.
Eschalot [esh-a-lot'], n.
Eschew [es-chōō'], v.
Escort [es'kort], n. [es-kort'],
Escritoire [es-kri-twar'], n.
Esculapius [es-kū-lā'pi-us], n.
Esculine [es'kūl-in], n.
Escutcheon [es-kuch'un], n.
Esoter'ic al [es-o-ter'ik-al], a
Espalier [es-pal'yēr], n. v.
Espe'cial ly [es-pe'shal-li], ?
Espial [es-pī'al], n.
Espionage [es'pi-on-āj], n.
Esplanade [es-plan-ād'], *
Espousal [es-powz'al], a
Espouse' ment [es-pov
Esprit [es'prē'], n.
Esprit de corps [es'p
Espy [es-pī'], v.
Esquimau [es'k
[es'ki-mōz], pl.
Esquire [es-kwi

Esquisse [es-kēs'], n.
Essay [es'sā], n. [es-sā'], v.
Essayer [es-sā'ér], n.
Essence [es'sens], n. v.
Essen'tial ly [es-sen'shal-li], ad.
Estab'lish er [es-tab'lish-ér], n.
Esteem' able [es-tēm'a-bl], a.
Esthetics [es-thet'iks], n.
Estimable [es'tim-a-bl], a. n.
Estimator [es'tim-āt-ér], n.
Estivation [es-tiv-ā'shun], n.
Estrange' ment [es-trānj'ment], n.
Estuary [est'ū-a-ri], a. n.
Etagère [ā'tä'zhär], n.
Eter'nal ly [e-tér'nal-li], ad.
Eternity [e-tér'ni-ti], n.
Ether [ē'thér], n.
Ethereal [e-thē'ri-al], a.
Ethiopian [ē-thi-ōp'i-an], a.
Ethnicism [eth'ni-sizm], n.
Etiquette [et'i-ket], n.
Etui [ā'twē'], n.
Etymology [et-i-mol'o-ji], n.
Eucharist [ū'ka-rist], n.
Euchre [ū'kér], n. A game of cards.
Eukairite [ū-kā'rit], n.
Eulogize [ū'lo-jīz], v.
Eunuch [ū'nuk], n. v.
Eupatorium [ū-pa-tō'ri-um],
Euphemism [ū'fem-izm], n.
Euphon'ic al [ū-fon'ik-al], a.
Euphonious [ū-fō'ni-us], a.
Euphonon [ū'fo-non], n.
Euphuism [ū'fu-izm], n.
European [ū-rō-pē'an], n.
Eustachian [ū-stā'ki-an], a.
Euterpe [ū-tér'pe], n.
Euthanasia [ū-than-ā'zi-a], n.
Euxanthine [ūks-anth'in], n.
Evacuator [e-vak'ū-āt-ér], n.
Evanescence [e-van-es'sens], n.
Evangel [e-van'jel], n.
Evangelical [ē-van-jel'ik-al], a.
Evangelist [e-van'jel-ist], n.
Evangelize [e-van'jel-iz], v.
Evaporate [e-vap'ér-āt], v.
Eva'sive ly [e-vā'siv-li], ad.
Evening [ē'vn-ing], a. n.
Event' ful [e-vent'fool], a.
Eventual [e-vent'ū-al], a.
Every [ev'ér-i], a.
Evict' ion [e-vik'shun], n.
Evidence [ev'i-dens], n.
Evil [ē'vl], a. ad. n.
Evince' ment [e-vins'ment], n.
Evincible [e-vins'i-bl], a.

Evolution [ev-o-lū'shun], n. v.
Ewe [ū], n.
Exaction [egz-ak'shun], n.
Exact' or [egz-akt'ér], n.
Exaggerator [egz-aj'ér-āt-ér], n.
Exalt' ation [egz-al-tā'shun], n.
Exalter [egz-alt'ér], n.
Exam'ine r [egz-am'in-ér], n.
Example [egz-am'pl], n.
Exas'perate r [egz-as'pér-āt-ér], n.
Excavator [eks'ka-vāt-ér], n.
Excel' lence [ek'sel-lens], n.
Excelsior [ek-sel'si-or], a. n.
Except' ion [ek-sep'shun], n.
Exceptor [ek-sept'ér], n.
Excess' ive [ek-ses'iv], a.
Exchequer [eks-chek'ér], n. v.
Excise [ek-sīz'], n. v.
Excitator [ek-si-tāt'ér], n.
Exclaim [eks-klām'], v.
Exclamation [eks-kla-mā'shun], n.
Exclusion [eks-klū'zhun], n.
Excoriate [eks-kō'ri-āt], v.
Excrement [eks'kre-ment], n.
Excrescence [eks-kres'ens], n.
Excretive [eks'kre-tiv], a.
Excruciate [eks-krōō'shi-āt], v.
Excur'sion ist [eks-kér'shun-ist], n.
Excusable [eks-kūz'a-bl], a.
Excusatory [eks-kūz'a-o-ri], a.
Execrable [ek'se-kra-bl], a.
Executant [egz-ek'ū-tant], n.
Execu'tion er [ek-se-kū'shun-ér], n.
Executive [egz-ek'ūt-iv], a. n.
Executor [egz-ek'ūt-ér], n.
Exegesis [eks-e-jē'sis], n.
Exeget'ic al [eks-e-jet'ik-al], a.
Exem'plar ily [egz'em-pla-ri-li], ad.
Exemplary [egz'em-pla-ri], a.
Exemplifier [egz-em'pli-fi-ér], n.
Exempt' ion [egz-em'shun], n.
Exercise [eks'ér-siz], n. v.
Exergue [egz-érg'], n.
Exert' ion [egz-ér'shun], n.
Exhalation [egz-ha-lā'shun], n.
Exhaust' er [egz-hast'ér], n.
Exhaustible [egz-hast'i-bl], a.
Exhib'it er [egz-hib'it-ér], n.
Exhilarate [egz-hil'a-rāt], v.
Exhortation [eks-hor-tā'shun], n.
Exhort' er [egz-hort'ér], n.
Exhume [egz-hūm'], v.
Exigency [eks'i-jen-si], n.
Exile [eks'il], n. [eks'il, egz-īl'], n. v.
Exist' ence [egz-ist'ens], n.
Exit [eks'it], n.

Exogamous [eks-og'a-mus], a.
Exogenous [eks-oj'en-us], a.
Exonerator [egz-on'ér-āt-ér], n.
Exorable [eks'o-ra-bl], a.
Exorbitance [egz-or'bit-ans], n.
Exorcise [eks'or-sīz], v.
Exordium [egz-or'di-um], n.
Expansible [eks-pans'i-bl], a.
Expatiator [eks-pā'shi-āt-ér], n.
Expatriate [eks-pā'tri-āt], v.
Expect' orate [eks-pek'to-rāt], v.
Expedient [eks-pē'di-ent], a. n.
Expedite [eks'pe-dīt], a. v.
Expeditious [eks-pe-di'shus], a.
Expel' ler [eks-pel'ér], n.
Expend' iture [eks-pend'i-tūr], n.
Experiment'al ly [eks-pe-ri-ment'-al-li], ad. [n.
Expe'riment er [eks-pe'ri-ment-ér].
Expert [eks-pért'], a. n.
Expiator [eks'pi-āt-ér], n.
Expirant [eks-pīr'ant], n.
Explain' er [eks-plān'ér], n.
Explanation [eks-pla-nā'shun], n.
Expletive [eks'ple-tiv], n.
Explicable [eks'pli-ka-bl], a.
Explicit [eks-plis'it], a.
Exploit [eks-ploit'], n.
Explosion [eks-plō'zhun], n.
Explosive [eks-plō'siv], n.
Exponent [eks-pō'nent], n.
Export [eks'pōrt], n. [eks-pōrt'], v.
Exporter [eks-pōrt'ér], n.
Exposé [eks'po'zā'], n.
Expose [eks-pōz'], v.
Exposition [eks-po-zi'shun], n.
Expositor [eks-poz'it-ér], n.

Expostulator [eks-post'ū-lāt-ér], n.
Express' er [eks-pres'ér], n.
Expugn' er [eks-pūn'ér], n.
Expurgator [eks-pér'gāt-ér], n.
Exquisite [eks'kwi-zit], a. n.
Extant [eks'tant], a.
Extemporaneous [eks-tem-po-rā'nē-us], a.
Extempore [eks-tem'po-re], a. ad.
Extemporize [eks-tem'po-rīz], v.
Extend' er [eks-tend'ér], n.
Extendible [eks-tend'i-bl], a.
Extensor [eks-rens'ér], n.
Extenuator [eks-ten'ū-āt-ér], n.
Exterminator [eks-tér'min-āt-ér], n.
Extern'al ly [eks-tèrn'al-li], ad.
Extinct' ion [ek-stingk'shun], n. [n.
Extin'guish er [ek-sting'gwish-ér].
Extirpate [eks-tér'pāt], v.
Extirpator [eks-tér'pa-tér], n.
Extol' ler [eks-tol'ér], n.
Extort' ion er [eks-tor'shun-ér], n.
Extra [eks'trä], a. n.
Extract' or [eks-trakt'ér], n.
Extraneous [eks-trā'ne-us], a. [ad. n.
Extraordinary [eks-trar'de-na-re], a.
Extravagance [eks-trav'a-gans], n.
Extremity [eks-trem'i-ti], n.
Exuberance [egz-ū'bér-ans], n.
Exude [egz-ūd'], v.
Exult' ant [egz-ult'ant], a.
Exultation [egz-ul-tā'shun], n.
Eye [ī], n. v. The organ of vision.
Eyre [ār], n. A circuit; the novel "Jane Eyre."
Eyry [ār'i, ā'ri, ē'ri], n. The place where birds of prey build their nests.

F.

miliarity [fa-mil-ye-ar-i-ti], n.
mine [fa'min], n.
mous [fam'us], a.
nat'ic ism [fa-nat'i-sizm], n
nciful [fan'si-fool], a.
ne [fan], n. A temple.
neuil [fan'el] American merchant.
Founder of Faneuil Hall, Boston.
nfare [fan'far], n.
ntasia [fan-ta'ze-a], n.
ntasy [fan'ta-si], n.
ntoocini [fan-to-che'ne], n pl.
rcical [fars'ik-al], a.
re [far], n. The price of passage;
food; condition.   v. To go; to be
in any state; to happen.
rewell [far'wel], n.
arina [fa-ri'na], n.
arinaceous [fa-rin-a'shus], a.
aro [far'o], n.
arrago [fa-ra'go], n.
arrier [fa'ri-er], n. v.
arrow [fa'ro], a. n. v.   [a. ad. v.
arther, Further [far'ther, fer'ther].
asces [fas'sez], n. pl.
ascialis [fash-i-a'lis], n.
ascicle [fas'si-kl], n.
ascinate [fas'sin-at], v.
ascine [fas-sen'], n.
ashionable [fa'shun-a-bl], a. n.

February [feb'roo-a-ri], n
Fec'und ate [fe'kund-at].
Feeble [fe'bl]
Feel er [fel'
Feign er [
Feint [fant
Felicitous   a.
Felon [fel'on], n.
Felonious [fe-lo'ni-us], a.
Felspar [fel'spar], n.
Felucca [fe-luk'a], n.
Femineity [fem-i-ne'i-ti],
Feminine [fem'i-nin], a.
Femininity [fem-i-nin'i-ti
   Femineity.
Femoral [fem'o-ral], a.
Femur [fe'mer], n.
Fenian [fe'ni-an], n.
Fennel [fen'nel], n.
Feoff [fef], n. v.
Ferment [fer'ment], n. [
Ferocious [fe-ro'shus], a
Ferret [fe'ret], n. v.
Ferrotype [fe'ro-tip], n.
Ferruginous [fe-roo'jin-
Ferrule [fe'rool], n. A r
Fertility [fer-til'i-ti], n.
Fertilizer [fer'til-iz-er],
Ferule [fer'ril], v. n.   A
Fervency [fer'ven-si], n.

Fibril lous [fi-bril'us], a.
Fibrine [fi'brin], n.
Fibroin [fib'ro-in], n.
Fibrolite [fib'rō-līt], n.
Fibrous [fī'brus], a.
Fibula [fib'u-la], n. **Fibula, pl.**
Fictile [fik'til], a.
Fiction [fik'shun], n.
Fictitious [fik-ti'shus], a.
Fidelity [fi-del'i-ti], n.
Fidget y [fij'et-i], a.
Fiduciary [fi-dū'shi-a-ri], a.
Field [fēld], n.
Fiend ish [fēnd'ish], a.
Fierce ly [fērs'li], ad.
Fieriness [fī'ē-ri-nes], n.
Fifteenth [fif'tēnth], a. n.
Fiftieth [fif'ti-eth], a. n.
Fight er [fīt'ēr], n.
Figurative [fig'ūr-āt-iv], a.
Figure [fig'ūr, fig'yēr], n. v.
Filament [fil'a-ment], n.
Filet de bœuf [fē'lā'de'bef'], Fr.
Fil'ial ly [fil'yal-li], ad.
Filibuster [fil'i-bus-tēr], n. v.
Filigree [fil'i-grē], a. n.
Fillet [fil'let], n. v.
Fillipeen [fil'li-pēn], n. **Same as Phi-**
lopena.
Film iness [film'i-nes], n.
Filoselle [fē'lō'zāl'], n. [Fr.]
Filth iness [filth'i-nes], n.
Finale [fē-nā'lā], n.
Fi'nal ity [fi-nal'i-ti], n.
Finance [fi-nans'], n. v.
Financial [fi-nan'shal], a.
Financier [fi-nan-sēr'], n. v.
Finesse [fi-nes'], n. v.
Fin'ical ly [fin'ik-al-li], ad.
Fin'ish er [fin'ish-ēr], n.
Finite [fī'nit], a.
Fiord [fē-ard'], n.
Fiorite [fī'o-rīt], n.
Firm ament [fērm'a-ment], n.
First [fērst], a.
Fissile [fis'sil], a.
Fissure [fi'shūr, fish'yēr], n. v.
Fistula [fis'tū-la], n.
Fitful [fit'fŭl], a.
Fixture [fiks'tūr, fikst'yōōr, fikst'-
yēr], n.
Flac'cid ity [flak'sid-i-ti], n.
Flagellate [fla'jel-lāt], a. v.
Flageolet [fla'jel-et], n.
Flagitious [fla-ji'shus], a.
Flagrancy [flā'gran-si], n.

Fla'grant ly [flā'grant-li], a.
Flail [flāl], n.
Flaire [dār], n. A fish.
Flambeau [flam'bō], n. **Flambeaux,**
Flambeaus, pl.
Flamboyant [flam-boi'ant], a.
Flamingo [fla-ming'gō], n.
Flannel [flan'nel], n.
Flat ten [flat'n], v.
Flatulency [flat'ū-len-si], n.
Flaunt [flänt], n. v.
Flautist [flat'ist], n.
Flavor [flā'vēr], n. v.
Flea [flē], n. An insect.
Flee [flē], v. To hasten.
Fleecy [flēs'i], a.
Fleet [flēt], a. n. v.
Fleur-de-lis [flēr'de'lē'], n.
Flew [flū], v.
Flexible [fleks'i-bl], a.
Flexion [flek'shun], n.
Flexuous [fleks'ū-us], a.
Flight [flīt], n.
Flimsily [flim'zi-li], ad.
Flippancy [flip'an-si], n.
Flirt atious [flērt-ā'shus], a.
Flitch [flich], n.
Float [flōt], n. v.
Floccose [flok-ōs'], a.
Floe [flō], n. A mass of ice.
Floor [flōr], n. v.
Florentine [flo'ren-tīn, flo'ren-tin], a. [n.
Florescence [flo-res'sens], n.
Floriculture [flō'ri-kult-ūr], n.
Flor'id ity [flor'id-i-ti], n.
Florin [flor'in], n.
Florist [flō'rist], n.
Flotilla [flō-til'la], n.
Flounce [flouns], n. v.
Flounder [floun'dēr], n. v.
Flour [flour], n. v. Meal.
Flour'ish er [flur'ish-ēr], n.
Flout er [flout'ēr], n.
Flower [flow'ēr], n. v. A blossom.
Flown [flōn], p. p.
Fluctuate [fluk'tū-āt], v.
Flue [flū], n. A passage for a chim-
ney; soft down or fur.
Fluellite [flū'el-līt], n.
Fluency [flū'en-si], n.
Flu'id ize [flū'id-īz], v.
Flummery [flum'mē-ri], n.
Flunk'y ism [flung'ki-izm], n.
Fluorine [flū'or-in], n.
Flute [flūt], n.
Foam y [fōm'i], a.

Po'cal ize [fō'kal-iz], v.
Focile [fō'sil], n.
Fog giness [fog'i-nes], n.
Foible [fōi'bl], n.
Foil [foil], n. v.
Foist [foist], v.
Follaceous [fō-li-ā'shus], a.
Foliage [fō'li-āj], n. v.
Folio [fō'li-ō], a. n.
Foliole [fō'li-ōl], n.
Folk [fōk], n.
Follicle [fol'li-kl], n.
Follicu ar [fol-lik'ū-lēr], a.
Fol'low er [fol'lō-ēr], n.
Foment' er [fō-ment'ēr], n.
Fomes [fō'mēz], n. Fomites [fō'mi-tēz], pl.
Fond le [fon'dl], v.
Font anel [font'a-nel], n.
Fool ery [fōōl'é-ri], n.
Fop pish [fop'ish], a.
Forage [for'āj], n. v.
Foray [for'ā], n.
Forbade [for-bad'], v.
Forbear [for-bār'], v.
Force ful [förs'fōōl], a.
Forceps [för'seps], n.
Forcible [förs'i-bl], a.
Ford able [förd'a-bl], a.
Fore bode [för-bōd'], v.
Forecastle [för'käs-sl], n.
Foreclosure [för-klō'zhur], n.
Forefather [för'fä-ᵗʰēr], n.
Forego [för-gō'], v.
Forehead [for'ed], n.
For'eign er [for'in-ēr], n.
Foren'sic al [fo-ren'sik-al], a.
For'est er [for'est-ēr], n.
For'feit ure [for'fit-ūr], n.
Forge [förj], n. v.
Forgery [för'jé-ri], n.
Forget' ful [for-get'fōōl], a.
For'mal ity [for-mal'i-ti], n.
Formidable [for'mi-da-bl], a.
Fornicator [for'ni-kāt-ēr], n.
Forsooth [for-sōōth'], ad. v.
Forswear [for-swār'], v.
Fortieth [för'ti-eth], a. n.
Fortifier [for'ti-fi-ēr], n.
Fortitude [för'ti-tūd], n.
Fortitudinous [for-ti-tūd'in-us], a.
Fortnight [fort'nit], n.
Fortress [fort'res], n. v.
Fortuitous [for-tū'it-us], a.
For'tunate ly [fort'ū-nāt-li], ad.
Fortune [for'tūn, fort'yōōn], n.

Fos'sil ize [fos'sil-iz], v.
Foul ly [fowl'li], ad.
Found ation [foun-dā'shun], n.
Foundry [found'ri], n.
Fount ain [fount'in], n.
Fourchette [fōōr-shet'], n.
Fourierism [fōō'ri-ēr-izm], n.
Fourneau [fōōr'nō'], n.
Four teenth [för'tenth], a. n.
Fourth ly [förth'li], ad.
Fowl [fowl], n. A bird. v. To hunt.
Fox y [foks'i], a.
Pracas [frā'kas], n.
Frac'tion al [frak'shun-al], a.
Fractious [frak'shus], a.
Fracture [frak'tūr, frakt'yōōr, frakt'yēr], n.
Fragile [fraj'il], a.
Fragility [fra-jil'i-ti], n.
Frag'ment ary [frag'ment-a-ri], a.
Fragrance [frā'grans], n.
Frail ty [frāl'ti], n.
Fraise [frāz], n. A military term.
Franc [frangk], n. A coin.
Fran'chise ment [fran'chiz-ment], n.
Franciscan [fran-sis'kan], a. n.
Francolin [frang'kol-in], n.
Frangible [fran'ji-bl], a.
Frangipane [fran-ji-pā'ni], n.
Frank incense [frangk'in-sens], n.
Frater'nal ly [fra-tēr'nal-li], ad.
Fraternity [fra-tēr'ni-ti], n.
Fraternize [fra'tēr-niz, fra-tēr'niz], v.
Fratricide [frat'ri-sid], n.
Fraud ulent [frad'ū-lent], a.
Fraught [frat], a.
Freak [frēk], n. v.
Freckle [frek'l], n. v.
Free dom [frē'dum], n. [geal.
Freeze [frēz], n. A frost. v. To con.
Freight age [frāt'āj], n.
Frenzy [fren'zi], n. v.
Frequency [frē'kwen-si], n. [v.
Frequent [frē'kwent], a. [frē-kwent'],
Frequenter [frē-kwent'ēr], n.
Fresco [fres'kō], n. v.
Friable [fri'a-bl], a.
Friar [fri'ēr], n.
Fricassee [fri-kas-sē'], n. v.
Fric'tion al [frik'shun-al], a.
Friend liness [frend'li-nes], n.
Frieze [frēz], n. A coarse cloth; the part of an entablature between the architrave and the cornice. v. To curl.
Frigate [fri'gāt], n.

], n.

itorian.

[a.
 tə'shus].

], n.

a.
n. v.

Fulness [fŏŏl'nes], n.
Fulsome [ful'sum], a.
Fumigate [fūm'i-gāt], v.
Fumitory [fū'mi-to-ri], n.
Punc'tion al [fungk'shun-al], a. n.
Fundamental [fun-da-ment'al], a. n.
Funeral [fū'nér-al], a. n.
Funereal [fū-nē'rē-al], a
Fungous [fung'gus], a.
Fungus [fun'gus], n. Fungi [fun'ji], [pl.
Funicle [fū'ni-kl], n.
Funiculus [fu-nik'ū-lus], n.
Funnel [fun'nel], n.
Funnily [fun'i-li], ad.
Furbelow [fèr'be-lō], n. v.
Fur'bish er [fèr'bish-ėr], n
Furioso [fū-ri-ō'zō], It.
Furious [fū'ri-us], a.
Furlough [fèr'lō], n. v.
Furnace [fèr'nas], n.
Fur'nish er [fèr'nish-ėr], n.
Furniture [fèr'ni-tūr], n.
Fur'ther ance [fèr'thèr-ans], n.
Fur'tive ly [fèr'tiv-li], ad.
Furze [fèrz], n.
Fusee [fū-zē'], n.
Fusible [fūz'i-bl], a.
Fu'sil eer [fū-zil-ēr'], n.
Fusillade [fū'zil-ād], n. v.
Fusion [fū'zhun], n.
Fuss iness [fus'i-nes], n
Fustian [fust'yan], a. n.
Futile [fū'til], a.
Futility [fū-til'i-ti], n.
Future [fū'tūr, fū'yŏŏr, fūt'yèr], a
Futurity [fu-tūr'i-ti], n.
Fuzz y [fuz'i], a.
Fyke [fīk], n.

], n.

a.
n. v.

G.

ɪ'], n.

{the Celts.
Pertaining to

ɪr of walking.

], n.
•

a. n.

Gallant [gal'lant], a. [gal-lant'],
Gallantry [gal'lant-ri], n.
Galleon [gal'le-un], n.
Gallery [gal'lè-ri], n.
Galley [gal'li], n.
Gallic [gal'lik], a. Pertaining t
 Gauls. [gal'lik], a. Noting an
Gallicism [gal'i-sizm], n.
Gallon [gal'lun], n.
Galloon [gal-lōōn'], n.
Gal'lop er [gal'lup-ėr], n.
Gallows [gal'lus], n. Gallov
Galoche [ga-losh'], n.

Galop [gă'lo'], n. A dance.
Galsome [gal'sum], a.
Gal'vanist [gal'van-ist], n.
Gambler [gam'blėr], n.
Gamboge [gam-bōō'], n.
Gambrel [gam'brel], n. v.
Game ster [găm'stėr], n.
Gamin [ga'man'], n.
Gamut [gam'ut], n.
Ganglion [gang'gli-on], n.
Gangrene [gang'grēn], n.
Gangrenous [gang'gre-nus], a.
Gaol er [jāl'ėr], n.
Gape [găp, gäp], n. v.
Garb age [gärb'āj], n.
Gar'den er [gär'dn-ėr], n.
Gargle [gär'gl], n. v.
Gargoyle [gär'goil], n.   [triot.
Garibaldi [gä-re-bäl'dē]. Italian pa-
Garish [gar'ish], a.
Garniture [gär'ni-tūr], n.
Garrison [ga'ri-sn], n. v.
Garrote [ga-rōt'], n. v.
Garrulity [ga-rōō'li-ti], n.
Garrulous [ga'rōō-lus], a.   [birds.
Garrulus [ga'rōō-lus], n. A genus of
Gas [gas], n.
Gaseous [gaz'e-us], a.
Gasometer [gaz-om'et-ėr], n.
Gastronomy [gas-tron'o-mi], n.
Gath'er er [gath'ėr-ėr], n.
Gauche rie [gōsh'rē'], n.
Gaud ily [gad'i-li], ad.
Gauge [gāj], n. v.
Gaunt let [gänt'let], n.
Gautier, Théophile [gō'tyā',tā'ō'fēl'].
  French littérateur and critic.
Gauze [gaz], n.
Gavel [gav'el], n.
Gavotte [ga-vot'], n.
Gawk y [gak'ĭ], a. n.
Gayety [gā'e-ti], n.
Gayly [gā'li], ad.
Gazelle [ga-zel'], n.
Gazette' er [ga-zet-tėr'], n.
Gear [gēr], n. v.
Gee [jē], v.
Gehenna [ge-hen'na], n.
Geikie [gē'ke]. British clergyman.
Gelatigenous [jel-a-tij'in-us], a.
Gelsemium [jel-sē'mi-um], n.
Gemini [jem'i-nī], n. pl.
Gemsbok [jemz'bok], n.
Gendarme [zhän'därm'], n.
Genealogical [jen-e-a-loj'ik-al], a.

Genealogy [jen-e-al'o-ji], n.
Gen'eral ize [jen'er-al-iz], v.
Generator [jen'ėr-āt-ėr], n.
Generic [je-ne'rik], a.
Generosity [jen-ėr-os'i-ti], n.
Generous [jen'ėr-us], a.
Genesis [jen'e-sis], n.
Genet [jen'et], n.
Ge'nial ity [jē-ni-al'i-ti], n.
Genital [jen'it-al], a.
Genitive [jen'it-iv], a. n.
Genitor [jen'it-ėr], n.   [es, pl.
Genius [jēn'yus], n. Talent. Genius-
Genius [jē'ni-us], n. A spirit. Genii
  [jē'ni-ī], pl.
Genoa [jen'o-á], n.
Genre [zhän'r'], n.
Genteel [jen-tēl'], a.
Gentian [jen'shan], n.
Gentile [jen'til], a. n.
Gentility [jen-til'i-ti], n.   [men, pl.
Gen'tle man [jen'tl-man], n. Gentle-
Genuflection [jē-nu-flek'shun], n.
Genuine [jen'ū-in], a.
Genus [jē'nus], n. Genera, pl.
Geographer [jē-og'ra-fėr], n.
Geologize [jē-ol'o-jiz], v.
Geometry [jē-om'e-tri], n.
Georgic [jor'jik], a. n.
Geranium [je-rā'ni-um], n.
Germane [jėr-mān'], a. Closely akin.
Germinal [jėrm'in-al], a.
Ger'und ive [je-rund'iv], n.
Gesticulate [jes-tik'ū-lāt], v.
Gesticulator [jes-tik'ū-lāt-ėr], n.
Gesture [jes'tūr, jest'yōōr, jest'yėr],
  n. v.
Gewgaw [gū'ga], a. n.
Geyser [gī'zėr], n.
Ghainorik [gä'nō-rik], n.
Ghastly [gast'li], a. ad.
Gherkin [gėr'kin], n.
Ghibelline [gib'el-in], n.
Ghost [gōst], n.
Ghoul [gōōl], n.
Gi'ant ess [jī'ant-es], n.
Giaour [jowr], n.
Gib'ber ish [gib'bėr-ish], a. n.
Gibbet [jib'bet], n. v.
Gibbous [gib'us], a.
Gibe [jib], n. v.
Giblets [jib'lets], n. pl.
Giddily [gid'i-li], ad.
Gigantean [ji-gan-tē'an], a.
Gigantic [ji-gan'tik], a.
Giggle [gig'l], n. v.

wōōl; ūse, us, ū, Fr.; g, get; j, jar; ñ, Fr. ton; ch, chain; th, then; th

Girl ish [...], a.
Girth [gẽrth], n.
Gist [jist], n.
Gizzard [giz'ẽrd], n.
Glacial [glā'shi-al], a.
Glacier [glas'i-ẽr], n. **Gladioli**
Gladiator [glad-i-āt-ẽr], n.
Gladiolus [glad-i'o-lus], n.
[glad-i'o-li], pl.
Glair [glār], n. The white of an egg.
Glamour [gla'mẽr, glä'mŏŏr], n.
Glance [glans], n. v.
Glass [glas], n.
Glassous [gla'kus], a.
Glaucous [glô'kus], a. n.
Glaucus [glô'zhẽr], n.
Glazier [glā'zhẽr], n.
Gleam [glēm], n. v.
Glean er [glēn'ẽr], n.
Glimmer [glim'mẽr], n.
Glimpse [glimps], n. v.
Glisten ing [glis'n-ing], a. n.
Gloam ing [glōm'ing], a. n.
Globous [glōb'us], a.
Globular [glob'ūl-ẽr], a.
Globule [glob'ūl], n.
Glomerous [glom'ẽr-us], a.
Gloom iness [glŏŏm'i-nes], n.
Gloriole [glō'ri-ōl], n.
Glorious [glō'ri-us], a.
Gloss ary [glos'a-ri], n.
Glottis [glot'is], n.
Gloucester [glos'tẽr] English duke.
Glove r [gluv'ẽr], n.
Gloze [glōz], n. v.
Glucose [glū'kōs], n.
Glue [glū], n. v.
Gluten [glū'ten], n.
Glut'ton ous [glut'n-us], a.
Glycerine [glis'ẽ-rin], n.
Gnarl y [närl'i], a.
Gnash [nash], v.
Gnat [nat], n.
Gnaw er [nô'ẽr], n.
Gneiss [nīs], n.
Gnome [nōm], n.
Gnostic [nos'tik], a. n.
Gnu [nū], n.
Goad [gōd], n. v.
Goal [gōl], n.

Gone [gon] [...]
Goose [gŏŏs] [...]
Gooseberry [gŏŏz'be...], a. n.
Gopher [gō'fẽr], n.
Gordian [gar'di-an], a.
Gorge ous [gar'jus], a.
Gorget [gar'jet], n.
Gorgon [gar'gon], n.
Gorilla [go-ril'a], n.
Gosling [goz'ling], n.
Gospel [gos'pel], a. n. v.
Gossamer [gos'a-mẽr], n.
Gos'sip er [gos'sip-ẽr], n.
Göttingen [get'ing-en] French music
Gounod [gŏŏ'no]. composer.
Gourd [gōrd, gŏŏrd], n.
Gourmand [gŏŏr'mänd], n.
Go'vern or [gu'vẽrn-ẽr], n.
Gown [gown], n.
Grace ful [grās'fŏŏl], a.
Gracious [grā'shus], a.
Graduator [grad'ū-āt-ẽr], n.
Grail [grāl], n. v.
Grain [grān], n. A unit of
Grammar [gram'mẽr], n.
Gramme [gram], n.
Granary [gran'a-ri], n.
Grand eur [grand'yẽr], n.
Grandiose [grand'i-ōs], a.
Grange r [grānj'ẽr], n.
Granite [gran'it], n.
Granula [gran'ū-la], n.
Granule [gran'ūl], n.
Graph'ic al [grafik-al], a
Graphite [graf'it], n.
Grass iness [grās'i-nes]. A frau
Grate [grāt], n.
Grateful [grāt'fŏŏl], a.
Gratifier [gra'ti-fi-ẽr], a. ad
Gratis [grā'tis], a. ad...
Gratuitous [gra-tū'i...
Gra'vel ly [gr...
Gravity [grav...
Grazier [grā'z...

āle, add, beär, ärm, åsk, fall; mē, met, thère, hèr; pin

Grease [grēs], n. [grēz], v.
Greasy [grēz'i], a.
Great [grāt], a. n.   Large ; chief.
Grecian [grē'shan], a. n.
Greed ily [grēd'i-ly], ad.
Gregarious [gre-gā'ri-us], a.
Grenade [gre-nād'], n.
Grenadier [gren-a-dēr'], n.
Grew some [grōō'sum], a.
Grey, Gray [grā], a. n.
Gridiron [grid'i-ern], n.
Grief [grēf], n.
Grievance [grēv'ans], n.
Grievous [grēv'us], a.
Grimace [gri-mās'], n. v.
Grimalkin [gri-mal'kin], n.
Grimy [grim'i], a.
Grind stone [grind'stōn], n.
Grisette [gri-zet'], n.
Grisly, Grizzly [griz'li], a.
Gristle [gris'l], n.
Groan [grōn], n. v.   To moan.
Groat [grät], n.
Grocer y [grō'sėr-i], n.
Grog gery [grog'ė-ri], n.
Grogram, Grogran [grog'ram, g
   ran], n.
Groin [groin], n. v.   [prea
Groove [grōōv], n.   E
Grosvenor [gro'ven-or].
Grotesque [gro-tesk'], a. n.
Grotto [grot'ō], n.
Ground sel [ground'sel], n.
Grouse [grows], n. v.
Grov'el ler [gro'vel-ėr], n.
Growl er [growl'ėr], n.
Growth [grōth], n.
Grudge [gruj], n.
Gruel [grōō'el], n.
Grumbler [grum'blėr], n.
Guaiacum [gwā'ya-kum], n
Guana [gwä'nä], n.   A bir
Guano [gwä'nō], n. v.   A
   [gar-an-tē'], n.

HALF.

Half [häf], a. ad. n. Halves [hävz], pl.
Half-wit ted [häf'wit-ed], a.
Halibut [hol'i-but], n.
Halleluiah [hal-le-loo'ya], inter. n.
Halloo [hal-loo'], inter. n. v.
Hallow-e'en [hal-lo'sin ät-er], n.
Hallucinator [hal-lu'sin-], n. v.
Halo [hā'lo], n.
Hame [hām], n.
Hammer [ham'mer], n. v.
Hammock [ham'mok], n.
Hand icap [hand'i-kap], a. n. v.
Handkerchief [bank'er-chif], n.
Handsome [hand'sum], a.
Haply [hap'li], ad. By accident.
Happily [hap'pi-li], ad. By good fortune.
Happiness [hap'pi-nes], n.
Harangue [ha-rang'], n. v.
Harass er [ha'ras-er], n.
Harbinger [här'bin-jer], n.
Harbor er [här'bor-er], n.
Hardiness [härd'i-nes], n.
Hare [hār], n. An animal.
Hare-lip ped [här'lip'd], a.
Harem [ha'rem], n.
Haricot [har'e-kō], n.
Harlequin [här'le-kwin], n. v.
Harmonica [här-mon'i-ka], n.
Harmonious [här-po'ni-us], a.
Harp oon [här-poon'], n. v.
Harpsichord [härp'si-kord], n.
Harridan [ha'ri-dan], n.
Harrier [ha'ri-er], n.
Hassock [has'sok], n.
Hasten er [hās'n-er], n.
Hatch et [hach'et], n.
Haughtily [haw'ti-li], ad.
Haul [hawl], n. A violent pull. v. To pull; to drag.
Hanneh [hänch], n.
Haunt [hänt], n. v.
Hautboy [hō'boi], n.
Hauteur [hō'tėr], n.
Havoc [ha'vok], n.
Hawk [hak], n. v.
Hawser [has'er, haz'er], n.
Hawthorn [ha'thorn], n.
Hazard ous [haz'ėrd-us], a.
Head ache [hed'āk], n.
Health ful [helth'fool], a.
Heard [hėrd], v.
Hearken [härk'n], n. v.
Hearse [hėrs], n. An organ of the body.
Heart [härt], n.
-th [härth], n.

Heat er [hēt'ėr], n.
Heathen [hē'then], a. n.
Heave [hēv], v.
Heaven [hev'n], n.
Heavily [he'be], ad.
Hebe [hē'be], n.
Hecatomb [he'ka-toom], n.
Hedge hog [hej'hog], n. A part of the foot. v. To put a heel to; to incline.
Heel [hēl], n.
Hegira [he-ji'ra, hej'i-ra], n.
Height [hit], n. German poet.
Heine [hī'ne], n.
Heinous [hā'nus], a.
Heir [ãr], n. v.
Helianthus [hē-li-an'thus], n.
Helioscope [hē'li-o-skōp], n.
Heliotrope [hē'li-o-trōp], n.
Heliotype [hē'li-o-tip], n.
Hellebore [hel'le-bōr], n.
Hellenic [hel-len'ik], a.
Helm et [helm'et], n.
Helot [he'lot, hel'ot], n.
Hemans, Mrs. [hem'anz], English poetess.
Hemiptera [he-mip'ter-a], n. pl.
Hemorrhage [hem'or-raj], n.
Hemorrhoids [hem'or-oidz], n. pl.
Hence [hens], ad.
Hepatica [he-pat'ik-a], n.
Hepateuch [hep'ta-tūk], n.
Heracleum [he-rak'le-um], n.
Heraldic [he-ral'dik], a.
Herald ry [he'rald-ri], n.
Herbaceous [herb-ā'shus], a.
Herb age [ėrb'aj, hėrb'aj], n.
Herbarium [hėr-bā'ri-um], n.
Herbivorous [hėr-biv'or-us], a.
Herculean [hėr-kū'le-an], a.
Here [hėr], ad. In this place.
Hereditary [he-red'it-a-ri], a.
Her'etic al [he'ri-ot], n.
Heriot [he'ri-ot], n.
Hermaphrodite [hėr-maf-ro-dite], n.
Hermeneutics [hėr-me-nū'tiks], n.
Her'mit age [hėr'mit-āj], n.
Hernia [hėr'ni-a], n.
Hero [he'rō], n.
Heroine [he'ro-in], n.
Heroism [he'ro-izm], n.
Herring [her'ing], n.
Hesitation [hez-i-tā'shun], n.
Heterodox [het'ėr-o-doks], a.
Heterogamu [het'ėr-o-gam], n.
Heterogenei [het-ėr-o-jē'ne-],
Heterogene [het-ėr-o-jē'ne-],

Heteropathy [het-er-op'a-thi], n.
Hew [hū], v.
Hexameter [heks-am'et-ėr], n.
Heyse [hi'ze]. German author.
Hiatus [hi-ā'tus], n.
Hibernate [hi'bėr-nāt], v.
Hibernicize [hi-bėr'ni-siz], n.
Hibiscus [hi-bis'kus], n.
Hiccup, Hiccough [hik'up], n. v.
Hickory [hik'ō-ri], n.
Hideous [hid'ē-us], a.
Hierarchy [hi'ėr-ärk-i], n.
Hi'eroglyph ic [hi-ėr-o-glif'ik], n.
Hilarious [hi-lā'ri-us, hi-lä'ri-us], a.
Hilarity [hi-lar'i-ti, hi-lar'i-ti], n.
Himalayan [him-a-lā'yan], a.
Hinderance, Hindrance [hin'dėr-ans, hin'drans], n.
Hindoo, Hindu [hin-dōō'], n.
Hippodrome [hip'pō-drōm], n.
Hippophagi [hip-pof'a-ji], n. pl.
Hippopotamus [hip-pō-pot'a-mus], n.
   Hippopotami [hip-pō-pot'a-mi], pl.
Hirsute [hėr-sūt'], a.
Historian [his-tō'ri-an], n.
Histrionics [his-tri-on'iks], n.
Hitch [hich], n. v.
Hith'er to [hi/h'ėr-tōō], ad.
Hoar y [hōr'i], ad.
Hoard er [hōrd'ėr], n.
Hoarse ness [hōrs'nes], n.
Hoax [hōks], n. v.
Hob'ble dehoy [hob'l-dē-hoi], n.
Hodometer [hod-om'et-ėr], n.
Hoe [hō], n. v. A tool ; a fish.
Hog gish [hog'ish], a.
Hogshead [hogz'hed], n.
Holden [hoi'den], a. n. v.
Hoist [hoist], n. v.
Hoi'ty toity [hoi'ti-toi'ti], a. inter.
Holiday [hol'i-dā], n.
Holiness [hō'li-nes], n.
Hollow [hol'lō], a. n. v.
Hol'ly hock [hol'li-hok], n.
Holocaust [ho'lo-kạst], n.
Homage [hom'āj], n. v.
Home ly [hōm'li], a. ad.
Homestead [hōm'sted], n.
Homicide [hom'i-sid], n.
Homœopathic [hō-mē-ō-path'ik], a.
Homœopathy [hō-mē-op'a-thi], n.
Homogeneity [hō-mō-je-nē'i-ti], n.
Homogeneous [hō-mō-jē'nē-us], a.
Homologous [hō-mol'og-us], a.
Hon'est y [on'est-i], n.
Hon'ey suckle [hun'i-suk-l], n.

Honi soit qui
   kē mai e po
Hon'or ariun
Hoof [hōōf].
Hook ah [hō
Hoop [hōōp].
Hooping-coug
   [hōōp'ing-k
Hoosier [hōō
Hoot [hōōt].
Hope fu [hō
Horary [hōr'
Horde [hōrd
Horehound
Horizon [hor
Horizontal
Horn blend
Hornet [hor
Horoscope [
Horrible [h
Horror [hor
Hors de co
Hortatory
Horticultur
Hosanna [h
Hosiery [h
Hospice [h
Hospitable
Hos'pital
Hospitalle
Host age
Hostelry [
Hostess [h
Hostile [h
Hostility
Hostler [o
Hottentot
Hough [h
Hound [h
Hour [ou
Houri [h
House wi
Hovel [h
Hover [h
Howadji
Howdah
Howitze
Howl [h
Huckab
Huckleb
Hue [hū
Huguen
Hullabs
Hu'ma
Humb
Hum!

], n. A bone of	**Hydropathist** [hī-dro′pa-thist], n.
	Hydrophane [hī′dro-fān], n.
l-tī], n.	**Hydrophobia** [hī-dro-fō′bi-a], n.
], n.	**Hydrophobic** [hī-dro-fob′ik], a.
:], n. [a.	**Hyena** [hī-ē′na], n.
~us, hū′mor-us],	**Hygiene** [hī′ji-ēn], n.
	Hygienic [hī-ji-en′ik], a.
dth], a. n.	**Hymen eal** [hī-me-nē′al], a.
i], ad.	**Hymn** [him], n. A song.
	Hyoscyamus [hī-os-sī′a-mus], n.
	Hypargyrite [hī-pär′ji-rīt], n.
er. v.	**Hyperbaton** [hī-pèr′ba-ton], n.
.], n.	**Hyperbola** [hī-pèr′bo-lä], n. A geo-
	metrical figure. [torical figure.
, n. v.	**Hyperbole** [hī-pèr′bo-le], n. A rhe-
.	**Hyperbolize** [hī-pèr′bol-īz], v.
	Hyperborean [hī-pèr-bō′rē-an], a. n.
	Hyphen [hī′fen], n. v.
er. v.	**Hypnotism** [hip′no-tizm], n.
], n.	**Hypobole** [hī-pob′o-li], n. [a. n.
n.	**Hypochondriac** [hip-ō-kon′dri-ak],
-izm], n.	**Hypochondriacal** [hip-ō-kon-drī′ak-
], v.	al], a.
]e-a], n.	**Hypocrisy** [hī-pok′ri-si], n.
n.	**Hypocritical** [hip-o-krit′i-kal], a.
ks], n.	**Hypothenuse** [hī-poth′e-nūs], n.
l], n.	**Hypothesis** [hī-poth′e-sis], n. Hy
ro-sē-fal′ik], a.	**potheses**, pl.
ro-sef′a-lus], n.	**Hypothetic** [hī-po-thet′ik], a.
], n.	**Hyssop** [his′sop], n.
u′et-èr], n.	**Hysteria** [his-tē′ri-a], n.

I.

	Ignominious [ig-nō-mi′ni-us], a.
	Ignoramus [ig-nō-rā′mus], n.
on], n.	**Ignorance** [ig′nō-rans], n.
	Iguana [ig-wä′na], n.
′o-ji], n.	**Iliad** [il′i-ad], n.
ii-o-sū′rus], n.	**Illegible** [il-lej′i-bl], a.
	Illegitimacy [il-le-jit′i-ma-si], n.
last], n.	**Illicit** [il-lis′it], a.
i], n.	**Illision** [il-lī′zhon], n.
:.	**Illiteracy** [il-lit′èr-a-si], n.
	Illude [il-lūd′], v.
	Illuminati [il-lū-mi-nā′tī], n.
′ik], n.	**Illuminator** [il-lū′mi-nāt-èr], n.
sin′kra-si], n.	**Illusion ist** [il-lū′zhun-ist], n.
n.	**Illusive** [il-lū′siv], a.
r], n.	**Illustrator** [il-lus′trāt-èr], n.
s], a.	**Illustrious** [il-lus′tri-us], a.
	Image ry [im′aj-è-ri], n.
t′ī-us], n. **Ig-**	**Imaginary** [im-aj′i-na-ri], a.
′ī-i], pl.	**Imbecile** [im′be-sil, im-be-sēl′], a.

ity [im-be-sil'i-ti], n.
lio [im-brō'lyō], n.
[im-bū'], v.
e [im'i-ta-bl], a.
ion ist [im-i-tā'shun-ist], n.
or [im'i-tāt-ér], n.
ulate [im-ma'kū-lāt], a. [ence.
ence [im'ma-nens], n. Inher-
diate [im-mē'di-āt], a.
morial [im-me-mō'ri-al], a.
nsity [im-mens'i-ti], n.
nsurable [im-men'sūr-a-bl], a.
er'sion ist [im-mér'shun-ist], n.
inence [im'mi-nens], n. Impend-
iscible [im-mis'i-bl], a. [ing.
olator [im'mo-lāt-ér], n.
unity [im-mū'ni-ti], n.
air [im-pár'], v.
ale [im-pāl'], v.
each' er [im-pēch'ér], n.
peccability [im-pek-a-bil'i-ti], n.
peccable [im-pek'ka-bl], a. [n.
pecuniosity [im-pe-kū-ni-os'i-ti],
pediment [im-ped'i-ment], n.
ipel'ler [im-pel'ér], n.
iperative [im-per'a-tiv], a. n.
aperious [im-pē'ri-us], a.
npertinence [im-pér'ti-nens], n.
npetuous [im-pet'ū-us], a.
npetus [im'pe-tus], n.
npious [im'pi-us], a.
nplacable [im-plā'ka-bl], a.
nplement [im'ple-ment], n. v.
nplicit [im-plis'it], a.
aport [im'pōrt], n. [im-pōrt'], v.
nportance [im-port'ans], n.
nporter [im-pōrt'ér], n.
nportune [im-por-tūn'], v.
nportunity [im-por-tūn'i-ti], n.
npostor [im-pos'ter], n. One who
imposes on others. [of an impostor.
nposture [im-pos'tūr], n. The act
npotence [im'pō-tens], n.
npoverish [im-pov'ér-ish], v.
nprecatory [im'pre-kāt-o-ri], a.
npress [im'pres], n. [im-pres'], v.
npression [im-pre'shun], n.
npromptu [im-promp'tū], a. ad. n.
nproviser [im-pro-vīz'ér], n.
nprovvisatrice [im-prov-vi-sa-trē'-
chā], n. fem.
ipudence [im'pū-dens], n.
ipugn' er [im-pūn'ér], n.
ipunity [im-pū'ni-ti], n.
iputation [im-pū-tā'shun], n.
amorata [in-a-mo-rā'ta], n. fem.

Inamorato [in-a-mo-rā'tō], n. mas.
Inanity [in-an'i-ti], n.
Inaugural [in-a'gū-ral], a. n.
Inauguration [in-a-gū-rā'shun], n.
Incarcerator [in-kár'se-rāt-ér], n.
Incarnation [in-kár-nā'shun], n.
Incendiarism [in-sen'di-a-rizm], n.
Incense [in'sens], n. v.
Incentive [in-sen'tiv], a. n.
Inceptor [in-sep'tér], n.
Incessant [in-ses'ant], a.
In'cest nous [in-sest'ū-us], a.
Inch [inch], a. n. v.
Inchoate [in'kō-āt], a. v.
Incidence [in'si-dens], n.
Incision [in-si'zhun], n.
Incisive [in-sī'siv], a.
Incisor [in-sīz'ér], n. A tooth.
Incisure [in-sizh'yōōr, in-sizh'ér], n.
Inclinable [in-klīn'a-bl], a.
Inclosure [in-klō'zhūr, in-klō'zhér].
Include [in-klūd'], v.
Incognito [in-kog'ni-tō], a. ad. n.
Incomparable [in-kom'pa-ra-bl], a.
Incongruity [in-kon-grōō'i-ti], n.
Incongruous [in-kong'grōō-us], a.
Increase [in'krēs], n. [in-krēs'], v.
Increment [in'kre-ment], n.
Incubator [in'kū-bā-tér], n.
Incubus [in'kū-bus], n.
Incur' sion [in-kér'shun], n.
Indecorous [in-de-kō'rus, in-dek'o-
rus], a.
Indefatigable [in-de-fat'i-ga-bl], a.
Indelible [in-del'i-bl], a.
Indemnity [in-dem'ni-ti], n. [n. v.
Indenture [in-dent'ūr, in-dent'yér],
Index [in'deks], n. Indexes, pl.
Indian [ind'yan, in'di-an], a. n.
India-rubber [in'jā-rub'ér], n.
Indicative [in-dik'a-tiv], a.
Indicator [in'di-kāt-ér], n.
Indicatory [in'di-ka-to-ri], a.
Indict' able [in-dīt'a-bl], a.
Indicter [in-dīt'ér], n.
Indigence [in'di-jens], n.
Indigenous [in-dij'en-us], a.
Indignation [in-dig-nā'shun], n.
Indignity [in-dig'ni-ti], n.
Indissoluble [in-dis'so-lū-bl], a.
Indite [in-dīt'], v. To compose; to
write.
Individ'ual ize [in-di-vid'ū-al-īz], v.
Individuator [in-di-vid'ū-āt-ér], n.
Indolence [in'dō-lens], n.
Indomitable [in-dom'it-a-bl], a.

Inexpiable
Inexplicable [in-eks-...], a.
Infamous [in'fam-s], a.
Infancy [in'fan-si-sid], n.
Infant icide [in-fant'i-sid], n.
In'fant [in'fant-il], a.
Infantile [in'fan-tin], a.
Infantine [in-fat'u-at], a. v.
Infatuate [in-fek'shus], a.
Infect' ious [in-fek'shus], a.
Infecund [in-fe'kund], a.
Inference [in'fer-ens], n.
Inferential [in-fer-en'shal], a.
Inferior ity [in-fer-i-or'i-ti], n.
Infe'rior ly [in-fer'nal-li], ad.
Infer'nal ly [in-fi-del'i-ti], n.
In'fidel ity [in'fi-nit], a. n.
Infinite [in-fin-i-tes'i-mal], a. n.
Infinitesimal [in-ferm'a-ri], n.
Infirm' ary [in-ferm'i-ti], n.
Infirmity [in-flam'a-bl], a.
Inflammable [in-flam-a'shun], n.
Inflammation [in-fla'tus], n.
Inflatus [in-flikt'er], n. v.
Inflict' er [in'flu-ens], n. v.
Influence [in-flu-en'shal], a
Influential [in-flu-en'za], n.
Influenza [in-fus'iv], a. [authoress.
Infusive [in'je-lo, jen]. English
Ingelow, Jean [in-jen'yus], a.
Ingenious [in-je-nu'i-ti], n.
Ingenuity [in-jen'u-us], a.
Ingenuous [in-gra'shi-at], v.
Ingratiate [in-grat'i-tud], n.
Ingratitude [in-gre'di-ent], n.
Ingredient [in'gres], n. v.
Ingress [in-hab'it-ant], n.
Inhab'it ant [in-hab'it], v.
Inhale [in-her'ent], a.
Inherent [in-her'it-er], n.
Inher'it or [in-im'ik-al], a.
Inimical [in-i'kwit-us], a.
Iniquitous

Inscription
Inscrutable [in-sk...
In'sect ivorous [in-ser'shun], n.
Insert' ion [in-ses-se'rez], n. p
Insessores [in-si'di-us], a.
Insidious [in-sig'nt-a], n.
Insignia [in-sin'u-at-er], n.
Insinuator [in-si-pid'i-ti], n
Insipid ity [in-sist'ens], n.
Insist' ence [in-sish'un], n.
Insition [in'sol-at], v.
Insolate [in'so-lens], n.
Insolence [in-som'ni-a], n.
Insomnia [in-spekt'er]
Inspect' or [in-spi-ra'shu
Inspiration [in-stal-
Install' ation [in-stal'ment
Instalment [in-stau
In'stant ancity [in-stan-
Instantaneous [in-ste...] ad.
Instead [in-sti-gat-e
Instigator [in-stil-
Instil' lation [in-stil'er], a
Instiller [in-stingkt']
Instinct [in-sti-tu-
Institution [in-sti-tut
Institutor [in-str
Instruct' or [in-str
In'strument al ist
al-ist], n.
Insular [in'su-ler'
Insulator [in'su-
Insult' er [in-
Insurance
Insurgent
Insurrec'
ist], n.

āle, add, beär, ärm, ȧsk, fạll, mē, met, thēre, he

Intaglio [in-tăl'yō], n.
Integral [in'te-gral], a. n.
Integrity [in-teg'ri-ti], n.
Integument [in-teg'ū-ment], n.
In'tellect ual [in-tel-lekt'ū-al], a.
Intelligence [in-tel'li-jens], n.
Intelligible [in-tel'li-ji-bl], a.
Intensity [in-tens'i-ti], n.
Inten'tion al [in-ten'shun-al], a.
Intercede [in-tér-sĕd'], v.
Intercept' er [in-tér-sept'ér], n.
Intercessor [in'tér-ses-ér], n.
Intercourse [in'tér-kôrs], n.
Interdict [in-tér-dikt'], n. v.
Interest [in'tér-est], n. v.
Interfere [in-tér-fēr'], v.
Interim [in'tér-im], n.
Inte'rior ity [in-tē-ri-or'i-ti], n.
Interjacent [in-tér-jā'sent], a.
Interjection [in-tér-jek'shun], n.
Interlocutor [in-tér-lok'ūt-ér], n.
Intermit' tent [in-tér-mit'ent], a. n.
Internal [in-tér'nal], a.
Interpolator [in-tér'pō-lāt-ér], n.
Inter'pret er [in-tér'pret-ér], n.
Interrogator [in-te'rō-gāt-ér], n.
Interrupt' er [in-tér-rupt'ér], n.
Intersperse [in-tér-spérs'], v.
Interstice [in'tér-stis], n.
Interval [in'tér-val], n.
Intervene [in-tér-vēn'], v.
Interventor [in-tér-vent'ér], n.
Intestinal [in-tes'ti-nal], a.
Intestine [in-tes'tin], a. n.
Intimacy [in'ti-ma-si], n.
Intimate [in'ti-mat], a. n. [in'ti-māt].
Intoxication [in-toks-i-kā'shun], n.
Intricacy [in'tri-ka-si], n.
Intrigue [in-trēg'], n. v.
Introduce [in-tro-dūs'], v.
Introduction [in-tro-duk'shun], n.
Introversion [in-tro-vér'shun], n.
Intrusion [in-trōō'zhun], n.
Intrusive [in-trōō'siv], a.
Intuition [in-tū-ĭ'shun], n.
Intuitive [in-tū'i-tiv], a.
Inundate [in-un'dāt], v.
Inure' ment [in-ūr'ment], n
Invalid [in-va'lid], a Not valid. [in'-
  va-lĕd, in'va-lid], a. n. Sick.
Invective [in-vek'tiv], a. n.
Inveigh [in-vā'], v.
Inveigle [in-vē'gl], v.
Invent' or [in-vent'ér], n.
Inventory [in'ven-tō-ri], **n v.**
Inverse [in-vérs'], a.

Investigator [in-ves'ti-gāt-ér], n.
Invidious [in-vī'di-us], a.
Invigoration [in-vig-or-ā'shun], n.
Invincible [in-vin'si-bl], a.
Involucre [in-vō-lū'kér], n.
Involution [in-vō-lū'shun], n.
Iodide [ĭ'o-dīd, ĭ'o-dĭd], n.
Iodine [ĭ'o-dīn], n.
Iolite [ĭ'o-līt], n.
Ionic [i-on'ik], a. n.
Ipecacuanha [ip-e-kak-u-an'a], n.
Iphigenia [if-i-je-nī'a]. Daughter of
  Agamemnon.
Irascibility [i-ras-i-bil'i-ti], n.
Irascible [i-ras'i-bl], a.
Irene [i-rē'ne], n.
Iridaceæ [i-rid-ā'sē-ē], n. pl.
Iridescence [ir-i-des'ens], n.
Iridium [i-rid'i-um], n.
Iron [ī'érn], a. n. v.
Irony [ī'érn-i], a. [ī'run-i], n.
Irrefragable [ir-ref'ra-ga-bl], a.
Irrefutable [ir-re-fūt'a-bl, ir-ref'ū-ta-
  bl], a.
Irreparable [ir-rep'a-ra-bl], a.
Irrevocable [ir-rev'o-ka-bl], a.
Irritable [ir'rit-a-bl], a.
Irritation [ir-rit-ā'shun], n.
Irruption [ir-rup'shun], n.
Ischiatic [is-ki-at'ik], a.
Ish'mael ite [ish'ma-el-īt], n.
Isinglass [ī'zing-glas], n.
Isis [ī'sis], n.
Is'lam ism [iz'lam-izm], n.
Island [ī'land], n.
Isle [īl], n. An island.
Isocheim [ī'sō-kīm], n.
Isochronous [i-sok'ro-nus], a.
Isolate [iz'o-lāt], v.
Isologous [i-sol'o-gus], a.
Isomerous [i-som'ér-us], a.
Isothere [ī'so-thér], n.
Isothermal [i-so-thér'mal], a.
Is'rael ite [iz'ra-el-īt], n.
Issuable [ish'ū-a-bl], a.
Issue [ish'ū], n. v.
Isthmian [ist'mi-an], a.
Isthmus [ist'mus], n.
Ital'ian ize [i-tal'yan-īz], v.
Italicize [i-tal'i-sīz], v.
Itch [ich], n. v.
Item [ī'tem], n. v.
Itinerancy [ī-tin'ér-an-si], n
Itnerite [ĭt'nér-īt], n. A mineral.
Ivory [ī'vo-ri], a. n. [the Lapithæ.
Ixion [iks-ī'on]. A fabulous king of

[jăk′al], n

apes [jak′a-nāps], n.

an [ja-kō′bē-an, jak-o-bē′an], Architectural term. [The first unciation is the Im. ; the sec- Wor.]

in [jak′o-bin], a. n.

erie [zhäk′rē′], n.

tor [jak′ū-lāt-ėr], n.

d [jag′ed], a. p.

r [jag-ū-är′], n.

[jăl′up], n.

jam], n. v. [or window.

[jam], n. The side of a door

ary [jan′i-za-ri], n.

ry [jan′ū-a-ri], n.

s [jā′nus], n.

ese [jap-an-ēz′], n.

r′ ner [ja-pan′ėr], n.

on elle [jar-gon-el′], n.

ine [jaz′min], n.

lice [jän′dis], n. v.

s ily [jän′ti-li], ad.

in [jav′lin], n. v.

us y [jel′us-i], n.

[jăn], n.

[jėr], n. v.

vah [je-hō′va], n.

e [je-jūn′], a.

d [jel′lid], a.

Joint [jint p

Jolliness [jol′li-nes],

Jonquil [jon′kwil], n.

Jostle [jos′l], v.

Jour′nal ism [jėr′nal-izm

Journey [jėr′ni], n.

Joust [just], n. v.

Jovial [jō′vi-al], n.

Jowl [jōl], n.

Joy ous [joi′us], a.

Jubilee [jū′bi-lē], n.

Judaic [ju-dā′ik], a.

Judaism [jū′dā-izm], n.

Judaize [jū′dā-iz], v.

Judge [juj], n. v.

Judgment [juj′ment], n.

Judicatory [jū′di-kā-tō-ri], a

Judicature [jū′di-kā-tūr], n.

Judi′cial ly [jū-dish′al-i], ad

Judiciary [jū-dish′i-er-i], a. r

Judicious [jū-dish′us], a.

Juggernaut [jug′ėr-nat], n.

Juggler [jug′lėr], n.

Jugular [jū′gu-lar], a. n.

Juice [jūs], n.

Juicy [jūs′i], a.

Julep [jū′lep], n.

Jumble [jum′bl], n. v.

Junction [jungk′shun], n.

Juncture [jungk′tūr, jung

K.

Kabala [kal'a-la], n. Same as Cab-
ala.
Kafir, Kaffer [kaf'ér], a. n.
Kale [kāl], n.
Kaleidoscope [ka-li'do-skōp], n.
Kaleidoscopic [ka-li-do-skop'ik], a.
Kangaroo [kang-ga-rōō'], n.
Kayak [kī'yak'], n. A light fishing-
boat used by the Esquimaux.
Keel [kēl], n. v.
Keelson [kel'sun, kēl'sun], n.
Keep er [kēp'ér], n.
Kelp ie [kel'pi], n.
Kennel [ken'nel], n. v.
Kerchief [kér'chif], n.
Kernel [kér'nel], n. v. A seed.
Kerosene [ker'o-sēn], n.
Kersey [kér'zi], a. n.
Ketchup [kech'up], n. Same as [Catchup.
Kettle [ket'l], n.
Key [kē], n. v.
Khan [kan], n.
Khedive [ka-dēv'], n.
Kid'nap per [kid'nap-ér], n.
Kidney [kid'ni], n.
Kiln [kil], n.
Kilogram [kil'o-gram], n.
Kilolitre [kil'o-lē-tr], n.
Kilometre [kil'o-mē-tér], n.
Kindle [kin'dl], v.
Kindred [kin'dred], a. n.
King dom [king'dum], n.
Kinkajou [king'ka-jōō], n.
Kiosk [ki-osk'], n.

Kioton
Kirtle
Kiss e
Kitche
Kitten
Knack
Knaps
Knave
Knavi
Knead
toget
Knee
Knell
Knicke
Knick-
Knife
Knight
Knit t
Knob
Knock
Knoll
Knosp
Knot
Knout
Know
Knowl
Knuck
Koran
Kossut
state
Kraal
Kreml
Kyani
Kyrie

L.

La'bel [lā'bel], n. v.
Labial [lā'bi-al], n.
Laboratory [lab'o-ra-tō-ri], n.
La'bor er [lā'bor-ér], n.
Laborious [la-bō'ri-us], a.
Laburnum [la-bér'num], n.
Labyrinth [lab'i-rinth], n.
Lacerate [las'ér-āt], v.
Lachesis [lak'ē-sis], n.
Lachrymose [lak'rim-ōs], a.
Lacinia [la-sin'i-a], n.
Lack ey [lak'i], n. v.

Lacon'
Laconi
Lacque
Lactes
Lactes
Lacun
Lacun
Ladde
Ladle
Lager
Lagg
Lag

Leeward
Legacy (leg'a-si) n.
Legal ize (le'gal-iz) v.
Legate (leg'at) n.
Legatee (leg-a-te') n.
Legation (le-ga'shun) n.
Legato (le-ga'to)
Legator (leg-a-tor') n.
Legend (le'jend, lej'end) n.
Legendary (lej'end-a-ri) n.
Legerdemain (lej'er-de-man') n.
Legible (lej'i-bl) a.
Legion ary (le'jun-a-ri) a. n.
Legislator (lej'is-lat-er) n.
Legislature (lej'is-lat-yur,
yer) n.
Legitimacy (le-jit'i-ma-si) n.
Legitimatize (le-jit'i-ma-tiz) v.
Legume (leg'um) n.
Leguminosæ (le-g-mi-no'sē).
Leisurely (le'zhur-li) ad.
Lem'on ade (lem-on-ad')
Lemur (le'mer) n.
Length y (length'i) a.

Leyd
Liais
Libel
Libera
Libern
Liberti
Lib
Libret
License
Licenti
Licenti
Lichen
Licorice
Lictor

all, mē, met, thêre, hêr; pine, pin

[lĕ'ni-en-si], n.
ĕ'ni-ent], a. n.
len'i-tiv], a.
n'i-ti], n.
], n. Lenses [lenz'ez], pl.
lent'en], a.
'til], n.
ĕ'o-nīn], a. n.
lep'ard], n.
'ér], n.
ra [lep-id-op'tér-a], n. pl.
ep'ro-si], n.
ep'rus], a.
es'n], v.
s'n], n.
'sąr], n.
[le-thär'jik], a.
[leth'är-jīz], v.
he], n.
le-thē'an], a.
et'is], n.
'sīt], n.
sa [lū-ko-rē'a], n.
'vant], a. [le-vant'], n. v.
[le-van'tin], a. n.
'el, n. v.
[lev'el-ér], n.
'ér], n.
[lev'ér aj], n.
[le-vī'a-than], n.
le-vit'i-kal], a.
], a.
pher [leks-i-kog'ra-fér], n.
eks'i-kon], n.
r [lī'dn-jär], n.
'ä'zoñ'], n.
[lī'bel-us], a.
st [lib'ér-al-ist], n.
[lib'ér-āt-ér], n.
[lib'ér-tin], a. n
[lī-brā'ri-an], n.
lī-bret'tō], n.
'sens], n. v.
[lī-sen'shi-āt], n. v.
[lī-sen'shus], a.
ken], n.
lik'or-is], n.
'tér], n.
A falsehood. v.
, a. n.
], n. A legal claim.
cy [lū-ten'an-si], n.
t [lū-ten'ant], n.
[lig'a-ment], n
lig'a-tūr], n.
lit'n], v.

Lightning [līt'ning], n.
Lightsome [līt'sum], a.
Ligneous [lig'ne-us], a.
Lilac [lī'lak], n.
Liliaceous [lil-i-ā'shus], a.
Limb [lim], n. v.
Lim'it ation [lim-it-ā'shun], n.
Limp et [lim'pet], n.
Limpid [lim'pid], a
Lin'eal ly [lin'ē-al-li], ad.
Lineament [lin'ē-a-ment], n. The outline of a body.
Linear [lin'ē-ér], a.
Linen [lin'en], a. n.
Lingual [ling'gwal], a. n.
Linguist [ling'gwist], n. [ment.
Liniment [lin'i-ment], n. An oint-
Linnet [lin'net], n.
Linoleum [li-nō'lē-um], n.
Linsey-woolsey [lin'si-wōol'si], n.
Li'on ize [lī'on-iz], v.
Liquefiable [lik'we-fī-a-bl], a
Li'quid ator [lik'wid-āt-ér], n.
Li'quor ice [lik'ér-is], n.
Lis'ten er [lis'n-ér], n.
Liszt [list]. Hungarian musician.
Litany [lit'an-i], n. v.
Lit'eral ize [lit'ér-al-iz], v.
Literati [lit-ér-ā'tī], n. pl.
Literature [lit'ér-a-tūr], n.
Lithe some [līth'sum], a.
Lith'ograph er [li-thog'raf-ér], n.
Litigator [li'ti-gāt-ér], n.
Litigious [li-tij'us], a.
Litre [lē'tr], n. [rary man.
Littérateur [lēt'tä'rä'tér], n. A lite-
Little [lit'l], a.
Liturgy [lit'ér-ji], n.
Live liness [līv'li-nes],
Livelong [liv'long], a.
Liv'er ed [liv'érd], a. [ery.
Liveried [liv'ér-id], a. Wearing liv-
Lizard [liz'érd], n.
Llama [lä'ma, lä'ma], n.
Loach [lōch], n.
Load stone [lōd'stōn], n.
Loaf [lōf], n. Loaves [lōvz], pl
Loam [lōm], n. v.
Loan [lōn], n. v. To lend.
Loath [lōth], a. Unwilling.
Loathe [lōth], v. To hate.
Loathsome [lōth'sum], a.
Lob'by ist [lob'bi-ist], n.
Lobelia [lō-bē'li-a], n.
Lobster [lob'stér], n.
Lo'cal ize [lō'kal-iz], v.

us ; ú, Fr. ; g, get ; j, jar ; h, Fr. ton : ch chain ; th, then ; th, t

Location [lō-kā'shun], n.
Lock et [lok'et], n.
Locomotive [lō-kō-mō'tiv], a. n.
Lodge [loj], n. v.
Lodgment [loj'ment], n.
Loft iness [lof'ti-nes], n.
Logarithm [log'a-rithm], n.
Log'ger head [log'er-hed], n.
Logical [loj'ik-al], a.
Logomachy [lo-gom'a-ki], n.
Loi'ter er [loi'ter-er], n.
Lollipop [lol'i-pop], n.
Lone ly [lōn'li], a.
Longitude [lon'ji-tūd], n.
Longitudinal [lon-ji-tūd'in-al], n.
Long-lived [long'livd], a.
Loop er [lōōp'er], n.
Loose ly [lōōs'li], ad.
Loquacious [lo-kwā'shus], a.
Loquacity [lo-kwas'i-ti], n.
Lose [lōōz], v.
Loth [lōth], a.
Lottery [lot'ter-i], n.
Loud ly [lowd'li], ad.
Lounge [lownj], n. v.
Louse [lows], n. Lice, pl.
Lovable [luv'a-bl], a.
Love ly [luv'li], a.
Lowliness [lō'li-nes], n.
Loy'al ist [loi'al-ist], n.
Loyally [loi'al-li], ad.
Lozenge [loz'enj], n.
Lubricator [lū'brik-āt-er], n.
Lu'cid ity [lū-sid'i-ti], n.

Lucifer [lū'si-fer], n.
Luck ily [luk'i-li], ad.
Lucrative [lū'kra-tiv], a.
Lucre [lū'ker], n.
Lu'cubrator y [lū'kū-brā-to-ri], a.
Ludicrous [lū'dik-rus], a.
Lug gage [lug'āj], n.
Lugubrious [lu-gū'bri-us], a.
Lumbar [lum'bar], a.
Lumber [lum'ber], n. v.
Luminary [lūm'in-a-ri], n.
Luminous [lūm'in-us], a.
Lunacy [lū'na-si], n.
Lunatic [lū'na-tik], a. n.
Lunch eon [lunsh'on], n. v.
Lupine [lū'pin], a. n.
Luscious [lush'us], a.
Lust ful [lust'fool], a.
Lustre [lus'ter], n.
Lustrous [lus'trus], a.
Lute [lūt], n.
Luxuriance [lug-zū'ri-ans], n.
Luxurious [lug-zū'ri-us], a.
Luxury [luks'ū-ri], n.
Lyceum [lī-sē'um], n.
Lycopodium [lī-kō-pō'di-um], n.
Lye [lī], n. A solution of alkali ; a railroad siding.
Lymph [limf], n.
Lynch [linsh], v.
Lynx [lingks], n.
Lyre [līr], n. A musical instrument.
Lyr'ic al [lir'ik-al], a.
Lyricism [lir'i-sizm], n.

M.

Ma'am [mäm], n.
Macadamize [mak-ad'am-īz], v.
Macaroni [mak-a-rō'ni], n.
Macaroon [mak-a-rōōn'], n.
Macaw [ma-ką'], n.
Macedonian [mas-e-dō'ni-an], a. n.
Macerate [mas'er-āt], v.
Machiavelian [mak-i-a-vēl'yan], a. n.
Machination [mak-i-nā'shun], n.
Machinator [mak'i-nāt-er], n.
Machine' ry [ma-shēn'er-i], n.
Machinist [ma-shēn'ist], n.
Mackerel [mak'er-el], n.
Mackintosh [mak'in-tosh], n.
Macrocosm [mak'ro-kozm], n.
Madam [mad'am], n.

Madame [mä'däm'], n. Fr. Mesdames [mä'däm'], pl.
Madeira [ma-dē'ra], n.
Mademoiselle [mádm'wä'zel'], n. Fr.
Madonna [ma-don'a], n.
Madrigal [mad'ri-gal], n.
Maelstrom [māl'strum], n.
Maestoso [mä-es-tō'zō], ad. It.
Maestro [ma-es'trō], n. It.
Magazine [mag-a-zēn'], n. v.
Magdalen [mag'da-len], n.
Magenta [ma-jen'ta], n.
Maggiore [maj-ō'rā], It.
Maggot [mag'ot], n.
Magi [mā'jī], n. pl.
Magian [mā'ji-an], n.

Mag'ic al [maj'ik-al], a.
Magisterial [maj-is-tē'ri-al], a.
Magistracy [maj'is-tra-si], n.
Magnanimity [mag-na-nim'i-ti], n.
Magnanimous [mag-nan'i-mus], a.
Magnate [mag'nāt], n.
Magnesia [mag-nē'zhi-a], n.
Mag'net ic [mag-net'ik], a.
Magnetize [mag'net-iz], v.
Magnificat [mag-nif'i-kat], n.
Magnificence [mag-nif'i-sens], n.
Magnifier [mag'ni-fi-ér], n.
Magniloquence [mag-nil'o-kwens], n.
Magnitude [mag'ni-tūd], n.
Magnolia [mag-nō'li-a], n.
Magpie [mag'pi], n.
Mahabarata, Mahabharatam [mä-ha-bä'rä-tä, mä-ha-bä'ra-tam], n.
Mahogany [ma-hog'a-ni], n.
Mahom'et an [ma-hom'e-tan], a. n.
Mahratta [ma-rat'ta], n.
Maid en [mād'n], a. n.
Maigre [mā'gr], a. n.
Mail [māl], v. n. Armor; a bag containing letters; a tribute.
Maim [mām], n. v.
Main [mān], a. Chief. n. The ocean; a continent.
Maintain' able [mān-tān'a-bl],
Maintenance [mān'te-nans], n.
Maize [māz], n.
Majes'tic ally [ma-jes'tik-al-li],
Majolica [ma-jol'i-kä], n.
Majority [ma-jor'i-ti], n.
Malacca [ma-lak'ka], a.
Malachite [mal'i-kīt], n.
Malady [mal'a-di], n.
Mal à propos [mál à pru'pō'], Fr.
Malaria [ma-lā'ri-a], n.
Malay [ma-lā'], a. n.
Malcontent [mal'kon-tent], a. n.
Male [māl], a. n. The sex that begets young.
Malediction [mal-e-dik'shun], n.
Malefactor [mal-e-fak'tér], n.
Malevolence [ma-lev'ō-lens], n.
Malfeasance [mal-fē'zans], n.
Malice [mal'is], n.
Malicious [ma-li'shus], a.
Malign [ma-lin'], a. v.
Malignancy [ma-lig'nan-si], n.
Malignity [ma-lig'ni-ti], n. [a walk.
Mall [mál], v. n. A hammer. [mal],
Malleable [mal'le-a-bl], a.
Malmsey [mäm'zi], n.
Maltreatment [mal-trēt'ment], n.

Malversation [mal-vér-sā'shun], n.
Mamma [ma-nä'], n.
Mammalia [mam-mā'li-á], n. pl.
Mammillary [mam'mil-a-ri], a. n.
Mam'mon ize [mam'mon-īz], v.
Mammoth [mam'moth], a. n.
Manacle [man'a-kl], n. v.
Man'age able [man'aj-a-bl], a.
Management [man'aj-ment], n.
Manatee [man-a-tē'], n.
Mandamus [man-dā'mus], n.
Mandarin [man-da-rēn'], n. v.
Mandible [man'di-bl], n.
Mandolin [man'dō-lin], n.
Mane [mān], n. The long hair on the neck of animals.
Manes [mā'nēz], n. pl.
Manganese [man-ga-bēz'], n.
Manger [mān'jér], n.
Manginess [mān'ji-nes], n.
Mangle [mang'l], n. v.
Mangy [mān'ji], a.
Maniac [mā'ni-ak], n.
Maniacal [ma-ni'ak-al], a.
Manicheism [man'i-ke-izm], n. [n.
Man'ifest ation [man-i-fes-tä'shun],
Manifold [man'i-fold], a. ad. n. v.
Manikin [man'i-kin], n.
Manipulator [ma-nip'ū-lāt-ér], n.
Manis [mā'nis], n.
Man'ner ism [man'nér-izm], n. [n v.
Manœuvre, Maneuver [ma-nōō'vér],
Manor [man'or], n.
Mansard [man'särd], n.
Mansion [man'shun], n.
Mantel [man'tel], n. A shelf.
Mantilla [man-til'la], n.
Mantle [man'tl], n. A cloak.
Mantua [man'tu-a], n.
Manual [man'u-al], a. n.
Manubrium [ma-nū'bri-um], n.
Manufactory [man-ū-fak'to-ri], a. n.
Manufacture [man-ū-fakt'yōōr, man-ū-fakt'yér], v.
Manumission [man-ū-mi'shun], n.
Manure [ma-nūr'], n. v.
Manx [mangks], a. n.
Many [men'i], a. n.
Maple [mā'pl], n.
Marabou [mar-a-bōō'], n.
Maranatha [mar-a-nath'ä], n.
Marasmus [ma-raz'mus], n.
Maraud' er [ma-rad'ér], n.
Mar'ble ize [mär'blīz], v.
Marchioness [mär'shun-es], n.
Margarite [mär'ga-tit], n. A mineral.

Mar'gin al [mär'jin-al], a.
Margravine [mär'gra-vin], n.
Marguerite [mär-ga-rēt'], n. A daisy.
Marigold [mar'i-gold], n.
Marine [ma-rēn'], a. n.
Mariner [mar'i-nér], n.
Mariolatry [mā-ri-ol'a-tri], n.
Marionette [mar-i-o-net'], n.
Marital [mar'i-tal], a.
Maritime [mar'i-tim], a.
Marjoram [mär'jo-ram], n.
Mark et [mär'ket], n.
Marmalade [mär'ma-lād], n.
Marmolite [mär'mo-lit], n.
Marmoset [mär'mo-zet], n.
Maroon [ma-rōōn'], a. n. v.
Marque [märk], n. A law term.
Marquee [mär-kē'], n. A tent.
Marquetry [mär'ket-ri], n.
Marquis [mär'kwis], n.
Mar'riage able [ma'rij-a-bl], a.
Marrow [mar'ō], n. v.
Marseillais [mär'sāl'yā'], a. mas.
Marseillaise [mär'sāl'yāz'], a. fem.
  "Marseillaise Hymn."
Mar'shal sea [mär'shal-sē], n.
Marsupialia [mär-sū-pi-ā'li-a], n. pl.
Marten [mär'ten], n.
Martial [mär'shal], a.
Martingal [mär'tin-gal], n.
Mar'tyr dom [mär'tér-dum], n.
Mar'vel ous [mär'vel-us], a. ad.
Masculine [mas'ku-lin], a. n.
Mask [mask], n. v.
Masquerade [mas'ker-ād], n. v.
Mass acre [mas'sa-ker], n. v.
Mast er [mas'tér], n. v.
Masticator [mas'ti-kāt-ér], n.
Mastiff [mas'tif], n.
Mastodon [mas'tō-don], n.
Matador [mat'a-dör], n.
Match [mach], n. v.
Mate [māt], n.
Mate'rial ize [ma-tē'ri-al-īz], v.
Maternal [ma-tér'nal], a.
Maternity [ma-tér'ni-ti], n.   [n.
Mathematician [math-e-ma-tish'an],
Matin [mat'in], a. n.
Matinée [mat-i-nā'], n.
Matricide [mat'ri-sid], n.
Matrimonial [mat-ri-mō'ni-al], a.
Matrix [mā'triks], n.
Matron [mā'tron], n.
Matronal [mat'ron-al, mā'tron-al], a.
Matronize [mat'ron-īz], v.
Mattress [mat'tres], n.

Maturity [ma-tūr'i-ti], n.
Matutinal [mat'ū-ti-nal], a.
Maudlin [mad'lin], a. n.
Maugre [ma'gér], prep.
Mausoleum [ma-sō-lē'um], n.
Mauve [mōv], n.
Mavis [mā'vis], n.
Mawkish [mak'ish], a.
Maxillary [maks'il-la-ri], a.
Max'im um [maks'i-mum], a. n.
  Maxima, pl.
Mayonnaise [mā'on'āz'], n.
May'or alty [mā'ér-al-ti], n.
Mazarine [maz-a-rēn'], n.
Mazily [māz'i-li], ad.
Mazurka [ma-zōōr'ká], n.   [ow
Mead [mēd], n. A beverage; a mead-
Meager, Meagre [mē'gér], a.
Meal y [mēl'i], a.
Mean [mēn], a. Wanting dignity or
  worth. n. Medium. v. To intend;
  to signify.
Measles [mē'zlz], n.
Measurably [mezh'yōōr-a-bli, mezh'-
  ér-a-bli], ad.
Measure [mezh'yōōr, mezh'ér], n. v.
Mechan'ic al [me-kan'ik-al], a.
Mechanician [mek-an-ish'an], n.
Mechanism [mek'an-izm], n.
Mechlin [mek'lin], a. n.
Med'al lion [me-dal'yun], n.
Medallurgy [med'al-ér-ji], n.
Med'dle some [med'l-sum], a.
Mediation [mē-di-ā'shun], n.
Me'diator ial [mē-di-ā-tō'ri-al], a.
Mediatrix [mē'di-āt-riks], n. fem.
Med'ical ly [med'ik-al-li], ad.
Medicament [med'i-ka-ment], n.
Medici de [dā med'e-chē], n. It.
Medicinal [me-dis'i-nal], a.
Medicine [med'i-sin], n.
Medieval [med-i-ē'val], a.
Mediocre [mē'di-ō-kér], n.
Mediocrity [mē-di-ok'ri-ti], n.
Meditation [med'i-tā'shun], n.
Mediterranean [med-i-te-rā'ne-an]
Medium [mē'di-um], a. n.
Medley [med'li], n.
Medulla [me-dul'la], n.
Medusa [me-dū'sa], n.
Meed [mēd], n. A reward.
Meek ness [mēk'nes], n.
Meerschaum [mēr'showm], n.
Meissonier [mā'sun'yā'],   F
  painter.
Melancholy [mel'an-kol-i],

Mêlée [mā'lā], n.
Meliorate [mēl'yor-āt], v.
Mellifluous [mel-lif'lū-us], ~.
Mellow [mel'lō], a. v.
Melodeon [me-lō'de-on], n.
Melodious [me-lō'di-us], a.
Melodrama [mel-o-drä'mä], n.
Melon [mel'on], n.
Melpomene [mel-pom'e-ne]. n.
Mem'brane ous, Membranous
 [mem-brā'ne-us, mem'bra-nus], a.
Memento [me-men'tō], n.
Memoir [mem'wor, mēm'wor], n.
Memorabilia [mem-or-a-bil'i-a], n.pl.
Memorandum [mem-o-ran'dum], n.
 Memoranda, pl.
Memo'rial ize [me-mō'ri-al-īz], v.
Memory [mem'o-ri], n.
Menace [men'as], n. v.
Manage [men-äzh'], n.
Menagery [me-nä'zhe-rē, me-naj'-
 ėr-i], n.
Mendacious [men-dā'shus], a.
Mendacity [men-das'i-ti], n.
Mendelssohn [men'dels-sōn] Musi-
 cal composer.
Mendicancy [men'di-kan-si], n.
Mendicity [men-dis'i-ti], n.
Menhaden [men-hā'den], n.
Menial [mē'ni-al], a. n.
Meningitis [men-in-jī'tis], n.
Mennonite [men'non-īt], n.
Menstrual [men'strōō-al], a.
Menstruum [men'strōō-um], n.
Mensurable [men'shōō-ra-bl], a.
Men'tion able [men'shun-a-bl], a.
Mentor [men'tor], n.
Mephitic [me-fit'ik], a.
Mephitis [me-fī'tis], n.
Mercantile [mėr'kan-til], a.
Mercenary [mėr'se-na-ri], a. n.
Merchandise [mer'chan-dīz], n.
er'chant able [mėr'chant-a-bl], a.
erciful ly [mėr'si-fōōl-li], ad.
erciless [mėr'si-les], a.
ercurial [mėr-kū'ri-al], a. n.
retricious [mer-e-tri'shus], a.
rganser [mėr-gan'sėr], n.
idian [me-rid'i-an], a. n.
ino [me-rē'no], a. n.
it orious [mer-i-tō'ri-us], a.
in [mėr'lin], n
iment [mer'i-ment], n.
atery [mes'en-tėr-i], n.
erize r [mez'mėr-iz-ėr], n.
ge [mes'saj], n.

Mess
Messi
Messi
Messi
 pist.
Met'al
Metam
Metam
Met'api
 ad.
Metaph
Mete [m
Metemp:
Me'teor
Meth'od
Methodiz
Metonym
Metre [na
Met'rical
Metronym
Metropolia
Metropolit:
Mew [mi],
Meyerbeer
Mezzotint [
Miargyrite
Miasma [mi
 [mi-as'ma-ta
Micaceous [u
Michaelmas [
Microcosm [n
Microphone [
Microscope [
Microscop'ic
Microscopy [
Microzyme [
Middle [mid'l
Midget [mij'e
Mid'wife ry
Might ily [m
Mignonette [
Migratory [u
Mikado [mi-k
Milan [mil'an
Milanese [mi
Milch [milsh]
Mildew [mil'd
Mile age [mi
Military [mil
Militia [mi-li
Millais [mil-la
Millena'rian
 izm], n.
Millennium
Millet [mě
Milliner

Million aire [mil-yon-âr'], n.
Mim'ic ry [mim'ik-ri], n.
Minaret [min'a-ret], n.
Min'eral ist [min'er-al-ist], n.
Mineralogy [min-er-al'o-ji], n.
Mingle [ming'gl], v.
Miniature [min'i-tūr], a. n.
Minimize [min'i-mīz], v.
Minion [min'yon], n.
Minister [min-is-tē'ri-al], n. v.
Ministerial [min-is-tē'ri-al], a.
Minority [mi-nor'i-ti], n. [a. n.
Min'strel sy [min'strel-si], n.
Minus [mī'nus], a. Small. [min'it],
Minute [mi-nūt'], a.
Miracle [mir'a-kl], n.
Miraculous [mi-rak'ū-lus], a.
Mirage [mi-räzh'], n.
Mirror [mir'er], n. v.
Mirth ful [mērth'fōol], a.
Misanthrope [mis'an-thrōp], n.
Misanthropic [mis-an-throp'ik], a.
Miscegenation [mis-se-je-nā'shun], n.
Miscellaneous [mis-sel-lā'ne-us], a.
Mischief [mis'chif], n.
Mischievous [mis'chiv-us], a.
Misconstrue [mis-kon-strōō'], v.
Miserable [miz'er-a-bl], a.
Miserere [miz-e-ri-ka'di-a], n.
Misericordia [mis-soj'i-nist], n.
Misogynist [mi-soj'i-nist], n.
Mis'sion ary [mi'shun-a-ri], a. n.
Mistakable [mis-tāk'a-bl], a.
Mistletoe [mis'l-tō], n.
Mitre [mī'tèr], n. v.
Mitten [mit'ten], n.
Mixture [miks'tūr, miks'yŏor, niks'yèr], n.
Mnemonics [nē-mon'iks], n.
Moan [mōn], n. v. To lament.
Moat [mōt], n. A ditch.
Mobile [mō-bēl', mō'bil], a. n.
Mobilize [mol'il-īz], v.
Moccasin [mok'a-sin], n.
Mock'er y [mok'er-i], n.
Mod'el er [mod'el-ér], n.
Moderator [mo'dèr-āt-ér], n.
Mo'dern ize [mo'dèrn-īz], v.
Mo'dest y [mo'des-ti], n.
Modifier [mo'di-fī-ér], n.
Modiste [mo-dēst'], n.
Modu...tor [...ar], n.

Molecular [mo-lek'ū-lèr], a.
Molecule [mol'e-kūl], n.
Molest' er [mo-lest'èr], n.
Mollière [mol'yār], French author.
Mollusk [mol'usk], n.
Moment ous [mo-ment'us], a.
Mo'ment oes [mon'a-kō], n.
Monaco [mon'a-kō], n.
Monad [mon'ad], n.
Mon'arch al [mon-ärk'al], a. [a.
Monastery [mon'ē-ta-ri, mun'ē-ta-ri],
Monetary [mun'ē-ta-ri],
Money [mun'i], n. v.
Monger [mung'gèr], n. v. a.
Mongrel [mung'grel], n.
Monitor [mon'i-tèr], n.
Monk ey [mung'ki], n.
Monacious [mo-nā'shus], a.
Monogamous [mo-nog'a-mus], a.
Monogram [mon'o-gram], n.
Monolith [mon'ō-lith], n.
Monologue [mon'ō-log], n.
Monomania [mon-o-mā'ni-a], n.
Monomaniac [mo-noj'ol-īz], a.
Monopolize [mo-nop'ol-īz], v.
Monosyllable [mon-o-sil-lab'ik], a.
Monotonous [mo-not'on-us], a.
Monsieur [mus'yèr], n. Fr. [Orthoe-
Monotony [mon-stros'i-ti], n. pist.]
Monstrosity [mon-stros'i-ti], n. ad.
Monstrous [mon'strus], a.
Monument al [mon-ū-ment'al], a.
Mon'ument [mod'ū'i-nes], n.
Mood iness [mo-rān'],
Moraine [mo-rān'], n.
Mo'ral ize [mo'ral-īz], v.
Morass [mo-ras'], n.
Morbid ity [mor-bid'i-ti], n.
Mordacious [mor-dā'shus], a.
Morganatic [mor-gan-at'ik], a.
Moribund [mor'i-bund], a.
Mor'mon ism [mor'mon-izm], n.
Morocco [mo-rok'ō], n.
Morpheus [mor'fūs], n.
Morphine [mor'fin], n.
Morsel [mor'sel], n.
Mor'tal ity [mor-tal'i-ti], n.
Mortar [mor'tèr], n.
Mortgage [mor'gāj], n. v.
Mortification [mor-ti-fi-kā'shun], n.
Mortise [mor'tis], n. v.
Mortuary [mor'tū-a-ri], a. n.
Mosaic [mo-zā'ik], a. n.
Moslem [moz'lem], n.
Mosque [mosk], n.
Mosquito [mos-kē'tō], n.
Moss y [mos'i], a.
Mote [mōt], n. A s...
Moth [moth], n.

Mother [mu*th*'ér], a. n. v.
Motion [mō'shun], n. v.
Motley [mot'li], a. n.
Mould er [mōld'ér], n.
Mouldiness [mōld'i-nes], n.
Mount'ain ous [moun'tin-us], a.
Mountebank [moun'ti-bangk], n.
Mourner [mōrn'ér], n.
Mouth [mowth], n. [mowth], v.
Movable [mōōv'a-bl], a. n.
Move ment [mōōv'ment], n. [poser.
Mozart [mōt'särt]. Musical com-
Mucilaginous [mū-si-laj'in-us], a.
Mucus [mū'kus], n.
Muezzin [mù-ed'zin], n.
Maff ler [muf'lér], n. [pl.
Mulatto [mu-lat'tō], n. Mulattoes,
Mulberry [mul'be-ri], n.
Mullen [mul'en], n.
Mullion [mul'yun], n.
Multifarious [mul-ti-fā'ri-us], a.
Multiple [mul'ti-pl], a. n.
Multiplicator [mul'ti-pli-kāt-ér], n.
Multiplicity [mul-ti-plis'i-ti], n.
Multiplier [mul'ti-plī-ér], n.
Multitudinous [mul-ti-tū'din-us], a.
Mummery [mum'ér-i], n.
Munchausen, Baron [mun-chaw'-
sen].
Mundane [mun'dān], a.
Munic'ipal ity [mū-nis-i-pal'i-ti], n.
Munificence [mu-nif'i-sens], n.
Munition [mū-ni'shun], n.
Mur'der er [mér'dér-ér], n.

Murderous [mér'dér-us], a. [
Murillo [mōō-rēl'yo]. Spanish pai
Mur'mur er [mèr'mèr-ér], n.
Murrain [mur'rin], a. n. A diseas
Muscadel, Muscadine [mus'ka-de
mus'ka-dīn], n.
Muscle [mus'l], n.
Muscovado [mus-ko-vā'do], a. n.
Muscular [mus'kū-lér], a.
Museum [mu-zē'um], n.
Mush room [mush'rōōm], n.
Musician [mu-zi'shan], n.
Muskallonge [mus'kal-lonj], n.
Musket [mus'ket], n.
Muslin [muz'lin], a. n.
Mussel [mus'el], n.
Musulman [mus'ul-man], n.
Mustache [mus-täsh'], n.
Mustard [mus'térd], n.
Mutability [mū-ta-bil'i-ti], n.
Mutilator [mū'ti-lāt-ér], n.
Mutineer [mū-ti-nēr'], n.
Mutinous [mū'ti-nus], a.
Mu'tual ly [mū'tū-al-i], ad.
Muzzle [muz'l], n. v.
Myriad [mir'i-ad], a. n.
Myrmidon [mér'mi-don], n.
Myrrh [mér], n.
Myrtle [mér'tl], n.
Mysterious [mis-tē'ri-ús], a.
Mys'tic ism [mis'ti-sizm], n.
Mystificator [mis'ti-fi-kāt-ér], n.
Myth ical [mith'ik-al], a.
Mythology [mith-ol'ō-ji], n.

N.

Neap [nēp], a. n.
Near ly [nēr'li], ad.
Neat ly [nēt'li], ad.
Nebula [neb'ū-lá], n. Nebulæ, pl.
Nebulous [neb'ū-lus], a.
Necessarily [ne'ses-sa-ri-li], ad.
Necrologic [nek-ro-loj'ik], a.
Necrology [ne-krol'o-ji], n.
Necromancer [nek'rō-man-sẽr], n.
Necrophorus [nek-rof'o-rus], n.
Necropolis [nek-rop'o-lis], n.
Nectarean [nek-tā're-an], a.
Nec'tar ine [nek'tar-in], n.
Need iness [nēd'i-nes], n.
Needle [nē'dl], n. v.
Ne'er [nãr], ad.
Nefarious [ne-fā'ri-us], a.
Negation [ne-gā'shun], n.
Negative [neg'a-tiv], n. v.
Neglect' ful [neg-lekt'fool], a.
Negligee [neg-li-zhā'], n.
Negligence [neg'li-jens], n.
Negotiable [ne-gō'shi-a-bl], a.
Negotiator [ne-gō'shi-āt-ẽr], n.
Negro [nē'grō], a. n. Negroes, pl.
Neigh [nā], n. v.
Neighbor [nā'bẽr], n.
Neither [nē'thẽr, ni'thẽr], a. conj.
  pron. [See note under Either.]
Nemesis [nem'e-sis], n.
Neophyte [nē'o-fīt], a. n.
Nepenthe [ne-pen'the], n.
Nephew [ne'vū, nef'fū], n.
Nephritic [ne-frit'ik], a. n.
Nepotism [nep'o-tizm], n.
Neptune [nep'tūn], n.
Nereid [nē're-id], n.
Neroli [ner'ō-li], n.
Nervine [nẽrv'in], n.
Nervous [nẽrv'us], a.
Nescience [nesh'i-ens], n.
Nestle [nes'l], v.
Nether [neth'ẽr], a.
Nettle [net'l], n. v.
Neuralgia [nū-ral'ji-a], n.
Neuralgic [nū-ral'jik], a.
Neuter [nū'tẽr], a. n.
Neu'tral ize [nū'tral-īz], v.
Newel [nū'el], n.
Newfoundland [nū-found'land], n.
Niagara [nī-ag'a-ra], n.
Nice ty [nīs'e-ti], n.
Niche [nich], n.
Nickel [nik'el], n.
Nicotine [nik'ō-tin], n.
Niece [nēs], n.

Niggard [nig'ẽrd], a. n.
Night ingale [nīt'in-gāl], n.
Nihilism [ni'hil-izm], n.
Nimble [nim'bl], a.
Ninth [ninth], a. n.
Niobe [ni'o-be], n.
Nipple [nip'l], n.
Nirvana [nir-vä'na], n.
Nitrogen [ni'trō-jen], n.
Nitrogenous [ni-troj'en-us], a.
Nitrous [ni'trus], a.
Nobility [nō-bil'i-ti], n.
No'ble ness [nō'bl-nes], n.   [Fr.
Noblesse oblige [nō'bles' o'blēzh'],
Noc'turn al [nok-tẽr'nal], a.
Noise less [noiz'les], a.
Noisily [noiz'i-li], ad.
Noisome [noi'sum], a.
Nomad [nom'ad], n.
Nomadic [no-mad'ik], a.
Nomenclature [nō'men-klāt-ẽr], n.
Nom'inal ly [nom'in-al-li], ad.
Nominative [nom'i-na-tiv], a. n.
Nominator [nom'in-āt-ẽr], n.
Nominee [nom-i-nē'], n.
Nonchalance [non'sha'lähs'], n.
Nondescript [non'de-skript], a. n.
None [nun], a. pron.
Nonentity [non-en'ti-ti], n.
Nonpareil [non-pa-rel'], n.
Nonplus [non'plus], n. v.
Nonsenrical [non-sen'si-kal], a.
Nook [nook], n.
Noose [nōōz], n. v.
Normal [nor'mal], a.
North ern [nor'thẽrn], a. n.
Nosology [no-sol'o-ji], n.
Nostril [nos'tril], n.
Notable [nōt'a-bl], a. n. Remarkable.
  [not'a-bl], a.   Careful and active.
Notation [nō-tā'shun], n.
Notch [noch], n. v.
Nothing [nu'thing], ad. n.
No'tice able [nō'tis-a-bl], a.
No'tion al [nō'shun-al], a.
Notoriety [nō-tō-rī'e-ti], n.
Notorious [nō-tō'ri-us], a.
Noun [nown], n.
Nour'ish er [nur'ish-ẽr], n.
Nov'el ist [nov'el-ist], n.
Novice [nov'is], n.
Novitiate [nō-vish'i-at], n.
Noxious [nok'shus], a.
Nozzle [noz'l], n.
Nucleus [nū'kle-us], n. Nuclei [nū-
  kle-ī'], pl.

Nude [nūd], a. n.
Nudge [nuj], n. v.
Nudity [nū'di-ti], n.
Nugatory [nū'ga-to-ri], a.
Nugget [nug'et], n.
Nuisance [nū'sans], n.
Nullifier [nul'i-fī-ėr], n.
Numb ness [num'nes], n.
Numeral [nūm'ėr-al], n.
Numerator [nū'mėr-āt-ėr], n.
Numerical [nū-mer'ik-al], a.

Numerous [nū'mėr-us], a.
Numismatics [nū-miz-mat'iks], n.
Nuncio [nun'shi-ō], n.
Nunnery [nun'ėr-i], n.
Nuptial [nup'shal], a. n.
Nurse ry [nėrs'ėr-], n. [n. v.
Nurture [nėr'tūr, nėrt'yōōr, nėrt'yėr],
Nutriment [nū'tri-ment], n.
Nutritious [nū-tri'shus], a.
Nympa [nimf], n.
Nymphæa [nim-fē'a], n.

O.

Oaf [ōf], n.
Oak en [ōk'n], a.
Oar [ōr], n. v.
Oasis [ō'ā-sis], n. Oasēs, pl.
Oath [ōth], n. Oaths [ōthzs], pl.
Obduracy [ob'du-ra-si], n.
Obedience [ō-bē'di-ens], n.
Obeisance [ō-bā'sans, ō-bē'sans], n.
Obelisk [ob'e-lisk], n.
Oberon [ob'ėr-on], n.
Obese [ō-bēs'], a.
Obesity [ō-bes'i-ti], n.
Obey' er [ō-bā'ėr], n.
Obfuscate [ob-fus'kāt], v.
Obituary [o-bit'ū-a-ri], a. n.
Objector [ob-jekt'ėr], n.
Objurgation [ob-jėr-gā'shun], n.
Oblation [ob-lā'shun], n.
Obligato [ob-le-gā'tō], a.
Obligatory [ob'li-ga-to-ri], a.
Oblige [ō-blīj'], v.
Oblique [ob-lēk', ob-līk'], a.
Obliquity [ob-lik'wi-ti], n.
Obliterate [ob-lit'ėr-āt], a. v.
Oblivious [ob-liv'i-us], a.
Obloquy [ob'lo-kwi], n.
Obnoxious [ob-nok'shus], a.
Obscene' ness, Obscenity [ob-sēn'-
nes, ob-sen'i-ti], n.
Obscuration [ob-skū-rā'shun], n.
Obscurity [ob-skū'ri-ti], n.
Obsequious [ob-sē'kwi-us], a. [pl.
Obsequy [ob'sē-kwi], n. Obsequies,
Observance [ob-zėrv'ans], n.
Observatory [ob-zėrv'a-tō-ri], n.
Obsolete [ob'sō-lēt], a.
Obstacle [ob'sta-kl], n.
Obstetrician [ob-ste-trish'an], n.
Obstinacy [ob'sti-na-si], n.
Obstruct' er [ob-strukt'ėr], n.

Obtain' able [ob-tān'a-bl], a.
Obtrusion [ob-trōō'zhun], n.
Obtuse [ob-tūs'], a.
Obverse [ob-vėrs'], a. [ob'vėrs], n.
Obviate [ob'vi-āt], v.
Ob'vious ly [ob'vi-us-li], ad.
Occa'sion al ly [ok-kā'zhun-al-li],ad.
Oc'cident al [ok-si-dent'al], a.
Occult' ation [ok-kul-tā'shun], n.
Occupancy [ok'kū-pan-si], n.
Occupier [ok'kū-pī-ėr], n.
Occur' rence [ok-kur'rens], n.
Ocean [ō'shan], a. n.
Oceanic [ō-shē-an'ik], a.
Ocelot [ū'se-lot], n.
Ochre [ō'kėr], n.
Ochrea [ō'kre-a], n.
Ochreous [ō'kre-us], a.
Octagon [ok'ta-gon], n.
Octagonal [ok-tag'on-al], a.
Octahedron [ok-ta-hē'dron], n.
Octameter [ok-tam'et-ėr], n.
Octave [ok'tāv], a. n.
Octavo [ok-tā'vō], a. n.
October [ok-tō'bėr], n.
Octogenarian [ok-tō-je-nā'ri-an], n.
Octogenary [ok-toj'e-na-ri], n.
Octopus [ok'tō-pus], n.
Octuple [ok'tū-pl], a.
Ocular [ok'ū-lėr], a. n.
Odd ly [od'li], ad.
Odeon [ō-dē'on], n.
Odious [ō'di-us], a.
Odometer [ō-dom'et-ėr], n.
Odontoid [ō-don'toid], a.
O'dor iferous [ō-dėr-if'ėr-us], a.
Odorous [ō'dėr-us], a.
Odyssey [od'is-se], n.
Œsophagus [e-sof'a-gus], n.
Of [ov], prep.

Off [of], a. ad. inter. prep. v.	**Opossum** [op-pos-...]
Offal [of'al], n.	**Opponent** [op-pō'nent], n.
Offence [of-fens'], n.	**Opportunity** [op-por-zi'shun], n.
Offend' er [of-fend'er], n.	**Opportune** [op-por-tūn'er], n.
Offer tory [of'fer-to-ri], n.	**Opposition or** [op-pres'er], n.
Officer [of'fis-er], n. v.	**Oppress** [op-pro'ri-us], a.
Official ly [of-fi'shal-li], ad.	**Opprobrious** [op-prō'bri-us], a.
Officiator [of-fi'shi-āt-er], n.	**Optical** [op'tik-al], a.
Officious [of-fi'shus], a.	**Optician** [op-tish'an], n.
Oft en [of'n], a. ad.	**Optimism** [op'ti-mizm], n.
Ogle [ō'gl], v.	**Option al** [op'shun-al], a.
Ogre [ō'ger], n.	**Opulency** [op'ū-len-si], n.
Oil y [oil'i], a.	**Oracle** [o-rak'ū-lēr], n.
Old en [ōld'n], a.	**Oracular** [or-enl-ad'], n.
Oleaginous [ō-le-aj'in-us], a.	**Orange ade** [ō-rang'oō-tang], n.
Oleander [ō-le-an'der], n.	**Orang-outang** [ō-rā-ter], n.
Olefiant [ō'le-fi-ant, o-lef'i-ant], a.	**Orator** [or-a-tor'ik-al], a.
Oleomargarine [ō-le-o-mär'ga-rin], n.	**Oratorical** [or-a-to'ri-ō], n.
Olfactory [ol-fak'to-ri], a.	**Oratorio** [or'a-to-ri], n.
Olibanum [o-lib'a-num], n.	**Oratory** [or-bik'ū-lēr], a.
Oligandrous [ol-i-gan'drus], a.	**Orb icular** [or'bit], n.
Oligarchy [ol'i-gär-ki], n.	**Orbit** [or'cherd], n.
Olive [ol'iv], a. n.	**Orchard** [or'kes-tra], a.
Olympiad [ō-lim'pi-ad], n.	**Orchestra** [or'kes-tral], a.
Omega [ō-mē'ga], n.	**Orchestral** [or-ki-dā'se-ē], n. pl.
Omelet [om'e-let], n.	**Orchid aceæ** [or-dān'er], n.
Omen [ō'men], n. v.	**Ordain' er** [or-dē-al'], n.
Ominous [om'i-nus], a.	**Ordeal** [or'di-nal], a. n.
Omission [ō-mi'shun], n.	**Ordinal** [or'di-nans], n.
Omnibus [om'ni-bus], n.	**Ordinance** [or-di-na-ti], n.
Omnipotence [om-nip'o-tens], n.	**Ordinary** [or-di-nā'shun], n.
Omniscience [om-ni'shi-ens], n.	**Ordination** [or'di-nāt-er], n.
Omnivorous [om-niv'o-rus], a.	**Ordinator** [or'gan-ist], n.
Once [wuns] ad.	**Organ ist** [or-gan-i-zā'shun], n.
Oneirocritic [o-ni-ro-krit'ik], a.	**Organization** [or'jiz], n. pl.
Oneiromancy [o-nī'ro-man-si], n.	**Orgies** [or'i-el], n. A window.
Onerous [on'er-us], a.	**Oriel** [ō-ri-en'tal-ist], n.
Onion [un'yun], n.	**Orient al ist** [ō-ri-fis], n.
Only [ōn'li], a. ad. con.	**Orifice** [ō-ri l-naf'i-ti], n.
Onomatology [on-o-ma-tol'o-ji], n.	**Oriflamb, Oriflamme** [ō-ri l-flam...]
Onslaught [on'slat], n.	**Original ity** [o-rij'i-nāt-er], n.
Onyx [ō'niks], n.	**Originator** [ō-ri-ōl], n. A bird.
Oolite [ō'o-līt], n. v.	**Oriole** [ō-ri'un], n.
Ooze [ōōz], n. v.	**Orion** [o-ri'zon], n.
Opal escent [ō-pal-es'ent], a.	**Orison** [or-na-men...], n.
Opaline [ō'pal-in], n.	**Ornament al** [or'nāt], a.
Opaque [ō-pāk'], a. n.	**Ornate** [or-ni-thol'o...]
Opera [op'e-rä], n.	**Ornithology** [ō'roid], n.
Operator [op'er-ā-ter], n.	**Oroide** [ō'ro-tund], a.
Operetta [op-er-et'tä], n.	**Orotund** [or'fan], a.
Ophicleide [of'i-klīd], n.	**Orphan age** [or'fē-an], a.
Ophthalmy [of'thal-mi], a. n. [of'thal-mi, op'thal-mi],	**Orphean** [or'fus, org...]
Opiate [ō'pi-āt], n.	**Orpheus** [or'tho...]
Opiniative [o-pin'ya-tiv, o-pin'ye-a-tiv], a.	**Orthodox y** [or'tho...]
Opin'ion ated [o-pin'yun-āt-ed], a.	**Orthoepist** [or'tho...]

āle, add, beär, ärm, âsk, fall; mē, met, thēre, hēr; pīne.

Orthoepy [or'tho-e-pī], n.
Orthography [or-thog'ra-fī], n.
Orycteropus [o-rik-ter'o-pus], n.
Oscillator [os'sil-lāt-ėr], n.
Osculation [os-ku-lā'shun], n.
Osier [ō'zhér], a. n.
Osprey [os'prā], n.
Osseous [os'sē-us], a.
Ossian [osh'an], n.
Ostensible [os-ten'si-bl], a.
Ostentatious [os-ten-tā'shus], a.
Ostler [os'lér], n. See *Hostler*.
Ostracize [os'tra-sīz], v.
Ostrich [os'trich], n.
Other [u*th*'ėr], a. pro.
Ottar [ot'tär], n. An essence.
Otter [ot'ėr], n. An animal.
Ottoman [ot'tō-man], a. n.
Ouch [ouch], n.
Ought [at], n. v.
Ounce [ouns], n.

Ous
Out
Out
Ora
Ova
O'v
Ove
Ove
Ove
Ovi
Ovi
Ow.
Ox
Ox
Ox
Ox
Ox
Oy
Oy
Oy
Os

P.

Pabulum [pab'ū-lum], a.
Pace [pās], n. v.
Pacha, Pasha [pa-shä'], n.
Pachyderm [pak'i-dėrm], n.
Pacification [pa-sif-i-kā'shun], n.
Pacific ator [pa-sif'i-kāt-ėr], n.
Pacifier [pas'i-fi-ėr], n.
Pack et [pak'et], n. v.
Paddle [pad'l], n. v.
Paddock [pad'ok], n.
Pæan [pē'an], n.
Paganini [pä-gä-nē'nē]. Italian violinist.
Pa'gan ize [pā'gan-īz], v.
Pageant [paj'ent], n.
Pagoda [pa-gō'da], n.
Pall [päl], n. A vessel.
Pain [pān], n. v. Suffering.
Paint er [pānt'ėr], n.
Pair [pár], n. A couple.
Palace [pal'as], n.
Palad [pal'a-din], n.
Palanquin, Palankeen [pal-an-kēn'], [n.
Palatable [pal'at-a-bl], a.
Palatine [pal'a-tīn], a. n.
Palaver [pa-lä'vėr], n. v.
Pale [pāl], a. n. v. Pallor ; a stake.
Palestine [pal'es-tīn], n.
Paletot [pal'e-tō], n.
Palfrey [pal'fri], n.

sh. | **Parol** [par'ol], a. n. Legal term.
Parole [pa-rōl'], n. Military term.
Paroquet, Parrakeet [par'o-ket, par'-a-kĕt], n.
Parotid [pa-rot'id], a. n.
Paroxysm [par'oks-izm], n.
Parquet [pär'kā'], n.
Parquetry [pär'ket-ri], n.
Parricide [par'-ri-sid], n.
Parrot [par'ot], n. v.

ĕ], | **Parsimonious** [pär-si-mō'ni-us], a.
Parsimony [pär'si mo-ni], n.

. | **Parsley** [pärs'li], n.
Parsnip [pärs'nip], n.
Par'son age [pär'sn-āj], n.
Parterre [pär-târ'], n.
Parthenon [pär'the-non], n.
Parthian [pär'thi-an], a.
Partial [pär'shal], a.
Partiality [pär-shi-al'i-ti], n.
Partible [pärt'i-bl], a.
Participant [pär-tis'i-pant], n.

ı. | **Participator** [pär-tis'i-pāt-ẽr], n.
Participial [pär-ti-sip'i-al], a. n.
Participle [pär'ti-si-pl], n.
Partic'ular ly [pär-tik'ū-lẽr-li], a
Partisan [pär'ti-zan], a. n.
Partition [pär-ti'shun], n. v.
Partner [pärt'nẽr], n
Partridge [pär'tri], n
Parturition [pär-tu-ri'shun], n.

pl. | **Parvenu** [pär've-nū], n.
n. | **Pasquinade** [pas-kwin-ād'], n. v.
Pass able [pas'a-bl], a.
Passenger [pas'en-jẽr], n.
Pas'sion ate [pa'shun-āt], a.
Passivity [pas-si'vi-ti], n.
Pastel [pas'tel], n. A crayon.
Pastil [pas'til], n. A lozenge.
Pas'tor al [pàs'tor-al], a. n.
Pasturage [pàs'tūr-āj, past'yŏŏr-ā' past'yẽr-āj], n.

?a- | **Patch** [pach], n. v.
pl. | **Patella** [pa-tel'la], n.
la, | **Patent** [pat'ent], a. n. v.
Patentee [pat-en-tē'], n
Paternal [pa-tẽr'nal], a.
Paternity [pa-tẽr'ni-ti], n.
Pater-noster [pā'tẽr-nos-
Pathetic [pa-thet'ik], a.
Pathology [pa-thol'o-ji]
Pathos [pā'thos], n.
Patience [pā'shens], ı
Patois [pat'wä'], n.
Patriarch [pā'tri-ärk
Patrician [pa-trish'a

Patrimony [pat'ri-mo-ni]. n.
Pa'triot ism [pā'tri-ot-izm], n.
Patrol [pa-trōl'], n. v.
Patron [pā'tron], a. n.
Patronage [pat'ron-āj], n.
Patronal [pat'ron-al], a.
Patroness [pā'tron-es], n.
Patronize [pat'ron-īz], v.
Patronymic [pat-ro-nim'ik], a. n.
Pattern [pat'ern], n. v.
Paucity [pa'si-ti], n.
Paunch [pänsh], n. v.
Pau'per ism [pa'pėr-izm], n.
Pave ment [pāv'ment], n.
Pavilion [pa-vil'yun], n. v.
Pea [pē], n. **Peas, Pease,** pl. [*Peas* is used when number is referred to; as, "Five *peas*," and *pease*, when species or quantity is denoted; as, " A peck of *pease*."
Peace able [pēs'a-bl], a.
Peach [pēch], n. v.
Peacock [pē'kok], n. [sickly.
Peak [pēk], n. A point. v. To look
Peal [pēl], n. A loud sound. v. To ring.
Pear [pâr], n. A fruit.
Pearl [pėrl], a. n.
Pearmain [pâr'mān], n.
Peas'ant ry [pez'ent-ri], n.
Peat [pēt], n. Fuel.
Peccadillo [pek-a-dil'ō], n.
Peccant [pek'ant], a.
Peculator [pek'ū-lāt-ėr], n.
Peculiar [pe-kūl'yar], a.
Peculiarity [pe-kūl-ye-ar'i-ti], n.
Pecuniary [pe-kūn'ya-ri], a.
Pedagogue [ped'a-gog], n.
Pedagogy [ped'a-go-ji], n.
Pedal [pē'dal], a. [ped'al].
Ped'ant ry [ped'ant-ri], n.
Peddle [ped'l], v.
Pedestal [ped'es-tal], n. v.
Pedestrian [pe-des'tri-an], n.
Pedicel [ped'i-sel], n.
Pedigree [ped'i-grē], n.
Pedler [ped'lėr], n.
Peek [pēk], v. To peep.
Peel [pēl], n. A rind. v. **To strip off.**
Peer ess [pēr'es], n.
Peevish [pē'vish], a.
Pegasus [peg'a-sus], n.
Pelargonium [pel-är-gō'ni-um], n.
Pelican [pel'i-kan], n.
Pellet [pel'et], n.
Pellucid [pel-lū'sid], a.

Pelvis [pel'vis], n.
Penal [pē'nal], a.
Penalty [pen'al-ti], n.
Penance [pen'ans], n.
Penates [pe-nā'tēz], n. pl.
Pencil [pen'sil], n.
Pendulous [pen'dū-lus], a.
Penelope [pe-nel'ō-pe], n.
Penetrable [pen'e-tra-bl], a.
Penetration [pen-e-trā'shun], n.
Penguin [pen'gwin], n.
Pen'itent ial [pen-i-ten'shal], a. n.
Penitentiary [pen-i-ten'sha-ri], n.
Pennon [pen'on], n.
Pen'sion er [pen'shun-ėr], n.
Pentameter [pen-tam'et-ėr], a. n.
Pentateuch [pen'ta-tūk], n.
Pen'tecost al [pen-tē-kos'tal], a. n.
Pē'nult imate [pe-nul'ti-māt], a. n.
Penurious [pe-nū'ri-us], a.
Penury [pen'ū-ri], n.
Peony [pē'o-ni], n.
People [pē'pl], n. v.
Pepper [pep'pėr], n. v.
Pepsin [pep'sin], n.
Peradventure [per-ad-vent'yŏor, per-ad-vent'yėr], ad.
Perambulator [pėr-am'bū-lā-tėr], **n.**
Perceivable [pėr-sēv'a-bl], a.
Perceive [pėr-sēv'], v.
Perceptible [pėr-sep'ti-bl], a.
Percolator [pėr'ko-lāt-ėr], n.
Percussion [pėr-kush'un], n.
Perdition [per-di'shun], n.
Peregrinator [per'e-grin-āt-ėr], n.
Peremptory [per'emp-to-ri], a.
Peren'nial ly [per-en'i-al-li], ad.
Per'fect ible [pėr-fekt'i-bl], a.
Perfec'tion ist [pėr-fek'shun-ist], n.
Perfidious [pėr-fid'i-us], a.
Perforator [pėr'for-āt-ėr], n.
Perform' able [pėr-form'a-bl], a.
Performer [pėr-form'ėr], n.
Perfume [pėr'fūm], n. [pėr-fūm'], v.
Perfunctory [pėr-funk'to-ri], a.
Perhaps [pėr-haps'], ad.
Perianth [per'i-anth], n.
Perigynium [per-i-jin'i-um], n.
Perigynous [pe-rij'i-nus], a.
Perihelion [per-i-hē'li-on], n. **Perihelia,** pl.
Pe'ril ous [pe'ril-us], a.
Pe'riod ic al [pe-ri'od'ik-al], a. n.
Periosteum [per-i-os'te-um], n.
Peripatetic [per-i-pa-tet'ik], a. n.
Periphery [pe-rif'er-i], n.

Periphrasis [pe-rif'ra-sis], n.
Periphyllia [per-i-fil'i-a], n. pl.
Pe'rish able [pe'rish-a-bl], a.
Peristaltic [per-i-stal'tik], a.
Perisystole [per-i-sis'to-le], n.
Peritonitis [per-i-to-ni'tis], n.
Perjurer [pèr'jùr-ėr], n.
Permanence [pèr'ma-nens], n.
Permeable [pèr'mē-a-bl], a.
Permission [pèr-mi'shun], n.
Permit' ter [pèr-mit'èr], n.
Pernicious [pèr-nish'us], a.
Pernicketty [per-nik'et-ti], a.
Peroration [per-ō-rā'shun], n.
Perpendic'ular ity [pèr-pen-dik-ū-lar'i-ti], n.
Perpetrator [pèr'pe-trā-tėr], n.
Perpet'ual ly [pèr-pet'ū-al-li], ad.
Perpetuity [pèr-pe-tū'i-ti], n.
Perplex' ity [pèr-pleks'i-ti], n.
Perquisite [pèr'kwi-zit], n.
Persecutor [pèr'se-kūt-ėr], n.
Perseus [pèr'sūs], n.
Perseverance [pèr-se-vē'rans] n.
Persian [pèr'shan], n.
Persiflage [pár'se'flāzh'], n.
Persimmon [pèr-sim'mon], n.
Persist' ence [pèr-sist'ens], n.
Per'sonal ity [pèr-son-al'i-ti], n.
Personator [pèr'son-āt-ėr], n.
Personnel [pèr-son-el'], n.
Perspective [pèr-spek'tiv], n.
Perspicacious [pèr-spi-kā'shus] a.
Perspicacity [pèr-spi-kas'i-ti], n.
Perspicuity [pèr-spi-kū'i-ti], n.
Perspicuous [pèr-spik'ū-us], a.
Perspirable [pèr-spi'ra-bl], a.
Perspiration [pèr-spi-rā'shun], n.
Persuasible [pèr-swā'zi-bl], a.
Persuasion [pèr-swā'zhun], n.
Persuasive [pèr-swā'siv], a.
Pertinacious [pèr-ti-nā'shus] a.
Pertinacity [pèr-ti-nas'i-ti], n.
Pertinent [pèr'ti-nent], a.
Perturbance [pèr-tèrb'ans], n.
Perturbator [pèr'tèrb-āt-ėr], n.
Peruke [per'ook], n.
Peruse [pe-rōōz'], v.
Perversity [pèr-vèr'si-ti], n.
Pervert' er [pèr-vèrt'èr], n.
Pessary [pes'a-ri], n.
Pessimism [pes'im-izm], n.
Pestiferous [pes-tif'ėr-us], a.
Pestilence [pes'ti-lens], n.
Pestilential [pes-ti-len'shal], a.
Pestle [pes'l], n. v.

Pet'al ous [pet'al-us], a.
Petiole [pet'i-ōl], n.
Peti'tion er [pe-tish'un-ėr], n.
Petrel [pet'rel], n.
Petrifiable [pet'ri-fi-a-bl], a.
Petroleum [pe-trō'le-um], n.
Petrous [pē'trus], a.
Pet'tifog ger [pet'ti-fog-ėr], n.
Petulance [pet'ū-lans], n.
Petunia [pe-tū'ni-a], n.
Pew ter [pū'tèr], a. n.
Phaeton [fā'e-ton], n.
Phalanx [fā'langks, fal'angks], n.
Phan'tasm agoria [fan-tas-ma-gō'ri-a], n.
Phantasmal [fan-taz'mal], a.
Phantom [fan'tom], n.
Pharisaical [far-i-sā'ik-al], a.
Pharisee [far'i-sē], n.
Pharmaceutics [fär-ma-sū'tiks], n.
Pharmacist [fär'ma-sist], n.
Pharmacopœia [fär-ma-ko-pē'ya], n.
Pharyngitis [fa-rin-ji'tis], n.
Pharynx [far'ingks], n.
Phase. [fāz], n.
Pheasant [fez'ant], n.
Phenomenon [fe-nom'e-non], n. Phenomena, pl.
Phial [fi'al], n. [a.
Philanthrop'ic al [fil-an-throp'ik-al],
Philanthropist [fi-lan'throp-ist], n.
Philippic [fi-lip'pik], n.
Philistine [fi-lis'tin], n.
Philology [fi-lol'o-ji], n.
Philosopher [fi-los'ō-fèr], n.
Philosophic [fil-o-sof'ik], a.
Philosophize [fi-los'ō-fīz], v.
Philter [fil'tèr], n. v. A love potion.
Phlegm [flem], n.
Phlegmatic [fleg-mat'ik], a.
Phlox [floks], n.
Phœnix [fē'niks], n.
Phonetics [fō-net'iks], n.
Phonics [fon'iks], n.
Phonograph [fō'nō-graf], n.
Phosphate [fos'fāt], n.
Phosphorescence [fos-fo-res'ens], n.
Phosphorous [fos'for-us], a.
Phosphorus [fos'for-us], n.
Photographer [fō-tog'raf-ėr], n.
Photography [fō-tog'ra-fi], n.
Phrase ology [frā-ze-ol'o-ji], n.
Phrenitis [fre-ni'tis], n.
Phrenologic [fren-o-loj']
Phrenology [fre-nol'o-y
Phthisic [tiz'ik], n.

āle, add, beâr, ärm, ásk, fall , mē met, thêre, hèr ; pine, pin , ç

Phthisis [thĭ'sĭs], n.
Phylactery [fĭ-lăk'tẽr-ĭ], n.
Phys'ic al ly [fĭz'ĭk-al-lĭ], ad
Physician [fĭ-zĭ'shan], n.
Physicist [fĭz'ĭ-sĭst], n.
Physiognomy [fĭz-ĭ-ŏg'no-mĭ], n.
Physiology [fĭz-ĭ-ŏl'o-jĭ], n.
Physique [fe-zēk'], n.
Pianist [pĭ-ăn'ĭst], n.
Piano-forte [pē-ä'nŏ-fōr'tä], n.
Piazza [pĭ-ăz'za], n.
Pibroch [pē'brok], n.
Pica [pī'ka], n.
Picayune [pĭk-a-yūn'], n.
Piccolo [pĭk'ko-lŏ], n.
Pickerel [pĭk'ẽr-el], n.
Pickle [pĭk'l], n. v.
Picnic [pĭk'nĭk], n. v.
Pictorial [pĭk-tō'rĭ-al], a.　　　[n. v.
Picture [pĭk'tūr, pĭkt'yŏŏr, pĭkt'yẽr],
Picturesque [pĭk-tūr-esk', pĭkt-yŏŏr-esk', pĭkt-yẽr-esk'], a.
Piebald [pī'bạld], a.
Piece [pēs], n. A fragment. v. To
　mend.
Pied [pīd], a.
Pier [pẽr], n. Masonry supporting
　an arch ; a jetty.
Pierce able [pẽrs'a-bl], a.
Piety [pī'e-tĭ], n.
Pigeon [pĭj'on], n.
Pigotite [pĭg'ŏt-ĭt], n.
Pilaster [pĭ-las'tẽr], n.
Pil'fer er [pĭl'fẽr-ẽr], n.
Pil'grim age [pĭl'grĭm-äj], n.
Pillion [pĭl'yun], n.
Pillory [pĭl'lo-rĭ], n. v.
Pillow [pĭl'lŏ], n. v.
Pimpernel [pĭm'pẽr-nel], n.
Pimple [pĭm'pl], n.
Pincers [pĭn'sẽrz], n. pl.
Pinch [pĭnsh], n. v.
Pine y [pīn'ĭ], a.
Pinnacle [pĭn'a-kl], n. v.
Pinnatifid [pĭn-nat'ĭ-fĭd], a.
Pioneer [pī-o-nẽr'], n. v.
Pious [pī'us], a.
Pippin [pĭp'ĭn], n.
Pipsissewa [pĭp-sĭs'se-wä], n.
Piquancy [pĭk'an-sĭ], n.
Piquant [pĭk'ant, pē'kant], a.
Pique [pēk], n. Displeasure. v. To
　stimulate ; to offend.
Piqué [pē'kā'], n. A dress fabric.
Piquet [pĭk'et], n. A game of cards.
Piquette [pē-ket'], n. Sour wine.

Piracy [pī'ra-sĭ], n.
Piratical [pĭ-rat'ĭk-al], a.
Pirogue [pĭ-rŏg'], n.
Pirouette [pĭr'ŏŏ-et], n. v.
Piscatory [pĭs'ka-to-rĭ], a.
Pia'til lary [pĭs'tĭl-la-rĭ], a.
Pistol [pĭs'tol], n. v. A firearm.
Piston [pĭs'ton], n.
Pitch er [pĭch'ẽr], n.
Piteous [pĭt'e-us], a.
Pitiable [pĭt'ĭ-a-bl], a.
Pitiful [pĭt'ĭ-fŏŏl], a.
Pittance [pĭt'ans], n.
Placable [plă'ka-bl], a.
Placard [pla-kärd', plak'ärd], n. v.
Place [plās], n. v.
Placenta [pla-sen'ta], n.
Placer [pla-sẽr'], n. A gold field.
Pla'cid ity [pla-sĭd'ĭ-tĭ], n.
Plagiarism [plă'jĭ-a-rĭzm], n.
Plagiarize [plă'jĭ-a-rīz], v.
Plague [plāg], n. v.
Plaice [plās], n. A fish.
Plaid [plad], a. n.
Plain ly [plān'lĭ], ad.
Plaint iff [plān'tĭf], n.
Plait [plāt], n. v.
Planchette [plan-shet'], n.
Plane [plān], n. A tool ; **a level sur-**
　face. v. To smooth.
Plan'et ary [plan'et-a-rĭ], a.
Plant ain [plan'tĭn], n.
Plantation [plan-tā'shun], n.
Plateau [plă'tŏ'], n.
Platina [plat'ĭ-na], n.
Platinum [plat'ĭ-num], n.
Platonic [pla-ton'ĭk], a. n.
Platonism [plă'ton-ĭzm], n.
Platoon [pla-tŏŏn'], n.
Plaudit [plâ'dĭt], n.
Plausibility [plâz-ĭ-bĭl'ĭ-tĭ], n.
Plead er [plēd'ẽr], n.
Pleas'ant ry [plez'ant-rĭ], n.
Pleasurable [plezh'ur-a-bl], a.
Pleasure [plezh'ur], n.
Plebeian [ple-bē'yan], a. n.
Pledge [plej], n. v.
Ple'iad es [plē'ya-dēz], n. pl.
Plenary [plen'a-rĭ, plē'na-rĭ], a.
Plenipotentiary [plen-ĭ-pŏ-ten'shĭ-a-rĭ], a. n.
Plenitude [plen'ĭ-tūd], n.
Plenteous [plen'te-us], a.
Plen'tiful ly [plen'tĭ-fŏŏl-lĭ], ad.
Plethora [pleth'o-ra], n.
Plethoric [ple-thor'ĭk], a.

]lūm'āj], n.
]lum'ẽr], n.
]m], n. v.
]plum'et], n.
plū-mōs'], a.
y [plū-ral'i-ti], n.
cs [nū-mat'iks], n.
ia [nū-mŏ'ni-à], n.
[pŏch'ẽr], n.
llum [pod-o-fil'lum], n.
ŏ'em], n.
al ly [pŏ-et'ik-al-li], ad.
cy [pol'nan-si], n.
r [point'ẽr], n.
]oiz], n. v.
[pol'zn], n. v.
ity [po-lar'i-ti], n.
ation [pol-ẽr-ĭ-zā'shun], n.
cs [pŏ-lem'iks], n.
[po-lēs'], n.
[po'li-si], n.
ness [pŏ-lit'nes], n.
cal ly [pŏ-lit'ik-al-li], ad.
cian [po-li-ti'shan], n.
l [pol'en], n.
tion [pol-lū'shun], n.
aise [pŏ-lo-nāz'], n.
ndria [po-li-an'dri-a], n.
nthus [po-li-an'thus], n.
mous [po-lig'a-mus], a.

Porpoise [...]
Porridge [por'ij], n.
Porringer [por'in-jẽr], n.
Port able [pōrt'a-bl], a.
Portal [pōrt'al], a. n.
Portcullis [pōrt-kul'is], n.
Porte-monnaie [pōrt'mon-na], n.
Portent ous [por-ten'tus], a.
Portfolio [pōrt-fō'li-ō], n.
Portière [par-ti'ãr'], n.
Por'tion er [pōr'shun-ẽr], n.
Portmanteau [pōrt-man'tō], n.
Por'trait ure [pōr'trāt-ūr], n.
Portray' al [pōr-trā'al], n.
Position [po-zish'un], n.
Positive [poz'i-tiv], a. n.
Possess ion [poz-zesh'un], n.
Possessor [poz-zes'ẽr], n.
Possibility [pos-i-bil'i-ti], n.
Posterior [pos-tē'ri-ẽr], a.
Posthumous [post'hu-mus], a.
Posture [pos'tūr, post'yōor, post
Potassium [po-tas'si-um], n.
Potato [po-tā'tō], n. Potatoes
Potentate [pō'ten-tāt], n.
Poten'tial ity [pŏ-ten-shi-al'i-t
Pot-pourri [pō'pōō'rē'], n.
Pottage [pot'āj], n.
Pot'ter y [pot'ẽr-i], n.
Pouch [powch], n. v.
Poultry [pōl'tri], n.

n al [pro-sesn-un-ai], ..
er [prō-klām'er], n.
tion [prok-la-mī'shun], n.
y [pro-kliv'i-tī], n.   [n.
inator [pro-kras'ti-nāt-ėr],
[prok'tėr], n.
tor [prok'ū-rāt'ėr], n.
as [pro-kūr'es], n.
il ity [prod-i-gal'i-tī], n.
ous [pro-dij'us], a.
[prod'i-ji], n.
e [prod'ūs], n. [pro-dūs'], v.
ible [pro-dūs'i-bl], a.
ct ion [pro-duk'shun], n.
nation [pro-fa-nā'shun], n.
nity [pro-fan'i-tī], n.
as' or [pro-fes'ėr], n.
ar [prof'ėr], n. v.
ciency [pro-fish'en-si], n.
le [prō'fēl, prō'fil], n. v.
it able [prof'it-a-bl], a.
ligacy [prof'li-ga-si], n.
ound [pro-found'], a. n.
undity [pro-fun-di-tī], n.
use' ly [pro-fūs'li], ad.
usion [pro-fū'zhun], n.
enitor [pro-jen'i-tėr], n.
eny [proj'e-ni], n.
nostic ator [prog-nos-ti-kāt'-
~ [prō'gram],n.

Pronunciamen... LF
tō], n
Pronunciation [pro-nun-she-ā'sl
Propagator [prop'a-gāt-ėr], n.
Propel' ler [pro-pel'ėr], n.
Propensity [pro-pen'si-tī], n
Prophecy [prof'e-si], n.
Prophesy [prof'e-si], v.
Proph'et ess [prof'et-es], n.
Propinquity [pro-ping'kwi-tī], n
Propitiator [pro-pish'i-āt-ėr], n.
Propitious [pro-pish'us], a.
Proportion [pro-pōr'shun], n.
Proposal [pro-pōz'al], n.
Proposition [prop-o-zi'shun], n.
Proprietary [pro-prī'e-ta-ri], a.
Proprietor [pro-prī'e-tėr], n.
Propriety [pro-prī'e-tī], n.
Prosaic [pro-zā'ik], a.
Proscenium [pro-sē'ni-um], n.
Prosecutor [pros'e-kūt-ėr], n.
Proselyte [pros'e-lit], n. v.
Proselytize [pros'e-lit-īz], v.
Prosily [prōz'i-li], ad.
Prosody [pros'o-di], n.
Pros'pect or [pros'pek-tėr]
Pros'per ity [pros-pe'ri-tī],
Prosperous [pros'pėr-us], a
Prostitutor [pros'ti-tūt-ėr],
Prostration [pros-trā'shun

Protuberance [pro-tū′bėr-ans], n.
Proud ly [prowd′li], ad.
Prove n [prōōv′n], v.
Provender [prov′en-dėr], n.
Prov′erb ial [pro-vėr′bi-al], a.
Providential [pro-vi-den′shal], a. n.
Provincial [pro-vin′shal], a. n.
Provision [pro-vizh′un], n. v.
Provisor [pro-vī′zor], n.
Provocation [pro-vŏ-kā′shun], n.
Provocative [pro-vŏk′a-tiv], a. n.
Provost [prov′ust], n.
Prow ess [prow′es], n.
Prowl er [prowl′ėr], n.
Proximity [prok-sim′i-ti], n.
Prudence [prōō′dens], n.
Pru′dent ial [prōō-den′shal], a. n.
Prunello [prōō-nel′lŏ], n. A fruit; a
    cloth.
Prurient [prōō′ri-ent], a.
Prussian [pru′shan, prōō′shan], n.
Prussic [prus′sik, prōōs′ik], a.
Psalm [sām], n.
Psalmody [sal′mo-di], n.
Psalter [sąl′tėr], n.
Pseudonym [sū′do-nim], n.
Pshaw [shą], inter.
Psychism [sī′kizm], n.
Psychology [sī-kol′o-ji], n.
Ptarmigan [tär′mi-gan], n
Ptolemaic [tol-e-mā′ik], a.
Pubescence [pū-bes′ens], n.
Publican [pub′li-kan], n.
Pub′lish er [pub′lish-ėr], n.
Puerile [pū′er-il], a.
Puerility [pū-ėr-il′i-ti], n.
Puerperal [pū-ėr′pėr-al], a.
Pugilism [pū′jil-izm], n.
Pugnacious [pug-nā′shus], a.
Puissance [pū′is-ans], n.
Pulley [pŏŏl′li], n. v.
Pulmonary [pul′mon-a-ri], a. n.
Pulpit [pŏŏl′pit], n.
Pulsation [pul-sā′shun], n.
Pulse [puls], n. v.
Pulverize [pul′vėr-iz], v.
Pumice [pum′is, pū′mis], n.
Pump kin [pump′kin], n.

Punch inello [punsh-i-nel′lo], n.
Punctilious [pungk-til′i-us], a.
Punc′tual ly [pungk′tū-al-li], ad.
Punctuation [pungk-tū-ā′shun], n.
Puncture [pungkt′yōōr, pungkt′yėr],
    n. v.
Pun′ish able [pun′ish-a-bl], a.
Punisher [pun′ish-ėr], n.
Pupil [pū′pil], n.
Purchase [pėr′chās], n. v.
Purgatory [pėr′ga-to-ri], n.
Purificator [pū-ri-fi-kā′tėr], n.
Purify [pū′ri-fī], v.
Pu′ritan ism [pū′ri-tan-izm], n.
Purlieu [pėr′lū], n.
Purloin′ er [pėr-loin′ėr], n.
Purple [pėr′pl], n. v.
Purport [pėr′port], n. v.
Purpose [pėr′pus], n. v.
Purse [pėrs], n. v.
Purslane [pėrs′lān], n.
Pursuance [pėr-sū′ans], n.
Pursue [pėr-sū′], v.
Pursuit [pėr-sūt′], n.
Pursuivant [pėr′swi-vant], n.
Purulent [pū′ru-lent], a.
Purvey′ or [pėr-vā′ėr], n.
Pusillanimity [pū-sil-la-nim′i-ti], n.
Pusillanimous [pū-sil-lan′im-us], a.
Pustule [pus′tūl], n.
Put [pŏŏt], v.
Putrefy [pū′tri-fī], v.
Putrescence [pū-tres′ens], n.
Pu′trid ity [pū-trid′i-ti], n.
Puzzle [puz′l], n. v.
Pyæmia [pī-ē′mi-a], n.
Pygmean [pig-mē′an], a.
Pygmy [pig′mi], a. n.
Pylorus [pī-lō′rus], n.
Pyr′amid al [pi-ram′id-al], a.
Pyre [pīr], n.
Pyrites [pi-rī′tēz], n.
Pyrotechnics [pir-ō-tek′niks], n.
Pythagorean [pi-thag-ō-rē′an], n.
Pythian [pith′i-an], a.
Python [pī′thon], n.
Pythoness [pith′on-es], n.
Pyx [piks].

Q.

Quack ery [kwak′ėr-i], n.
Quadrangle [kwod-rang′gl], n.
Quadrille [ka-dril′], n.
Quadroon [kwod-rōōn′], n.

Quadruped [kwod′rōō-ped], a. n.
Quadrupedal [kwod-ru-pē′dal, kwod-
    rōō′pe-dal], a.
Quadruple [kwod′rōō-pl], a. n. v.

Quaff [kwȧf], v.
Quagga [kwag'a], n.
Quaggy [kwag'i], a.
Quagmire [kwag'mir], n.
Quail [kwāl], n. v.
Quaint [kwānt], a.
Quak'er ism [kwāk'ér-izm], n.
Qualifier [kwol'i-fī-èr], n.
Quality [kwol'i-ti], n.
Qualm [kwäm], n.
Quandary [kwon-dā'ri, kwon'da-ri], n. v.
Quantity [kwon'ti-ti], n.
Quarantine [kwor'an-ten], n. [kwor-an-tēn'], v.
Quar'rel some [kwor'el-sum], a.
Quarry [kwor'i], n. v.
Quarter [kwȧr'tér], n. v.
Quartz [kwȧrts], n.
Quash [kwosh], v.
Quassia [kwosh'i-a], n.
Quaternary [kwa-ter'na-ri], a.
Quaternion [kwa-tér'ni-on], n.
Quaver [kwā'vér], n.
Quay [kē], n. v.
Queen [kwēn], n. v.
Queer [kwēr], a.
Quell [kwel], v.
Quench able [kwensh'a-bl], a.
Querist [kwēr'ist], n.
Querulous [kwer'u-lus], a.

Query [kwē'ri], n. v.
Question er [kwest'yun-èr], n.
Queue [ku], n. Fr. of Cue.
Quib ble [kwib'l], n. v.
Quick'en er [kwik'n-èr], n.
Quiescent [kwi-es'ent], a. n.
Qui'et ism [kwi'et-izm], n.
Quietus [kwi-ē'tus], n.
Quill [kwil], n. v.
Quilt er [kwilt'ér], n.
Quince [kwins], n.
Quinine [kwi-nin', kwi'nin], n.
Quinsy [kwin'zi], n.
Quintain [kwin'tān], n.
Quintessence [kwin-tes'ens], n.
Quintet, Quintette [kwin-tet'].
Quintillion [kwin-til'li-on], n.
Quire [kwir], n. Twenty-four s of paper.
Quite [kwit], ad.
Quittance [kwit'ans], n.
Qui vive [kē'vēv'], n.
Quixotic [kwik-sot'ik], a.
Quiz zer [kwiz'èr], n.
Quizzical [kwiz'ik-al], a.
Quoin [kwoin], n.
Quoit [kwoit], n.
Quorum [kwō'rum], n.
Quotation [kwō-tā'shun], n.
Quoth [kwōth], v.
Quotient [kwō'shent], n.

R.

Rabbet [rab'bet], v. n. A groove.
Rabbi [rab'bi, rab'bī], n.
Rabbit [rab'bit], n. An animal.
Rabble [rab'l], n. v.
Rabelais [rä'blā'], French satirist.
Rabies [rā'bi-ēz], n.
Raccoon [rak-kōōn'], n.
Race [rās], n. v.
Raceme [ra-sēm'], n.
Racine [ras'sēn'], French poet.
Raciness [rā'si-nes], n.
Radiance [rā'di-ans], n.
Radiator [rā'di-āt-èr], n.
Rad'ical ism [rad'i-kal-izm], n.
Radicle [rad'i-kl], n. Botanical term.
Radish [rad'ish], n.
Radius [rā'di-us], Radii, pl.
Raffle [raf'l], n. v.
Ragamuffin [rag-a-muf'in], n.
Ragged [rag'ed], n.

Ragout [rä'gōō'], n.
Raid [rād], n.
Raillery [ral'èr-i], n.
Rail way [rāl'wā], n.
Raiment [rā'ment], n.
Rain y [rān'i], a.
Raise [rāz], v.
Raisin [rā'zn], n.
Raisonné [rā'zon'nā'].
Rajah [rä'ja, rä'jä], n.
Rakish [rāk'ish], a.
Rambler [ram'blér], n.
Ramification [ram-i-fi
Rampacious [ram-pā
Ranch [ransh], n.
Ran'cid ity [ran-s
Ran'cor ous [ran
Random [ran'dom
Ransom [ran'sum
Rant er [rant'èr

Ranunculaceæ [ra-nun-kū-lā'se-ē], n.
Rapacious [ra-pā'shus], a. [pl.
Rapacity [ra-pas'i-ti], n.
Raphaelite [raf'a-el-īt], n.
Raphilite [raf'i-līt], n. A mineral.
Rap'id ity [ra-pid'i-ti], n.
Rapier [rā'pi-ėr], n.
Rapine [rap'in], n.
Rapport [rap-pōrt'], n.
Raptores [rap-tō'rēz], n. pl.
Rapture [rap'tūr, rapt'yŏŏr, rapt'-
  yėr], n. v.
Rapturous [rapt'yŏŏr-us, rapt'yėr-
  us], a.
Rare fy [râr'e-fī], v.
Rarity [rā'ri-ti], n. Uncommonness.
  [rar'i-ti], n. Thinness.
Ras'cal lion [ras-kal'yun], n.
Rasores [ra-sō'rēz], n. pl.
Raspberry [raz'be-ri], n.
Ratchet [rach'et], n.
Rather [ra'h'ėr], ad.
Ratio [rā'shi-ō], n.
Ration [rā'shun], n. v.
Rationale [rash-i-o-nā'le, rā-shi-o-nā'-
  le], n.
Ra'tional ize [rash'un-al-īz], v.
Rat'tle snake [rat'l-snāk], n.
Rav'el ing [rav'el-ing], n.
Raven [rā'vn] a. n. A bird. [rav'en],
  n. v. Plunder.
Ravenous [rav'en-us], a.
Ravine [ra-vēn'], n.
Rav'ish er [rav'ish-ėr], n.
Razor [rā'zor], n.
Reach [rēch], n. v.
Read er [rēd'ėr], n.
Readily [red'i-li], ad.
Re'al ism [rē'al-izm], n.
Realization [rē-al-i-zā'shun], n.
Really [rē'al-li], ad.
Realm [relm], n.
Reap er [rēp'ėr], n.
Rear ward [rēr'wård], a. n.
Rea'son able [rē'zn-a-bl], a.
Rebel [reb'el], a. n. [re-bel'], v.
Rebellion [re-bel'yon], n.
Rebellious [re-bel'yus], a.
Rebut' tal [re-but'al], n.
Recalcitrant [rē-kal'si-trant], a.
Recede [re-sēd'], v.
Receipt' or [re-sēt'or], n.
Receivable [re-sēv'a-bl], a.
Receive [re-sēv'], v.
Receptacle [re-sep'ta-kl], n.
Receptible [re-sep'ti-bl], a.

Reception [re-sep'shun], n.
Receptivity [res-ep-tiv'i-ti], n.
Recess' ion [re-se'shun], n.
Rechabite [rē'kab-īt], n.
Recherché [re'sher-shā'], a.
Reciprocal [re-sip'rō-kal], a. n.
Reciprocity [res-i-pros'i-ti], n.
Recital [re-sīt'al], n.
Recitation [res-i-tā'shun], n.
Recitative [res-i-ta-tēv'], a. n.
Reclaim' er [re-klām'ėr], n.
Reclamation [rek-la-mā'shun], n.
Recluse [re-klūs'], a. n.
Recognition [rek-og-ni'shun], n.
Recognizable [rek'og-nīz-a-bl], a.
Recognizance [re-kog'ni-zans, re-
  kon'i-zans], n.
Recognize [rek'og-nīz] v.
Recollect' ion [rek-ol'lek-shun], n.
Recommend' ation [rek-om-mend-
  ā'shun], n.
Recompense [rek'om-pens], n. v.
Reconcilable [rek'on-sīl-a-bl], a. [n.
Reconciliation [rek-on-sil-i-ā'shun],
Recondite [rek'on-dīt], a.
Reconnoissance [re-kon'nis-sāns], n.
Reconnoiter [rek-on-noi'tėr], v.
Record [rek'ord], n. [re-kord'], v.
Recorder [re-kord'ėr], n.
Recourse [re-kōrs'], n.
Recov'er y [re-kuv'ėr-i], n.
Recreant [rek're-ant], a. n.
Recreate [rek're-āt], v.
Recruit' er [re-krōōt'ėr], n.
Rectifier [rek'ti-fī-ėr], n.
Rectitude [rek'ti-tūd], n.
Rec'tor y [rek'to-ri], n.
Recumbency [re-kum'ben-si], n.
Recuperative [re-kū'pėr-a-tiv], a.
Recusant [re-kū'zant], n.
Red dish [red'ish], a.
Redeem' able [re-dēm'a-bl], a.
Redeemer [re-dēm'ėr], n.
Redemption [re-dem'shun], n.
Redhibition [red-hi-bi'shun], n.
Redolence [red'o-lens], n.
Redoubt' able [re-dowt'a-bl], a.
Reducible [re-dūs'i-bl], a.
Reduction [re-duk'shun], n.
Redundance [re-dun'dans], n.
Reed [rēd], n. A plant; a musical
  tube; an instrument used by weav-
  ers.
Reef [rēf], n. v.
Reel [rēl], n. v.
Refection [re-fek'shun], n.

Refectory [re-fek'to-ri], n.
Referable [ref'ĕr-a-bl], a.
Refer' ee [ref-ĕr-ē'], n.
Referrible [re-fĕr'ri-bl], a.
Refine' ry [re-fīn'ĕr-i], n.
Reflect' or [re-flekt'ĕr], n.
Reflex [rē'fleks], a. n.
Refluent [ref'lu-ent], a.
Reform' able [re-form'a-bl], a.
Reformer [re-form'ĕr], n.
Refract' ory [re-frakt'ĕr-i], a.
Refractoriness [re-frak'to-ri-nes], n.
Refragable [ref'ra-ga-bl], a.
Refrain [re-frān'], n. v.
Refrigerator [re-frij'ĕr-ā-tĕr], n.
Ref'uge e [ref-ū-jē'], n.
Refusal [re-fū'zal], a. n. [re-fūz'], v.
Refuse [ref'ūs], n.
Refutable [re-fūt'a-bl], a.
Refutation [ref-ū-tā'shun], n.
Regalia [re-gā'li-a], n. pl.
Re'gal ly [rē'gal-li], ad.
Regatta [rĕ'gat'ta], n.
Regency [rē'jen-si], n.
Regicidal [rej'i-sīd], a.
Regicide [rej'i-sīd], n.
Régime [rā'zhēm'], n.
Regimen [rej'i-men], n.
Register [rej'is-tĕr], n. v.
Registrar [rej'is-trär], n.
Regnancy [reg'nan-si], n.
Regress' ion [re-gre'shun], n.
Regular ity [reg-ū-la'ri-ti], n.
Regulator [reg'ū-lāt-ĕr], n.
Rehabilitate [rē-ha-bil'i-tāt], v.
Rehearsal [re-hĕrs'al], n.
Reign [rān], n. v. To rule.
Reimburse [rē-im-bĕrs'], v.
Rein [rān], n. v. The strap of a bridle.
Reindeer [rān'dĕr], n.
Reiteration [rē-it-ĕr-ā'shun], n.
Reject' ion [re-jek'shun], n.
Rejoice [re-jois'], v.
Rejuvenate [re-jū've-nāt], v.
Rejuvenescence [re-jū-ve-nes'ens], n.
Relation [re-lā'shun], n.
Relax' ation [re-lak-sā'shun], n.
Release [re-lēs'], n. v.
Relegation [rel-e-gā'shun], n.
Relevance [rel'e-vans], n.
Reliable [re-lī'a-bl], a.
Reliance [re-lī'ans], n.
Relief [re-lēf'], n.
Relieve [re-lēv'], v.
Religious [re-lij'us], a. n.
Relin'quish er [re-ling'kwish-ĕr], n.

Reliquary [rel'i-kwa-ri], n.
Relish [rel'ish], n. v.
Reluctance [re-luk'tans], n.
Remain' der [re-mān'dĕr], n.
Remedial [re-mē'di-al], a. re-medi-
Remediless [rem'e-di-les, rem'e-di-
les], a.
Remembrance [re-mem'brans], n.
Reminiscence [rem-i-nis'sens], n.
Remiss' ion [re-mi'shun], n.
Remit' tance [re-mit'ans], a.
Remittent [re-mit'ent], a.
Remonstrance [re-mon'strans], n.
Remorse' ful [re-mors'fool], a.
Remuneration [re-mū-nĕr-ā'shun], n.
Renaissance [re-nās'säns'], n.
Rendezvous [ren'de-vōō], n. v.
Rend ition [ren-di'shun], n.
Renegade [ren'e-gād], n.
Rennet [ren'net], n.
Renounce [re-nowns'], n. v.
Renown [re-nown'], n. v.
Renunciation [re-nun-shi-ā'shun], n.
Repair' er [re-pâr'ĕr], n.
Reparable [rep'a-ra-bl], a.
Repartee [rep-är-tē'], n.
Repeal [re-pēl'], n. v.
Repeat' er [re-pēt'ĕr], n.
Repel' ler [re-pel'ĕr], n.
Repent' ance [re-pent'ans], n.
Répertoire [rā'pâr'twär'], n.
Repertory [rep'ĕr-to-ri], n.
Repetition [rep-e-ti'shun], n.
Repletion [re-plē'shun], n.
Replevin [re-plev'in], n.
Replica [rep'li-ka], n.
Report' er [re-pōrt'ĕr], n.
Repository [re-poz'i-to-ri], n.
Repoussé [re-pōōs'ā'], a.
Reprehend' er [rep-re-hend'ĕ
Reprehensible [rep-re-hen'si-
Represent' ative [rep-re-zen
a. n.
Repress' ion [re-pre'shun], n. v.
Reprieve [re-prēv'], n. v.
Reprimand [rep'ri-mand], n.
Reprisal [re-prī'zal], n.
Reproach' ful [re-prōch'f
Reprobate [rep'rō-bāt], a.
Reptile [rep'til], a. n.
Republican [re-pub'li-ka
Repudiator [re-pū'di-āt
Repugnance [re-pug'na
Repulsion [re-pul'shu
Reputable [rep'ū-ta-b
Requiem [rē'kwi-em'

Requirable [re-kwir'a-bl], a.
Require' ment [re-kwir'ment], n.
Requisite [rek'wi-zit], a. n.
Requisition [rek-wi-zi'shun], n. v.
Requisitor [re-kwiz'i-tėr], n.
Requital [re-kwit'al], n.
Reredos [rēr'dos], n.
Rescission [re-si'zhun], n.
Rescuable [res'kū-a-bl], a.
Rescue [res'kū], n. v.
Research [re-sérch'], n.
Resemblance [re-zem'blans], n.
Reservation [rez-ėr-vā'shun], n.
Reservoir [rez-ėr-vwar'], n.
Residence [rez'i-dens], n.
Residuary [re-zid'ū-a-ri], a.
Residue [rez'i-dū], n.
Resign [re-zin], v.
Resignation [rez-ig-nā'shun], n.
Res'in ous [rez'in-us], a.
Resist' ance [re-zist'ans], n.
Resoluble [rez'o-lū-bl], a.
Resolution [rez-o-lū'shun], n.
Resolvable [re-zolv'a-bl], a.
Resonance [rez'o-nans], n.
Resource [re-sōrs'], n.
Respect' able [re-spekt'a-bl], a.
Respirable [re-spir'a-bl], a.
Respiration [res-pi-rā'shun], n.
Respirator [res'pi-rāt-ėr], n.
Respiratory [re-spir'a-to-ri], a.
Respite [res'pit], n. v.
Resplendence [re-splen'dens], n.
Respond' ent [re-spon'dent], a. n.
Responsible [re-spons'i-bl], a.
Restaurant [res'tō'rn̄ā', res'to-rant],
    n. ["In speaking English, to pro-
    nounce this word à la française is
    in questionable taste : it smacks of
    edantry." — Orthoëpist.]
Restaurateur [res'tōr-ā'tėr], n. Wb.
Restitution [res-ti-tū'shun], n.
Restoration [res-tō-rā'shun], n.
Restorative [re-stōr'a-tiv], n.
Restrain' er [re-strān'ėr], n.
Restrict' ion [re-strik'shun], n.
Result' ant [re-zult'ant], a. n.
Résumé [rā'zū'mā'], n. A summing
    up. [re-zūm'], v.
Resurrection [rez-ėr-rek'shun], n.
Resuscitate [re-sus'i-tāt], v.
Retail [rē'tāl], n. [rē-tāl'], v.
Retain' er [re-tān'ėr], n.
Retaliation [re-tal-i-ā'shun], n.
Retch [rēch, rech], v. To make an
    effort to vomit.

Retention [re-ten'shun], n.
Reticence [ret'i-sens], n.
Reticule [ret'i-kūl], n.
Retina [ret'i-na], n.
Retinue [ret'i-nū], n.
Retire' ment [re-tir'ment], n.
Retort [re-tort'], n. v.
Retract' or [re-trak'tėr], n.
Retreat [re-trēt'], n. v.
Retrench [re-trensh'], v.
Retribution [ret-ri-bū'shun], n.
Retributive [re-trib'ū-tiv], a.
Retrievable [re-trēv'a-bl], a.
Retrieve [re-trēv'], v.
Retrocede [rē'tro-sēd, ret'ro-sēd], v.
Retrocession [rē-tro-se'shun, ret-ro-
    se'shun], n.
Retrograde [ret'ro-grād], a. v.
Retrogression [ret-ro-gre'shun], n.
Retrospect [ret'ro-spekt], n.
Reveal' er [re-vēl'ėr], n.
Reveille [re-vāl'yā], n.
Rev'el er [rev'el-ėr], n.
Revenge' ful [re-venj'fool], a.
Revenue [rev'e-nū], n.
Reverberator [re-vėr'bėr-āt-ėr], n.
Reverence [rev'er-ens], n. v.
Rev'erent ial [rev-er-en'shal], a.
Reversal [re-vėrs'al], n.
Reversible [re-vėrs'i-bl], n.   [n.
Revery, Reverie [rev'er-i, rev-er-ē'],
Reviv'al ist [re-viv'al-ist], n.
Revocable [rev'ō-ka-bl], a.
Revolt' er [re-vōlt'ėr], n.
Revolu'tion ize [rev-ō-lū'shun-īz], v.
Revolver [re-volv'ėr], n.
Revulsion [re-vul'shun], n.
Reynard [ren'ard, rā'nard], n.
Rhapsodist [rap'sod-ist], n.
Rhetoric [ret'or-ik], n.
Rhetorician [ret-o-ri'shan], a. n.
Rheum atism [rōō'ma-tizm], n.
Rhinoceros [ri-nos'e-ros], n.
Rhizoma [ri-zō'ma], n.
Rhododendron [rō-dō-den'dron], n.
Rhomb oid [rom'boid], a. n.
Rhubarb [rōō'bärb], n.
Rhyme [rim], n.
Rhythm [rithm], n.
Rib'ald ry [rib'ald-ri], n.
Ribbon [rib'on], n. v.
Rickets [rik'ets], n.
Ricochet [rik-o-shā'], a. n. [rik-o-
    shet], v.
Riddance [rid'ans], n.
Ridicule [rid'i-kūl], n. v.

Ridiculous [ri-dik'ů-lus], a.
Rifle [ri'fl], n. v.
Right eous [rit'yus], a
Righter [rit'er], n. One who sets right.
Rig'id ity [ri-jid'i-ti], n.
Rigmarole [rig'ma-rōl], a. n.
Rig'or ous [rig'or-us], a.
Rime [rīm], n. Frost. v. To freeze.
Rind [rind], n.
Rinse [rins], v.
Ri'ot er [ri'ot-er], n.
Riotous [ri'ot-us], a.
Ripple [rip'l], n. v.
Rise [rīs], n. [rīz], v.
Risible [riz'i-bl], a.
Rissole [re-sōl'], n.
Rite [rīt], n. A ceremony.
Rit'ual ism [rit'ů-al-izm], n.
Ri'val ry [ri'val-ri], n.
Rivet [riv'et], n. v.
Roach [rōch], n.
Road way [rōd'wā], n.
Roam er [rōm'ér], n.
Roar er [rōr'er], n.
Roast [rōst], a. n. v.
Robin [rob'in], n.
Robust [rō-bust'], a.
Rochet [roch'et], n.
Rock ery [rok'er-i], n.
Rodeo [ro-dā'o], n.
Roe [rō], n. The spawn of fish; the female of the hart.
Rogatory [rog'a-to-ri], a.
Rogue ry [rōg'er-i], n.
Roguish [rōg'ish], a.
Roll y [roil'i], a.
Rois'ter er [rois'ter-ér], n.
Rôle [rōl], n. A dramatic character.
Rollic [rol'lik], v.
Romance [rō-mans'], n. v.
Ro'man esque [rō-man-esk'], a. n.
Roman'tic ism [rō-man'ti-sizm], n.
Roof [rōōf], n.
Rook ery [rōōk'er-i], n.
Roost er [rōōst'er], n.
Root [rōōt], n. v.
Rosaceæ [ro-zā'sē-ē], n. pl.
Rosary [rō'za-ri], n.
Roseate [rō'ze-āt], a.
Roseola [ro-zē'o-lä], n.
Rosetta-stone [rō-zet'a-stōn], n.
Rosette [rō-zet'], n.
Rosicrucian [roz-i-krōō'shi-an], a. n.
Rosin [roz'in], n. v.

Rostrum [ros'trum], n.
Rotation [rō-tā'shun], n.
Rota'tor y [rō'tá-to-ri], a.
Rotchet [roch'et], n.
Rot ten [rot'n], a.
Rotunda [rō-tun'da], n.
Rotund' ity [rō-tun'di-ti], n.
Roué [rōō-ā'], n.
Rouge [rōōzh], n. v.
Rouge-et-noir [rōōzh'e'nwär'], n.
Rough ly [ruf'li], ad.
Roulade [rōō-läd'], n.
Roulette [rōō-let'], n.
Round about [rownd'a-bout], a. n.
Roundelay [rown'de-lā], n.
Rout [rowt], n. v.
Route [rōōt], n. Road.
Routine [rōō-tēn'], n.
Row er [rō'er], n. One who rows.
Roy'al ist [roi'al-ist], n.
Rub ber [rub'ér], n.
Rubbish [rub'ish], n.
Rubeola [ru-bē'o-lä], n.
Rubinstein [rōō-bin-stin']. Russian musician.
Rubric [rōō'brik], n. v.
Ruche [rōōsh], n.
Rudder [rud'ér], n.
Ruddiness [rud'i-nes], n.
Rude [rōōd], a.
Rudiment [rōō'di-ment], n.
Ruffian [ruf'yan], a. n.
Ruffle [ruf'l], n. v.
Rugged [rug'ed], a.
Ru'in ous [rōō'in-us], a.
Rulable [rōōl'a-bl], a.
Ruler [rōōl'ér], n.
Ruminator [rōō'min-āt-ér], n.
Rummage [rum'āj], n. v.
Rumor [rōō'mér], n. v.
Run ner [run'ér], n.
Rupture [rup'tūr, rupt'yōōr, yér], n. v.
Ru'ral ism [rōō'ral-izm], n.
Ruse [rōōz], n.
Russet [rus'et], a. n.
Russian [rush'an, rōō'shan].
Rustic [rus'tik], a.
Rusticity [rus-tis'i-ti], n.
Rustle [rus'sl], n. v.
Ruthenium [ru-thē'ni-um]
Ruth less [rōōth'les], a.
Rutidosia [rōō-ti-dō'si-] ?
Rye [rī], n. A grain.
Rytina [rit'i-nä], n.

S.

Sabbatarian [sab-ba-tā'ri-an], a.
Sabbath [sab'bath], n.
Sabre [sā'bėr], n. v. [a.
Saccharine [sak'ka-rīn, sak'ka-rin],
Sacerdotal [sas-ėr-dō'tal], a.
Sachem [sā'chem], n.
Sack, Sacque [sak], n. A garment.
Sac'rament al [sak-ra-ment'al], a.
Sacrifice [sak'ri-fīz], n. v.
Sacrificial [sak-ri-fish'al], a.
Sacrilege [sak'ri-lej], n.
Sacrilegious [sak-ri-lē'jus], a.
Sacristan [sak'ris-tan], n.
Sacrum [sā'krum], n.
Saddle [sad'l], n. v.
Safe ty [sāf'ti], n.
Saffron [saf'frun], a. n.
Sagacious [sa-gā'shus], a.
Sagacity [sa-gas'i-ti], n.
Sagamore [sag'a-mōr], n.
Sagittal [saj'it-al], a.
Said [sed], v.
Sail er [sāl'ėr], n. A ship.
Sailor [sāl'ėr], n. A seaman.
Saint ly [sānt'li], a.
Salable [sāl'a-bl], a.
Salad [sal'ad], n.
Salamander [sal-a-man'dėr], n.
Salary [sal'a-ri], n. v.
Sale [sāl], n. The act of selling.
Saleratus [sal-e-rā'tus], n.
Salicine [sal'i-sin], n.
Salicylic [sal-i-sil'ik], a.
Salient [sā'li-ent], a.
Saline [sa-līn'], a. n.
Saliva [sa-lī'va], n.
Salmon [sam'un], n.
Salsify [sal'si-fi], n.
Salubrious [sa-lū'bri-us], a.
Salutatorian [sa-lū-ta-tō'ri-an], n.
Salutatory [sa-lū'ta-to-ri], a.
Salvable [sal'va-bl], a.
Salvation [sal-vā'shun], n.
Salve [sāv], n. v.
Salver [sal'vėr], n. A plate.
Samaritan [sa-mar'i-tan], a. n.
Samphire [sam'fėr, sam'fir], n.
Sample [sam'pl], n. v.
Sanatorium [san-a-tō'ri-um], n. [n.
Sanctification [sangk-ti-fi-kā'shun],
Sanctimonious [sangk-ti-mō'ni-us], a.

Sanction [sangk'shun], n. v.
Sanctity [sangk'ti-ti], n.
Sanctuary [sangk'tū-a-ri], n.
Sandal [san'dal], n.
Sandwich [sand'wich], n. v
Sang-froid [sang'frwa'], n.
Sanguigenous [sang-gwij'e-nus], a.
Sanguinary [sang'gwi-na-ri], a. n.
San'guine ous [sang-gwin'e-us], a.
Sanguinity [sang-gwin'i-ti], n.
Sanhedrim [san'he-drim], n.
Sanitary [san'i-ta-ri], a.
Sans-culotte [sänz'koo'lot'], n.
Sanskrit, Sanscrit [san'skrit], n.
Sap'id ity [sa-pid'i-ti], n.
Sapience [sā'pi-ens], n.
Saponaceous [sap-o-nā'shus], a.
Sapphire [saf'fėr, saf'fir], a. n.
Sar'acen ic [sar-a-sen'ik], a.
Sarcasm [sär'kazm], n.
Sarcenet [särs'net], n.
Sarcophagus [sär-kof'a-gus], n. Sar-
cophagi [sär-kof'a-ji], pl.
Sardine [sär'dēn], n. A fish.
Sardonyx [sär'do-niks], n.
Sarsaparilla [sär-sa-pa-ril'la], n.
Sassafras [sas'sa-fras], n.
Sā'tan ic [sa-tan'ik], a.
Satchel [sach'el], n.
Satellite [sat'el-līt], n.
Satiate [sā'shi-āt], v.
Satiety [sa-tī'e-ti], n.
Satin [sat'in], n.
Satire [sat'īr], n.
Satirical [sa-tir'ik-al], a. [n.
Satisfactoriness [sat-is-fak'to-ri-nes],
Satrap [sā'trap], n.
Saturation [sat-ū-rā'shun], n.
Saturday [sat'ėr-dā], n.
Saturnalia [sat-ėr-nā'li-a], n. pl.
Saturnine [sat'ėr-nīn], a.
Satyr [sā'tėr], n.
Sauce r [sa'sėr], n.
Saucy [sa'si], a.
Sauer-kraut [zow'ėr-krout], n.
Saun'ter er [sän'tėr-ėr], n.
Sauria [sa'ri-a], n. pl.
Sausage [sa'sāj], n.
Sav'age ry [sav'āj-ri], n.
Savant [sā'vän'], n.
Saviour [sāv'yėr], n.

Savonarola [sä-vo-nä-ro′lä].   Italian monk.
Savor [sā′vèr], n. v.
Sawyer [sa′yèr], n.
Saxifrage [sak′si-frāj], n.
Saxon [sak′son], a. n.
Saxophone [sax′o-fōn], n.
Says [sez], v.
Scabbard [skab′ärd], n. v.
Scabious [skā′bi-us], a. n.
Scabrous [skā′brus], a.
Scaffold [skaf′old], n. v.
Scagliola [skal-yi-ō′la], n.
Scald [skald], n. v.
Scalene [ska-lēn′], a. n.
Scal′lop ed [skol′lupt], a.
Scan′dal ize [skan′dal-īz], v.
Scan′dalous [skan′dal-us], a.
Scandinavian [skan-di-nā′vi-an],a.n.
Scansores [skan-sō′rēz], n. pl.
Scant iness [skant′i-nes], n.
Scapular [skap′ū-lèr], a. n.
Scarabæus [skar-a-bē′us], n.   A genus of insects.
Scarabee [skar′a-bē], n.   A beetle.
Scaramouch [skar′a-mowch], n.
Scarce ly [skärs′li], ad.
Scarify [skar′i-fī], v.
Scarlatina [skär-la-tē′na], n.
Scarlet [skär′let], a. n.
Scath, Scathe [skath, skāth], n. v.
Scatter [skat′tèr], v.
Scavenger [skav′en-jèr], n.
Scene ry [sēn′èr-i], n.
Scenic [sen′ik], a.
Scep′tic ism [skep′ti-sizm], n.
Sceptre [sep′tèr], n. v.
Schedule [sked′yūl], n. v.
Scheelstine [shēl′e-tin], n.
Scheererite [shēr′èr-īt], n.
Scheme [skēm], n. v.
Scherzo [skert′sō], n.
Schism atic [siz-mat′ik], a. n.
Schol′ar ly [skol′èr-li], a.
School [skōōl], n. v.
Schooner [skōōn′èr], n.
Schubert [shōō′bert].   German musical composer.
Schurz, Carl [shōōrts].   German orator and general, and American citizen.
Sciat′ic a [sī-at′ik-a], n.
Science [sī′ens], n.
Scientific [sī-en-tif′ik], a.
Scientist [sī′ent-ist], n.
Scion [sī′on], n.

Scission [si′zhun], n.
Scissors [siz′èrs], n. pl.
Scoff er [skof′èr], n.
Sconce [skons], n.
Scorbutic [skor-bū′tik], a. n.
Scorch [skorch], v.
Scoria [skō′ri-a], n.   Scoriæ, pl.
Scorn ful [skorn′fōōl], a.
Scorpion [skor′pi-on], n.
Scotch [skoch], a. n.
Scotticism [skot′ti-sizm], n.
Scoundrel [skown′drel], a. n.
Scourge [skèrj], n. v.
Scout [skowt], n. v.
Scowl [skowl], n. v.
Scrabble [skrab′l], n. v.
Scrag gy [skrag′i], a.
Scramble [skram′bl], n. v.
Scratch [skrach], n. v.
Scrawl [skral], n. v.
Scrawny [skra′ni], a.
Scream er [skrēm′èr], n.
Screech [skrēch], n. v.
Screen [skrēn], n. v.
Screw [skrōō], n. v.
Scribble [skrib′l], n. v.
Scriptural [skrip′tūr-al, skript′yōōr-al, skript′yèr-al], a.
Scripture [skrip′tūr, skript′yōōr, skript′yèr], n.
Scrivener [skriv′nèr], n.
Scrofula [skrof′ū-la], n.
Scrofulous [skrof′ū-lus], a.
Scruple [skrōō′pl], n. v.
Scrupulous [skrōō′pū-lus], a.
Scrutable [skrōō′ta-bl], a.
Scrutinize [skrōō′tin-īz], v.
Scuffle [skuf′l], n. v.
Scullery [skul′èr-i], n.
Scullion [skul′yon], n.
Sculpin [skul′pin], n.
Sculptor [skulp′tor], n.
Sculpture [skulp′tūr, skulpt′yōōr, skulpt′yèr], n. v.
Scurrility [skur-ril′i-ti], n.
Scurrilous [skur′ril-us], a.
Scurvy [skur′vi], a. n.
Scuttle [skut′l], n. v.
Scythe [sīth], n. v.
Scythian [sith′i-an], a. n.
Sea [sē], n.   The ocean.
Seal [sēl], n. v.   [n.
Seam stress [sēm′stres, sem′stres],
Séance [sā′äns], n.
Sear [sēr], a. Dry. v. To wither.
Search er [sèrch′èr], n.

 āle, add, beâr, ärm, ásk, fạll ; mē, met, thère, hèr ; pīne, pin ; ōld, odd, nōōn,

Sea'son able [sē'zn-a-bl], a.
Sebaceous [se-bā'shus], a.
Secancy [sē'kan-si], n.
Secede [sē-sēd'], v.
Seces'sion ist [se-se'shun-ist], n.
Seckel [sek'l], n.   A pear.
Seclusion [se-klū'zhun], n.
Sec'ond ary [sek'und-a-ri], a. n.
Secrecy [sē'kre-si], n.
Secretary [sek're-ta-ri], n.
Secretion [se-krē'shun], n.
Secretory [se-krē'to-ri], a.
Sec'tion al [sek'shun-al], a.
Sec'ular ize [sek'ū-lėr-īz], v.
Security [se-kū'ri-ti], n.
Sedan [se-dan'], n.
Sedative [sed'a-tiv], a. n.
Sedentary [sed'en-ta-ri], a. n.
Seditious [se-di'shus], a.
Sedlitz [sed'lits], n.
Seducible [se-dū'si-bl], a.
Seduction [se-duk'shun], n.
Sedulous [sed'ū-lus], a.
Seed iness [sēd'i-nes], n.
Seem [sēm], v.   To appear.
Seersucker [sēr'suk-ėr], n.
Seethe [sēth], v.
Segregation [seg-re-gā'shun], n.
Seigneurial [sēn-yū'ri-al], a.
Seign'ior age [sēn'yėr-āj], n. [river.
Seine [sēn], n.   A net.   [sān]   The
Seismic, Seismal [sīs'mik, sīs'mal], a.
Seismology [sīs-mol'o-ji], n.
Seize [sēz], v.
Seizure [sēz'ūr], n.
Seldom [sel'dom], ad.
Select' or [se-lekt'ėr], n.
Self ish [self'ish], a.
Selvedge [sel've], n.
Semblance [sem'blans], n.
Semen [sē'men], n.
Semi [sem'i], A prefix.
Seminal [sem'i-nal], a.
Seminary [sem'i-na-ri], a. n.
Seminole [sem'i-nōl], a. n.
Semitic [se-mit'ik], a.
Sempstress [sem'stres], n. The same
   as Seamstress.
Senator [sen'a-tor], n.
Senatorial [sen-a-tō'ri-al], a.
Senescence [se-nes'sens], n.
Seneschal [sen'e-shal], n.
Senile [sē'nil], a.
Sen'ior ity [sēn-yor'i-ti], n.
Senna [sen'na], n.   [n.
Sensa'tion al ist [sen-sā'shun-al-ist],

Sensibility [sens-i-bil'i-ti], n.
Sensorium [sen-sō'ri-um], n.
Sen'sual ize [sen'shū-al-īz], n.
Sensuous [sen'shū-us], a.
Sentence [sen'tens], n. v.
Sententious [sen-ten'shus], a.
Sentient [sen'shi-ent], a. n.   [v.
Sen'timent al ize [sen-ti-ment'al-īz],
Sentinel [sen'ti-nel], n. v.
Sepal [sē'pal], n.
Sepalous [sep'al-us], a.
Separable [sep'a-ra-bl], a.
Separation [sep-a-rā'shun], n.
Separatist [sep'a-ra-tist], n.
Separator [sep'a-rāt-ėr], n.
Sepia [sē'pi-a], n.
Septicidal [sep-ti-sī'dal], a.
Septuagint [sep'tu-a-jint], a. n.
Sepulchral [se-pul'kral], a.
Sepulchre [sep'ul-kėr], n.   [sep-ul'-
   kėr], v.
Sepulture [sep'ul-tūr], n.
Sequel [sē'kwel], n.
Sequence [sē'kwens], n.
Sequester [se-kwes'tėr], v.
Sequestrate [se-kwes'trāt], v.
Sequestrator [sek'wes-trāt-ėr], n.
Seraglio [se-ral'yō], n.
Ser'aph ic [se-raf'ik], a.
Seraphim [ser'a-fim], n. pl.
Serapis [se-rā'pis], n.
Serenade [ser-e-nād'], n. v.
Serenity [se-ren'i-ti], n.
Serf [sėrf], n.   A slave.
Sergeancy [sär'jan-si], n.
Sergeant [sär'jant, sėr'jant], n.
Serial [sē'ri-al], a. n.   Belonging to a
   series.   [pl.
Series [sē'ri-ēz, sē'rēz], n. sing. and
Serious [sē'ri-us], a.
Ser'mon izer [sėr'mon-īz-ėr], n.
Serous [sē'rus], a.
Ser'pent ine [sėr'pen-tīn], a. n.
Serrate [ser'rāt], a.
Serum [sē'rum], n.
Servable [sėrv'a-bl], a.
Servant [sėr'vant], n.
Ser'vice able [sėr'vis-a-bl], a.
Ser'vile ly [sėr'vil-li], ad.
Servility [sėr-vil'i-ti], n.
Servitor [sėr'vi-ter], n.
Servitude [sėr'vi-tūd], n.
Sesame [ses'a-me], n.
Sessile [ses'sil], a.
Sexterce [ses'tėrs], n.
Setaceous [se-tā'shus], a.

Settee [set·tē′], n.
Set′tle ment [set′l-ment], n.
Sev′en teenth [sev′n-tēnth], n.
Seventieth [sev′n-ti-eth], a. n.
Sev′eral ty [sev′ẽr-al-ti], n.
Severance [sev′ẽr-ans], a. n.
Severity [se-ver′i-ti], n.
Sew [sō], v. To stitch.
Sew′er age [sū′ẽr-āj], n.
Sex′ual ize [seks′ū-al-īz], v.
Sexually [seks′ū-al-li], ad.
Shabbily [shab′i-li], ad.
Shackle [shak′l], n. v.
Shadiness [shā′di-nes], n.
Shad′ow y [shad′ō-i], a.
Shah [shä], n.
Shale [shāl], n.
Shallop [shal′lop], n.
Shallow [shal′lō], a. n.
Sha′n't [shänt], v. Shall not.
Shame ful [shām′fŏŏl], a.
Shampoo [sham-pŏŏ′], n. v.
Sheaf [shēf], n. Sheaves [shēvz], pl.
Shears [shērz], n. pl.
Sheath [shēth], n.
Sheathe [shēth], v.
Sheep ish [shēp′ish], a.
Sheer [shēr], a. n. v. To deviate.
Sheet [shēt], n. v.
Sheik [shēk], n.
Shekel [shek′l], n.
Shelf [shelf], n. Shelves [shelvz], pl.
Shep′herd ess [shep′ẽrd-es], n.
Sheriff [sher′if], n.
Shew-bread [shō′bred], n.
Shibboleth [shib′bō-leth], n.
Shield [shēld], n. v.
Shilling [shil′ing], n.
Shingle [shing′gl], n. v.
Shire [shẽr, shīr], n.
Shoal [shōl], n. v.
Shoe [shŏŏ], n. v.
Shone [shon, shōn], v.
Shoot [shŏŏt], v.
Short′en er [short′n-ẽr], n.
Short-lived [short′līvd], a.
Shoulder [shōl′dẽr], n. v.
Shout er [showt′ẽr], n.
Shovel [shuv′vl], n. v.
Show [shō], v.
Shower [show′ẽr], n. v.
Shrewd [shrŏŏd], a.
Shrew ish [shrŏŏ′ish], a.
Shriek [shrēk], n. v.
Shrill [shril], a.
Shrine [shrīn], n.

Shrink age [shringk′āj], n.
Shrivel [shriv′el], v.
Shroud [shrowd], n. v.
Shrub bery [shrub′ẽr-i], n.
Shrug [shrug], n.
Shrunk en [shrungk′n], a. p.
Shudder [shud′ẽr], n. v.
Shuffle [shuf′l], n. v.
Shuttle [shut′l], n. v.
Siam [sī-am′], n.
Sibilancy [sib′i-lan-si], n.
Sib′yl line [sib′il-līn], a.
Sicilian [si-sil′i-an], a.
Sickle [sik′l], n.
Sidereal [si-dē′re-al], a.
Siderolite [sid′ẽr-ō-līt], n.
Siege [sēj], n. v.
Sierra [si-er′a], n.
Siesta [si-es′ta], n.
Sieve [siv], n.
Sigh [sī], n. v.
Sight-seer [sīt′sē-ẽr], n.
Sigillaria [sij-il-lā′ri-a], n.
Sig′nal ize [sig′nal-īz], v.
Signature [sig′na-tūr], n.
Signet [sig′net], n.
Significance [sig-nif′i-kans], n.
Significator [sig-nif′i-kāt-ẽr], n.
Silence [sī′lens], n. v.
Silesia [si-lē′shi-a], n.
Silhouette [sil′ŏŏ-et′], n.
Silica [sil′i-ka], n.
Silicic [si-lis′ik], a.
Silicify [si-lis′i-fī], v.
Silicle [sil′i-kl], n.
Sillabub [sil′la-bub], n.
Silphidæ [sil′fi-dē], n. pl.
Sil′ver y [sil′vẽr-i], a.
Sim′ilar ity [sim-i-lar′i-ti], n.
Simile [sim′i-lē], n.
Similitude [si-mil′i-tūd], n.
Simony [sim′o-ni], n.
Simoom, Simoon [si-mŏŏm′, si-mŏŏn′], n.
Simous [sī′mus], a.
Sim′ple ton [sim′pl-ton], n.
Simplicity [sim-plis′i-ti], n.
Simulator [sim′ū-lāt-ẽr], n.
Simultaneous [sī-mul-tā′ne-us], a.
Since [sins], ad. con. prep.
Sincere′ ly [sin-sēr′li], ad.
Sincerity [sin-ser′i-ti], n.
Sinciput [sin′si-put], n.
Sinecure [sī′ne-kūr], n. v.
Sine die [sī′ne-dī′e], Lat.
Sin′ew y [sin′ū-i], a.

Sing'ular ity [sing-gū-lar'i-ti], n.
Sinister [sin'is-tẽr], a.
Sinistrous [sin'is-trus], a.
Sin ner [sin'ẽr], n.
Sinuous [sin'ū-us], a.
Siphon [si'fon], n. v.
Sir [sẽr], n.
Siren [si'ren], a. n.
Sirloin [sẽr'loin], n.
Sirrah [sir'ra], n.
Sirup [sir'up], n.
Sistine [sis'tin], a.
Site [sit], n. Situation.
Situation [sit-ū-ā'shun], n.
Sitz-bath [sits'bath], n.
Six teenth [siks'tēnth], a. n.
Sixth [siksth], a. n.
Sizable [siz'a-bl], a.
Skate [skāt], n. v.
Skedaddle [skē-dad'l], v.
Skein [skān], n.
Skel'eton ize [skel'e-ton-īz], v.
Sketch er [skech'ẽr], n.
Skew er [skū'ẽr], n. v.
Skiff [skif], n.
Skil'ful ly [skil'fool-li], ad.
Skill [skil], n.
Skillet [skil'let], n.
Skim mer [skim'ẽr], n.
Skip per [skip'ẽr], n.
Skir'mish er [skẽr'mish-ẽr], n.
Skittish [skit'ish], a.
Sky [ski], n.
Slabber [slab'bẽr], n. v. [Colloq. slobber.]
Slain [slān], p.
Slan'der er [slan'dẽr-ẽr], n.
Slanderous [slan'dẽr-us], a.
Slant [slant], n. v.
Slate [slāt], n.
Slattern [slat'tẽrn], a. n.
Slaugh'ter ous [sla'tẽr-us], a. [ter.
Slav'er er [slav'ẽr-ẽr], n. A drivel-
Sleazy [slē'zi], a.
Sledge [slej], n. v.
Sleek [slēk], a. v.
Sleep er [slēp'ẽr], n.
Sleet [slēt], n.
Sleeve [slēv], n.
Sleigh [slā], n. A sled.
Sleight [slīt], n. A trick.
Slew [slū], v.
Slice [slīs], n. v.
Slight [slīt], a. n. v.
Slip per [slip'ẽr], n.
Silver [sliv'ẽr, sli'vẽr], n. v.

Sloop [sloōp], n.
Slope [slōp], n. v.
Sloth [slōth], n.
Slouch [slowch], n. v.
Slough [sluf], n. v. The cast skin of a serpent; a scab. [slow], n. A quagmire.
Slov'en liness [sluv'en-li-nes], n.
Slug gard [slug'ard], a. n.
Sluggish [slug'ish], a.
Sluice [slūs], n. v.
Slum'ber ous [slum'bẽr-us], a.
Small ness [smal'nes], n.
Smash er [smash'ẽr], n.
Smear [smēr], n. v.
Smilax [smi'laks], n.
Smirch [smẽrch], v.
Smirk [smẽrk], n. v.
Smithery, Smithy [smith'ẽr-i, smith-i], n.
Smock [smok], n.
Smoke [smōk], n. v.
Smooth ly [smoōth'li], ad.
Smother [smuth'ẽr], n. v.
Smoulder [smōl'dẽr], v.
Smudge [smuj], n. v.
Smuggle [smug'l], v.
Smutch [smuch], n. v.
Smyrnium [smẽr'ni-um], n.
Snail [snāl], n.
Snatch [snach], n. v.
Sneak [snēk], n. v.
Sneer [snēr], n. v.
Sneeze [snēz], n. v.
Snob bery [snob'ẽr-i], n.
Snooze [snooz], n. v.
Snout [snowt], n.
Snuff [snuf], n. v.
Snug gle [snug'l], v.
Soak er [sōk'ẽr], n.
Soap [sōp], n. v.
Soar [sōr], n. v. To fly.
Sobriety [sō-bri'e-ti], n.
Sobriquet [sob'rē'kā'], n.
Sociability [sō-shi-a-bil'i-ti], n.
Sociable [sō'shi-a-bl], a. n.
So'cial ism [sō'shal-izm], n.
Society [sō-si'e-ti], n.
Sociology [sō-shi-ol'o-ji], n.
Socratic [sō-krat'ik], a.
Sodden [sod'n], a. v.
Sofa [sō'fa], n.
Soft en [sof'n], v.
Soil [soil], n. v.
Soirée [swä'rā'], n.
Sojourn er [sō'jẽrn-ẽr], n.

nder

Soup [sōōp], n.
Soupçon [sōōp'sôṅ'], n.
Sour [sowr], a. v.
Source [sŏrs], n.
Souse [sows], n. v.
South [sowth], a. ad. n. v.
Southern [suᵗʰ'ĕrn], a.
Souvenir [sōōv'nĕr], n.
Sovereign [suv'ĕr-in], a. n.
Spacious [spā'shus], a.
Spadiceous [spa-dish'us], ɛ
Spaniard [span'yĕrd], n.
Spaniel [span'yel], a. n.
Spare [spâr], a. v.
Spark le [spar'kl], n. v.
Sparrow [spa'rō], n.
Spartan [spär'tan], a.
Sparterie [spär'tĕr-i], n.
Spasm odic [spaz-mod'ĭk]
Spathe [spâth], n.
Spavin [spav'in], n. v.
Spawn [spạn], n. v.

[a.
som'bĕr].
um'ĕr-salt,
[n.
n'bŭ-lizın],
, n.

Speak er [spēk'ĕr], n.
Spear er [spēr'ĕr], n.
Spearmint [spēr'mint], n.
Spec'ial ist [spesh'al-ist]
Speciality, Specialty [s;
    spesh'al-ti], n.
Species [spē'shez], n. ;
Specific [spe-sif'ik], a. n
Specification [spes-i-fi-]
Specimen [spes'i-men],
Specious [spē'shus], a.
Spectacle [spek'ta-kl],
Spectacular [spek-tak
Spectator [spek-tā'toı

[-tĕr], n.
,
n.
-us], a.
n.

Spectral [spek'tral], ɛ
Spectre [spek'tĕr], n.
Spectrum [spek'trum
Speculator [spek'ū-l
Speculum [spek'u-lu
Speech ifier [spēch'
Speed ily [spēd'i-lī
Spell er [spel'ĕr], ;
Spencer [spen'sĕr],
Spend thrift [speı
Spenserian [spen-ı
Sperm aceti [spĕ
Spew [spū], v.
Sphagnum [sfag'ı
Sphenoid [sfē'noı
Sphere [sfēr], n.
Spherical [sfer'ï
Spheroid [sfēr'ı
Sphinx [sfingk
Spicy [spis'ï].

; mē, met, thêre, hèr ; p

Spider [spī'dèr], n.
Spigelia [spī-jē'lī-a], n.
Spigot [spig'ot], n.
Spike nard [spīk'närd], n.
Spill [spil], n. v.
Spinach, Spinage [spin'āj], n.
Spinal [spī'nal], a.
Spindle [spin'dl], n.
Spinet [spin'et], n.
Spin ner [spin'èr], n.
Spinous [spin'us], a.
Spinster [spin'stèr], n.
Spiræa [spī-rē'a], n.
Spi'ral ly [spī'ral-li], ad.
Spir'it ual ism [spir'it-ū-al-izm], n.
Spirituous [spir'it-ū-us], a.
Spit tle [spit'l], n.
Spittoon [spit-tōōn'], n.
Splash er [splash'èr], n.
Spleen y [splēn'ī], a.
Splendid [splen'did], a.
Splendor [splen'dèr], n.
Splenetic [splen'e-tik], a.
Splice [splis], n. v.
Splint er [splin'tèr], n. v.
Spoil er [spoil'èr], n.
Spoliator [spō'li-āt-èr], n.
Spondyl [spon'dil], n.
Sponge [spunj], n. v.
Sponsor [spon'sor], n.
Spontaneity [spon-ta-nē'i-ti], n.
Spontaneous [spon-tā'ne-us], a.
Spoon ful [spōōn'fōōl], n. Spoon- fuls, pl.
Sporadic [spo-rad'ik], a.
Spouse [spowz], n.
Spout [spowt], n. v.
Sprain [sprān], n. v.
Sprawl [spral], v.
Spread [spred], n. v.
Spright liness [sprīt'li-nes], n.
Sprinkle [spring'kl], n. v.
Sprite [sprīt], n. A spirit.
Sprout [sprowt], n. v.
Spruce [sprōōs], a. n. v.
Spurious [spū'ri-us], a.
Spurt [spèrt], n.
Squabble [skwob'l], n. v.
Squad ron [skwod'ron], n.
Squalid [skwol'id], a.
Squall y [skwal'i], a.
Squalor [skwā'lor], n.
Squan'der er [skwon'dèr-èr], n.
Square [skwår], n. v.
Squash [skwosh], n. v.
Squat ter [skwot'èr], n.

Squaw [skwa], n.
Squawk [skwak], v.
Squeak er [skwēk'èr], n.
Squeal [skwēl], n. v.
Squeamish [skwē'mish], a.
Squeezable [skwēz'a-bl], a.
Squeeze [skwēz], n. v.
Squib [skwib], n.
Squid [skwid], n.
Squint [skwint], n. v.
Squire [skwīr], n. v.
Squirrel [skwir'rel], n.
Squirt [skwèrt], n. v.
Stab ber [stab'èr], n.
Stability [sta-bil'i-ti], n.
Staccato [stak-kä'tō], n.
Stadium [stā'di-um], n. Stadia [stā'- di-a], pl.
Staff [staf], n. Staves [stāvz, stävz].
Stag ger [stag'èr], n. v.
Stagnant [stag'nant], a.
Staid [stād], a. p.
Stain [stān], n. v.
Stair case [stār'kās], n.
Stake [stāk], n. A stick; money pledged or wagered. v. To mark off; to wager.
Stalactite [sta-lak'tīt], n.
Stalagmite [sta-lag'mīt], n.
Stale [stāl], a. n.
Stalk er [stak'èr], n.
Stall [stal], n. v.
Stallion [stal'yun], n.
Stalwart [stal'wèrt], a.
Stamen [stā'men], n.
Stamina [stam'i-na], n. pl.
Stammer [stam'èr], n. v.
Stampede [stam-pēd'], n. v.
Stanch [stänsh], a. v.
Stanchion [stan'shun], n.
Stand ard [stand'ard], a. n.
Stanza [stan'za], n.
Staple [stā'pl], a. n. v.
Starch y [stärch'i], a.
Star ling [stär'ling], n.
Start le [stär'tl], n. v.
Starvation [stär-vā'shun], n.
Statics [stat'iks], n.
Sta'tion er [stā'shun'èr], n.
Statistician [stat-is-tish'an], n.
Statistics [sta-tis'tiks], n.
Statuary [stat'ū-a-ri], n.
Statue [stat'ū], n.
Statuesque [stat-ū-esk'], a.
Statuette [stat-ū-et'], n.
Statu quo [stā'tu-kwō], Lat.

wōōl; ūse, us; ū, Fr.; g. get; j. jar; ñ, Fr. ton; ch, chain; th, then; t'

Stature [stat′yōōr, stat′yẽr], n.
Status [stā′tus], n.
Statute [stat′ūt], n.
Staves [stāvz, stăvz], n. pl.
Stead ily [stĕd′i-li], ad.
Steak [stāk], n. A slice of meat.
Steal [stēl], n. v. To pilfer.
Stealth ily [stelth′i-li], ad.
Steam er [stēm′ẽr], n.
Stearine [stē′a-rin], n.
Steatite [stē′a-tīt], n.
Steed [stēd], n.
Steel yard [stēl′yärd], n.
Steep le [stēp′l] n.
Steer age [stēr′āj], n.
Stellaria [stel-lā′ri-a], n.
Sten′cil ler [sten′sil-ẽr], n.
Stenographer [sten-og′ra-fẽr], n.
Stenographic [sten-ō-graf′ik], a.
Stentorian [sten-tō′ri-an], a.
Steppe [step], n. An extensive plain.
Stereopticon [ster-e-op′ti-kon], n.
Stereoscope [stē′re-o-skōp, ster′e-o-
skōp], n. [a. n. v.
Stereotype [stē′re-o-tīp, ster′e-o-tīp].
Sterile [ster′il], a.
Sterility [ste-ril′i-ti], n.
Sterling [stẽr′ling], a. n.
Stertorous [stẽr′tor-us], a.
Stethoscope [steth′o-skōp], n.
Stew′ard ess [stū′ẽrd-es], n.
Stick ler [stik′lẽr], n.
Stiff′en er [stif′n-ẽr], n.
Stifle [stī′fl], n. v.
Stig′ma tize [stig′ma-tiz], v.
Stilbite [stil′bīt], n.
Stiletto [sti-let′tō], n. v.
Stimulant [stim′ū-lant], n.
Stimulator [stim′ū-lāt-ẽr], n.
Stimulus [stim′ū-lus], n. Stimūli, pl.
Stint [stint], n. v.
Sti′pend iary [sti-pen′di-a-ri], a. n.
Stipulator [stip′ū-lāt-ẽr], n.
Stipule [stip′ūl], n.
Stir rup [stẽr′rup], n.
Stitch er [stich′ẽr], n.
Stock ade [stok-ād′], n. v.
Sto′ic al [stō′ik-al], a.
Stoicism [stō′i-sizm], n.
Stoker [stōk′ẽr], n.
Stolid [stol′id], a.
Stomach [stum′ak], n.
Stomacher [stum′a-chẽr], n.
Stomachic [sto-mak′ik], a. n.
Stony [stōn′i], a.
Stoop [stōōp], n. v.

Stop per [stop′ẽr], n.
Storage [stōr′āj], n.
Storied [stō′rid], a.
Stout ly [stowt′li], ad.
Straggler [strag′lẽr], n.
Straight [strāt], a. Direct; narrow
ad. Immediately.
Straighten [strāt′n], v.
Strain er [strān′ẽr], n.
Strait [strāt], a. Narrow ; difficul
n. A pass ; distress.
Stramonium [stra-mō′ni-um], n.
Strange ly [strānj′li], ad.
Strangulation [strang-gū-lā′shun],
Strangury [strang′gū-ri], n.
Stratagem [strat′a-jem], n.
Strategic [stra-tej′ik], a.
Stratify [strat′i-fī], v.
Stratum [strā′tum], n. Strāta, pl.
Strawberry [strą′be-ri], n.
Streak [strēk], n. v.
Stream [strēm], n. v.
Street [strēt], n.
Strength′ en er [strength′en-ẽr], n
Strenuous [stren′ū-us], a.
Stretch er [strech′ẽr], n.
Strew [strōō, strō], v. [n
Strict ure [strikt′yōōr, strikt′yẽr]
Stroll er [strōl′ẽr], n.
Strophe [strō′fe], n.
Structure [strukt′yōōr, strukt′yẽr],n
Struggle [strug′l], n. v.
Strumpet [strum′pet], a. n.
Strychnia, Strychnine [strik′ni-a
strik′nin, strik′nin], n.
Stubble [stub′l], n.
Stubborn [stub′orn], a.
Stucco [stuk′kō], n. v.
Student [stū′dent], n.
Studied [stud′id], a. p.
Studio [stū′di-ō], n.
Studious [stū′di-us], a.
Stuff [stuf], n. v.
Stumble [stum′bl], n. v.
Stun ner [stun′ẽr], n.
Stupefaction [stū-pe-fak′shun], n.
Stupefier [stū′pe-fī-ẽr], n.
Stupendous [stū-pen′dus], a.
Stu′pid ity [stū-pid′i-ti], n.
Stupor [stū′por], n.
Sturdily [stẽr′di-li], ad.
Sturgeon [stẽr′jun], n.
Stygian [stij′i-an], a.
Style [stīl], n. A pencil ; diction
title ; manner ; fashion ; a filame
of a pistil. v. To denominate.

āle, add, beår, ärm, ásk, fạll ; mē, met, thêre, hèr ; pīne, pin ; ōld, odd,

Suasory [swā'so-ri], a.
Suavity [swav'i-ti], n. [n.
Subaltern [sub'al-tèrn, sub-al'tèrn],
Subdue [sub-dū'], v.
Subjacent [sub-jā'sent], a. [v.
Subject [sub'jekt], a. n. [sub-jekt']
Subjection [sub-jek'shun], n.
Subjugator [sub'ju-gāt-èr], n.
Subjunctive [sub-jungk'tiv], a. n.
Sublimate [sub'li-māt], n. v.
Sublimity [sub-lim'i-ti], n.
Sublunary [sub'lu-nā-ri], a.
Submitter [sub-mit'èr], n.
Suborn er [sub-orn'èr], n.
Subpœna [sub-pē'na], n. v.
Subriguous [sub-rig'ū-us], a.
Subscribe [sub-skrīb'], v.
Subscription [sub-skrip'shun], n.
Subsequent [sub'se-kwent], a.
Subservience [sub'sèr'vi-ens], n.
Subsidence [sub-sīd'ens], n.
Subsidiary [sub-sid'i-a-ri], a. n.
Subsidize [sub'si-dīz], v.
Subsist ence [sub-sis'tens], n.
Substantial [sub-stan'shal], a.
Substantiate [sub-stan'shi-āt], v.
Substantive [sub'stan-tiv], a. n.
Substitution [sub-sti-tū'shun], n.
Subterfuge [sub'tèr-fūj], n.
Subterranean [sub-tèr-rā'ne-an], a.
Subtile ly [sub'til-li], ad. Thinly; finely.
Subtility [sub'til-ti], n. Thinness.
Subtle ty [sut'l-ti], n. Cunning; craftiness.
Subtly [sut'li], ad. Slyly.
Subtract ion [sub-trak'shun], n.
Subtrahend [sub'tra-hend], n.
Suburb an [sub-èr'ban], a. n.
Subvert er [sub-vèrt'èr], n.
Subvertible [sub-vèrt'i-bl], a.
Succeed er [suk-sēd'èr], n.
Success ful ly [suk-ses'fool-li], ad.
Succession [suk-se'shun], n.
Successor [suk-ses'or], n.
Succinct [suk-singkt'], a.
Succor er [suk'èr-èr], n.
Succotash [suk'ko-tash], n.
Succulence [suk'kū-lens], n.
Succumb [suk-kumb'], v.
Such [such], a.
Suction [suk'shun], n.
Sudatory [sū'da-to-ri], n.
Sudden ly [sud'en-li], ad.
Suet [sū'et], n.
Suffer able [suf'fèr-a-bl], a.

Sufferance [suf'fer-ans], n.
Sufferer [suf'fèr-èr], n.
Suffice [suf-fīz'], v.
Sufficiency [suf-fi'shen-si], n.
Suffocation [suf-fo-kā'shun], n.
Suffocative [suf-fo-kāt'iv], a.
Suffrage [suf'frāj], n.
Suffragist [suf'fra-jist], n.
Suffuse [suf-fūz'], v.
Suffusion [suf-fū'zhun], n.
Sugar y [shoo'gér-i], a.
Suggest er [sug-jest'èr], n.
Suicidal [sū-i-sīd'al], a.
Suicide [sū'i-sīd], n.
Suit able [sūt'a-bl], a.
Suite [swēt], n. A retinue; a set, particularly of apartments.
Suitor [sūt'or], n.
Sullen [sul'en], a.
Sulphate [sul'fāt], n.
Sulphide [sul'fīd], n.
Sulphuret ted [sul'fu-ret-ed], a.
Sulphuric [sul-fū'rik], a.
Sulphur ous [sul'fèr-us], a.
Sultan [sul'tan], n.
Sultana [sul-tā'na, sul-tä'na], n.
Sultriness [sul'tri-nes], n.
Sultry [sul'tri], a.
Sumac [shoo'mak, sū'mak], n.
Summarily [sum'a-ri-li], ad.
Summation [sum-ā'shun], n.
Summer sault [sum'èr-salt], n.
Summit [sum'it], n.
Summon er [sum'on-èr], n.
Sumptuous [sump'tū-us], a.
Sundries [sun'drīz], n. pl.
Sun ny [sun'i], a.
Superable [sū'pér-a-bl], a.
Superannuation [sū-pér-an-nu-ā'shun], n.
Superciliary [sū-pér-sil'i-a-ri], a.
Supercilious [sū-pér-sil'i-us], a.
Supererogation [sū-pér-er-ō-gā'shun], n.
Supererogatory [sū-pér-e-rog'a-to-ri], a. [n.
Superficial ity [sū-pér-fish-i-al'i-ti],
Superficies [sū-pér-fish'e-ēz, sū-pér-fish'ēz], n. sing. and pl.
Superfluity [sū-pér-flū'i-ti], n.
Superfluous [sū-pér-flū-us], a.
Superintend ence [sū-pér-in-ten'dens], n.
Superintender [sū-pér-in-tend'èr], n.
Superior ity [sū-pér-i-or'i-ti], n.
Superlative [sū-pér-la'tiv], a. n.

Supernal [sū-pér'nal], a.
Supernumerary [sū-pér-nū'me-ra-ri], a. n. [n.
Superscription [sū-pér-skrip'shun],
Supersede [sū-pér-sēd'], v.
Superstition [sū-pér-sti'shun], n.
Superstitious [sū-pér-sti'shus], a.
Supervene [sū-pér-vēn'], v.
Supervisor [sū-pér-viz'ér], n.
Supine [sū-pīn'], a. [sū'pīn], n.
Supple [sup'l], a. v.
Sup'plement al [sup-le-men'tal], a.
Suppliant [sup'li-ant], a. n.
Supplicator [sup'li-kāt-ér], n.
Support' able [sup-port'a-bl], a.
Supporter [sup-port'ér], n.
Suppose [sup-pōz'], v.
Supposition [sup-pō-zish'un], n.
Supposititious [sup-poz-i-tish'us], a.
Suppository [sup-poz'i-to-ri], n.
Suppress' or [sup-pres'ér], n.
Suppuration [sup-pu-rā'shun], n.
Supremacy [sū-prem'a-si], n.
Surcease [sér-sēs'], v.
Surcingle [sér'sing-gl], n. v.
Sure ly [shōōr'li], n. v.
Surface [sér'fās], n. v.
Sur'feit er [sér'fit-ér], n.
Surgeon [sér'jun], n.
Surgery [sér'jér-i], n.
Surname [sér'nām], n. [sér-nām'], v.
Surplice [sér'plis], n.
Surprise [sér-prīz'], n. v.
Surren'der or [sér-ren'dér-ér], n.
Surreptitious [sér-rep-tish'us], a.
Surrogate [sér'rō-gāt], n.
Surtout [sér-tōō'], n.
Surveillance [sér-vāl'yans], n.
Survey [sér'vā], n. [sér-vā'], v.
Surveyor [sér-vā'ér], n.
Survival [sér-vīv'al], n.
Survivor [sér-vīv'ér], n.
Susceptibility [sus-sep-ti-bil'i-ti], n.
Susceptivity [sus-sep-tiv'i-ti], n.
Suspect' er [sus-pekt'ér], n.
Suspend' er [sus-pend'ér], n.
Suspension [sus-pen'shun], n.
Suspicion [sus-pi'shun], n.
Suspicious [sus-pish'us], a.
Sustain' able [sus-tān'a-bl], a.
Sustainer [sus-tān'ér], n.
Sustenance [sus'ten-ans], n.
Sustentation [sus-ten-tā'shun], n.
Suttee [sut-tē'], n.
Suture [sūt'yōōr, sūt'yér], n.
Suz'erain ty [sōō'ze-rān-ti], n.

Swab ber [swob-ér], n.
Swaddle [swod'l], n. v.
Swagger [swag'ér], n. v.
Swain [swān], n.
Swallow [swol'lō], n. v.
Swamp [swomp], n. v.
Swap [swop], ad. v.
Sward [swōrd], n. v.
Swarm [swärm], n. v.
Swarthy [swärth'i], a.
Swash [swosh], n. v.
Swath [swäth], n.
Swathe [swāth], v.
Swear er [swâr'ér], n.
Sweat [swet], n. v. [n.
Swedenborgian [swē-den-bor'ji-an],
Sweep er [swēp'ér], n.
Sweet en [swēt'n], v.
Swell [swel], n. v.
Swerve [swérv], v.
Swift ly [swift'li], ad.
Swim mer [swim'ér], n.
Swindler [swin'dlér], n.
Swingel [swin'jel, swing'gl], n.
Switch [swich], n. v.
Swivel [swiv'el], n. v.
Swoon [swōōn], n. v.
Sword [sōrd], n.
Sybarite [sib'a-rīt], n.
Sycamore [sik'a-mōr], n.
Sycophant [sik'o-fant], n.
Syenite [sī'en-it], n.
Syllabic [sil-lab'ik], a.
Syllable [sil'la-bl], n. v.
Syllogism [sil'lō-jizm], n.
Sylph [silf], n.
Sylvan [sil'van], a. n.
Sym'bol ism [sim'bol-izm], n.
Symmetrical [sim-met'rik-al], a.
Symmetry [sim'me-tri], n.
Sympathize [sim'pa-thīz], v.
Symphony [sim'fo-ni], n.
Symposium [sim-pō'zi-um], posia, pl.
Symp'tom atology [simp-e-ji], n.
Synæresis [sin-er'e-sis], n.
Synagogue [sin'a-gog], n.
Synchronism [sink'ro-nizm]
Synchronous [sink'ro-nus]
Syncope [sing'ko-pe], n.
Syndicate [sin'dik-āt], r
Synecdoche [si-nek'do
Synod [sin'od], n.
Synonym [sin'o-n
Synopsis [si-nop'

Syntax [sin'taks], n.
Synthesis [sin'the-sis], n. Syntheses, pl.
Syphilis [sif'i-lis], n.
Syringa [si-ring'ga], n.
Syringe [sir'inj], n. v.

Syrup [sir'up], n.
Sys'tem atic [sis-te-mat'ik], a.
Systematize [sis'tem-at-iz], v.
Systole [sis'to-le], n.
Systyle [sis'til], a.
Syzygy [siz'i-ji], n.

T.

Tabard [tab'ärd], n.
Tabernacle [tab'er-na-kl], n. v.
Tablature [tab'la-tūr], n.
Tableau [tab-lō'], n. Tableaux [tab-lōz'], pl.
Table d'hôte [tä'bl'dōt'], n.
Tablet [tab'let], n.
Tac'it urnity [tas-i-tērn'i-ti], n.
Tack le [tak'l], n. v.
Tact ics [tak'tiks], n.
Tænia [tē'ni-a], n.
Tail [tāl], n. An appendage.
Tailor [tā'lêr], n.
Taint [tānt], n. v.
Talc [talk], n.
Talcose [tal-kōs'], a.
Tale [tāl], n. A story ; a reckoning.
Talisman [tal'iz-man], n.
Talk ative [tak'a-tiv], a.
Tallow [tal'lō], n. v.
Tal'mud ic [tal-mud'ik], a.
Tamarind [tam'a-rind], n.
Tambour [tam'bōōr], n. v.
Tambourine [tam-bo-rēn'], n.
Tame able [tām'a'bl], a.
Tanager [tan'a-jêr], n.
Tanagra [tan'a-gra], n.
Tanagrinæ [tan-a-grī'nē], n. pl.
Tangency [tan'jen-si], n.
Tangible [tan'ji-bl], a.
Tank ard [tang'kärd], a. n.
Tan nable [tan'a-bl], a.
Tan'ner y [tan'êr-i], n.
Tantalize [tan'ta-līz], v.
Taper [tā'pêr], a. Conical. n. A small wax candle. v. To diminish toward one end.
Tapestry [tap'es-trī], n. v.
Tapioca [tap-i-ō'ka], n.
Tapir [tā'pêr], n. An animal.
Tapis [ta'pē'], n.
Tarantella [tar-an-tel'la], n.
Tarantula [ta-ran'tu-la], n.
Tardiness [tär'di-nes], n.

Target [tär'get], n.
Tariff [tar'if], n. v.
Tar'nish er [tär'nish-êr], n.
Tarpaulin [tär-pa'lin], n.
Tarpeian [tär-pē'yan], a.
Tartan [tär'tan], a. n.
Tartar [tär'tar], n.
Tartarean [tar-tä're-an], a.
Tartareous [tar-tä're-us], a. Pertaining to Tartarus ; consisting of tartar.
Tartaric [tar-tar'ik], a.
Tartarous [tär'tar-us], a. Containing tartar.
Tartarus [tär'ta-rus], n. The infernal regions.
Tassel [tas'sel], n. v.
Taste ful [tāst'fŏŏl], a.
Tatouay [tat'ōō-ā], n.
Tatouhou [tat'ōō-hōō], n.
Tat'ter demalion [tat-têr-de-mal'-yun], n.
Tattoo [tat-tōō'], n. v.
Taught [tat], v. To teach. a. Tight [same as Taut].
Taunt [tänt], n. v.
Taurus [ta'rus], n.
Taut [tat], a. Tight.
Tautology [ta-tol'o-ji], n.
Tavern [tav'êrn], n.
Tawdry [ta'dri], a.
Tax able [taks'a-bl], a.
Taxation [taks'ā-shun], n.
Taxidermy [taks'i-der-mi], n.
Teach able [tēch'a-bl], a.
Teak [tēk], n.
Teal [tēl], n.
Team ster [tēm'stêr], n.
Tear [tēr], n. A drop of lachrymal fluid. [tär], n. A rent. v. To sever.
Tease [tēz], n. v.
Teat [tēt], n.
Technic [tek'nik], a. n.
Tech'nical ity [tek-ni-kal'i-ti], n.
Tedious [tē'di-us, ted'yus], a.

of

nt], n.

n.

i], a.

ti], n.

n.

z], n. pl.

'shun],n.

, n.

Terminator [tẽr'min-āt-ẽr], n.
Terminus [tẽr'min-us], n. **Termini**
[tẽr'mi-nī], pl.
Tern [tẽrn], a. Threefold. n. A bird.
Terpsichore [tẽrp-sik'o-rē].
Terpsichorean [tẽrp-si-ko-rē'an], a.
Terrace [ter'ras], n. v.
Terrapin [ter'a-pin], n.
Terraqueous [ter-āk'we-us], a.
Terrestrial [ter-res'tri-al], a. n.
Terrible [ter'ri-bl], a.
Terrier [ter'i-ẽr], n.
Terrific [ter-rif'ik], a.
Terrigenous [ter-rij'en-us], a.
Territory [ter'ri-to-ri], n.
Ter'ror ism [ter'ror-izm], n.
Tertiary [tẽr'shi-a-ri], a. n.
Tessellated [tes'sel-lāt-ed], a.
Tes'tament ary [tes-ta-men'ta-ri], a.
Testator [tes-tāt'or], n.
Testatrix [tes-tāt'riks], n.
Testify [tes'ti-fī], v.
Testily [tes'ti-li], ad.
Testimonial [tes-ti-mō'ni-al], n.
Tetanus [tet'a-nus], n.
Tête-à-tête [tāt'à'tāt'], a. ad. n.
Tetradynamia [tet-ra-di-nā'mi-a], n.
Tetragynia [tet-ra-jin'i-a], n.
Tetrarch [tē'trärk], n.
Teu'ton ic [tū-ton'ik], a. n.
Text ile [teks'til], n.
Texture [teks'tūr, tekst'yōōr, tekst'-
yẽr], n.
Thanksgiving [thanks'giv-ing], n.
Thatch [thach], n. v.
Thaumaturgic [tha-ma-tẽr'jik], a.
Theatre [thē'a-tẽr], n.
Theatrical [thē-at'rik-al], a.
Thee [thē], pron.
Their [thār], a.
Theme [thēm], n.
Thence [thens], ad.
Theocracy [thē-ok'ra-si], n.
Theodicy [thē-od'i-si], n.
Theologue [thē'o-log], n.
Theorist [thē'o-rist], n.
Theosophist [thē-os'o-fist], n
Therapeutics [ther-a-pū'tiks]
There [thēr], ad.
Therefore [thēr'fōr], ad. c
Thereof [thēr-of'], ad.
Therewith [thēr-with'],
Thermal [thẽr'mal], a.
Thermometer [the
Thesaurus [the-s
Thesis [thē'sis], n.

Theurgy [thē'ér-ji], n.
Thew [thū], n.
Thick et [thik'et], n.
Thief [thēf], n. Thieves [thēvz], pl.
Thiers [te'er]. French historian.
Thievish [thēv'ish], a.
Thigh [thī], n.
Thim'ble ful [thim'bl-fŏŏl], n.
Thine [thīn], a.
Think able [thingk'a-bl], a.
Thirst ily [thérs'ti-li], ad.
Thirteenth [thèr'tènth], a. n.
Thirtieth [thèr'ti-eth], a. n.
Thistle [this'l], n.
Thither [thith'ér], ad.
Thoracic [tho-ras'ik], n.
Thorax [thō'raks], n.
Thor'ough fare [thur'ō-fâr], n.
Thought ful [thạt'fŏŏl], a.
Thousand [thow'zand], n.
Thraldom [thrạl'dom], n.
Thrall [thrạl], n.
Thrash, Thresh [thrash, thresh], v.
Thread bare [thred'bâr], a.
Threat en [thret'n], v.
Three-legged [thrē'legd], a.
Threshold [thresh'ōld], n.
Threw [thrŏŏ], v.
Thrice [thris], ad.
Thrift iness [thrif'ti-nes], n.
Thrill [thril], n. v.
Throat [thrōt], n.
Throne [thrōn], n. v.
Throng [throng], n. v.
Throstle [thros'l], v.
Throttle [throt'l], v.
Through [thrŏŏ], a. ad. prep.
Thrush [thrush], n.
Thule [thū'le], n.
Thun'der er [thun'dèr-ér], n.
Thunderous [thun'dér-us], a.
Thurible [thū'ri-bl], n.
Thuringite [thū-rin'jit], n.
Thurl [thérl], n.
Toursday [thérz'dā], n.
Thwack [thwak], n. v.
Thwart [thwạrt], a. n. v.
Thayine [thī'in], n.
Thyme [tīm], n.
Thyroid [thī'roid], a.
Thyrsus [thér'sus], n.
Tiara [ti-ā'ra], n.
Tibia [tib'i-a], n.
Ticdouloureux [tik-dŏŏ'lŏŏ-rŏŏ], n.
Tick et [tik'et], n. v.
Tickle [tik'l], v.

Ticklish [tik'lish], a.
Tidal [tī'dal], a.
Tidbit [tid'bit], n.
Tidology [ti-dol'o-ji], n.
Tier [tēr], n. A row ; a rank.
Tierce [tèrs], n.
Tight [tīt], n.
Till age [til'āj], n.
Timber [tim'bér], n. Wood.
Timbre [tim'br], n. Musical term.
Time liness [tīm'li-nes], n.
Tim'id ity [ti-mid'i-ti], n.
Timorous [tim'or-us], a.
Tinamou [tin'a-mŏŏ], n.
Tincture [tingkt'yŏŏr, tingkt'yèr], n. v.
Tinea [tin'e-a], n.
Tinkle [ting'kl], n. v.
Tinsel [tin'sel], a. n. v.
Tiny [tī'ni], a.
Tippet [tip'et], n.
Tirade [ti-rād'], n.
Tire some [tir'sum], a.
Tissue [tish'ŭ], n. v.
Tithable [tith'a-bl], a.
Tithe [tith], n. v.
Title [tī'tl], n. v.
Titular [tit'ū-lèr], a. n.
Toad [tōd], n.
Toady [tōd'i], n. A flatterer. v. To flatter ; to fawn upon.
Toast er [tōst'ér], n.
Tobac'co nist [tō-bak'kō-nist], n.
Tocsin [tok'sin], n.
Toddle [tod'l], v.
Tody [tō'di], n. A bird.
Toe [tō], n. v.
Together [to-geth'èr], ad.
Toilet [toi'let], n.
Tolerable [tol'èr-a-bl], a.
Tolerance [tol'èr-ans], n.
Tolerator [tol'èr-āt-ér], n.
Toll [tōl], n. v.
Tomahawk [tom'a-hạk], n. v.
Tomato [tō-mā'to, to-mä'to], n.
Tomb [tŏŏm], n. v.
Tome [tōm], n.
Tongs [tongz], n.
Tongue y [tung'i], a.
Tonic [ton'ik], n.
Ton nage [tun'āj], n.
Ton'sil itis [ton-sil-i'tis], n.
Tonsorial [ton-sō'ri-al], a.
Tonsure [ton'shŏŏr, ton'sher], n.
Tontine [ton-tēn'], a. n.
Too [tŏŏ], ad.

Tool [tōōl], n. v.
Tooth [tōōth], n. Teeth, pl.
Toothache [tōōth'āk], n. [Not Teeth-
ache.]
Topaz [tō'paz], n.
Tophet [tō'fet], n.
Topiary [top'i-a-ri], a.
Top'ic al [top'ik-al], a.
Topographic al [top-o-graf'i-kal], a.
Topography [to-pog'ra-fi], n.
Toque [tōk], n.
Toreutic [to-rū'tik], a.
Torment [tor'ment], n. [tor-ment'], v.
Tormenter [tor-ment'ér], n.
Tornado [tor-nā'dō], n. Tornadoes,
pl.
Torpedo [tor-pē'dō], n. Torpedoes,
pl.
Torpesence [tor-pes'ens], n.
Tor'pid ity [tor-pid'i-ti], n.
Tortoise [tor'tiz, tor'tis], n.
Tortuous [tor'tū-us], a.
Torture [tort'yōōr, tort'yér], n. v.
Toss [tos], n. v.
To'tal ity [tō-tal'i-ti], n.
Totaninæ [to-ta-ni'nē], n. pl.
Totter er [tot'ér-ér], n.
Toucan [tow'kan, tōō'kan], n.
Touch able [tuch'a-bl], a.
Tough [tuf], a.
Tour ist [tōōr'ist], n.
Tourmalin [tōōr'ma-lin], n.
Tournament [tōōr'na-ment], n.
Tourniquet [tōōr'ni-ket], n.
Tourney [tōōr'ni], n.
Tournure [tōōr'nōōr'], n.
Tout-ensemble [tōōt'ah'sah'bl], n.
Toward [tō'érd], a. ad. prep.
Tow'el ing [tou'el-ing], n.
Town [town], a. n.
Trace able [trās'a-bl], a.
Trachea [trā'kē-a], n. Tracheæ, pl.
Trachenchyma [trā-ken'ki-ma], n.
Tracheotomy [trā-ke-ot'o-mi], n.
Trachyte [trā'kīt], n.
Tract able [trak'ta-bl], a.
Tractile [trak'til], a.
Tradescantia [tra-des-kan'shi-a], n.
Tradi'tion al [tra-di'shun-al], a.
Traducible [tra-dūs'i-bl], a.
Traf'fic ker [traf'ik-ér], n.
Tragacanth [trag'a-kanth], n.
Tragedian [tra-jē'di-an], n.
Trag'ic al ly [traj'ik-al-li], ad.
Train er [trān'ér], n.
Trai'tor ous [trā'tér-us], a.

Tram'mel er [tram'mel-ér], n.
Tramontane [tra-mon'tan, tram'on
tān], a. n.
Trance [trans], n. v.
Tran'quil lity [tran-kwil'i-ti], n.
Tranquillizer [tran'kwil-īz-ér], n.
Transact' or [trans-ak'tér], n.
Transcend' ent [trans-sen'dent], a. n.
Transcendental ist [tran-sen-den'
tal-ist], n.
Transept [tran'sept], n.
Trans'fer able [trans-fér'a-bl], a.
Transference [trans-fér'ens], n.
Transgress' or [trans-gres'ér], n.
Transient [tran'shent], a.
Transit [tran'sit], n. v.
Transition [tran-sizh'un], n.
Transitive [trans'i-tiv], a. n.
Translator [trans-lāt'ér], n.
Translucence [trans-lū'sens], n.
Transmigrate [trans'mi-grāt], v.
Transmit' ter [trans-mit'ér], n.
Transmittible [trans-mit'i-bl], a.
Transparency [trans-pā'ren-si], n.
Transpire [trans-pīr'], v.
Transposing [trans-pōz'ing], a.
Trapeze [tra-pēz'], n.
Trapezium [tra-pē'zi-um], n.
Trapezoid [trap'e-zoid], n.
Trap per [trap'ér], n.
Travail [trav'il], n. Parturition.
Trav'el er [trav'el-ér], n. One w
journeys.
Traversable [trav'ers-a-bl], a.
Travertine [trav'ér-tin], n.
Travesty [trav'es-ti], n. v.
Trawl [tral], n. v.
Treacherous [trech'ér-us], a.
Treacle [trē'kl], n.
Tread [tred], n. v.
Trea'son able [trē'zon-a-bl], a.
Treas'ure r [trezh'ur-ér], n.
Treat ise [trē'tiz], n.
Treble [treb'l], n.
Tree [trē], n. v.
Trefoil [trē'foil], n.
Trellis [trel'is], n.
Tremble [trem'bl], n. v.
Tremendous [trē-men'dus]
Tremolo [trem'o-lō], n.
Tremor [trē'mur], n.
Tremulous [trem'ū-lus],
Trench er [trensh'ér],
Trepan' ning [tre
Trephine [tre-fin',
Trepidation [trep

Trepidity [tre-pid'i-ti], n.
Tres'pass er [tres'pas-ér], n.
Trestle [tres'l], n.
Triad [tri'ad], n.
Trib'al ism [trib'al-izm], n.
Tribulation [trib-ū-lā'shun], n.
Tribunal [tri-bū'nal], n.
Tribune [trib'ūn], n.
Trichina [tri-ki'na], n.
Trichiniasis, Trichinosis [trik-i-ni'a-sis, trik-i-nō'sis], n.
Trichopteran [tri-kop'tér-an], n.
Trickle [trik'l], v.
Triclinium [tri-klin'i-um], n.
Triennial [tri-en'ni-al], a.
Trifle [tri'fl], n. v.
Trifolium [tri-fō'li-um], n.
Trigeminous [tri-jem'in-us], a.
Trigonometry [trig-o-nom'et-ri], n.
Trillion [tril'yon], n.
Trilobite [tri'lo-bit], n.
Trim mer [trim'ér], n.
Trinitarian [trin-i-tā'ri-an], n.
Trio [tri'ō], n. [Webster, The Imperial, and Stormonth give tre'ō as an allowable pronunciation.]
Tripartite [trip'ar-tit], a.
Triphthong [trif'thong, trip'thong], n.
Triple [trip'l], a. v.
Tripod [tri'pod], n.
Trisyllable [tris'sil-la-bl], n.
Tri'umph er [tri'um-fér], n.
Triumvir [tri-um'vér], n.
Triune [tri'ūn], a.
Triv'ial ity [triv-i-al'i-ti], n.
Troche [trō'kē], n. A lozenge.
Trochee [trō'kē], n. A poetic foot of two syllables.
Troglodyte [trog'lo-dit], n.
Troll er [trōl'ér], n.
Trombone [trom'bōn], n.
Troop er [trōōp'ér], n.
Trope [trōp], n.
Trophy [trō'fi], n.
Trop'ic al [trop'ik-al], a.
Troth [troth], n.
Trot ter [trot'ér], n.
Troubadour [trōō'ba-dōōr], n.
Trouble [trub'l], n. v.
Troublous [trub'lus], a.
Trough [trof], n.
Trounce [trowns], v.
Troupe [trōōp], n. A troop.
Trousers [trow'zérz], n. pl.
Trousseau [trōō'sō'], n.

Trout [trowt], n.
Trow [trō], v.
Truant [trōō'ant], n.
Truculence [trōō'kū-lens], n.
True [trōō], a. v.
Truffle [trōō'fl], n.
Truly [trōō'li], ad.
Trum'pet er [trum'pet-ér], n.
Truncheon [trun'shun], n. v.
Trundle [trun'dl], n. v.
Trust ee [trus-tē'], n.
Truth [trōōth], n.
Tryst [trist], n. v.
Tu'ber cle [tū'bér-kl], n.
Tubercular [tū-bér'kū-lér], a.
Tuberose [tūb'rōz, tū'bér-ōz], n.
Tuesday [tūz'di], n.
Tuileries [twē'le'rē'], Fr.
Tuition [tū-i'shun], n.
Tulip [tū'lip], n.
Tumid [tū'mid], a.
Tumor [tū'mor], n.
Tu'mult uous [tū-mult'ū-us], a.
Tune [tūn], n. v.
Tunnel [tun'el], n. v.
Turban [tér'ban], n.
Turbid [tér'bid], n.
Turbine [tér'bin], n.
Turbot [tér'bot], n.
Turbulence [tér'bū-lens], n.
Tur'gid ity [tér-jid'i-ti], n.
Turkey [tér'ke], n.
Turmoil [tér'moil], n. v.
Turnip [tér'nip], n.
Turpentine [tér'pen-tin], n.
Turquoise [tér-koiz'], n.
Tur'ret ed [tér'et-ed], a. p.
Turtle [tér'tl], n.
Tutelage [tū'tel-āj], n.
Tutor [tū'tor], n. v.
Twaddle [twad'l], n. v.
Tweak [twēk], n. v.
Tweed [twēd], n.
Tweezers [twē'zérs], n. pl.
Twelfth [twelfth], a. n.
Twilight [twi'lit], n.
Twinge [twinj], n. v.
Twinkle [twing'kl], n. v.
Twitch [twich], n. v.
Twit'ter ing [twit'ér-ing], n.
Tympanitis [tim-pa-ni'tis], n.
Tympanum [tim'pa-num], n.
Type [tip], n.
Typhoid [ti'toid], a.
Typhoon [ti-fōōn'], n.
Typhus [ti'fus], n.

Typical [tip′ik-al], a.
Typographer [tĭ-pog′raf-ẽr, tĭ-pog′-raf-ẽr], n.
Typographical [tĭ′po-graf′i-kal, tip-o-graf′i-kal], a.
Tyran′nic al [tĭ-ran′ni-kal], a.

Tyrannicide [tĭ-ran′ni-sīd], n.
Tyrannize [tir′an-īz], v.
Tyranny [tir′an-ni], n.
Tyr′ol ese [tir′ol-ēz], a.
Tzar [zär], n.
Tzarina [zä-rē′nȧ], n.

U.

Ubiquitarian [û-bik-we-tā′re-an], n.
Ubiquitous [û-bik′wĭ-tus], a.
Udometer [û-dom′e-tẽr], n.
Ugliness [u̯g′li-nes], n.
Ukase [û-kās′], n.
Ul′cer ous [ul′ser-us], a.
Uliginous [û-lĭj′i-nus], a.
Ullmannite [ul′man-īt], n.
Ulmaceous [ul-mā′shus], a.
Ulmine [ul′min], n.
Ulterior [ul-tē′ri-or], a.
Ultima Thule [ul′te-mȧ thū′le]
Ultimatum [ul-ti-mā′tum], n. Ultimata [ul-ti-mā′tä], pl.
Ultramontane [ul-tra-mon′tān], a. n.
Umbelliferæ [um-bel-lif′ẽr-ē], n. pl.
Umbilic, Umbilical [um-bil′ik, um-bil′i-kal], a.
Umbilicus [um-bi-lī′kus], n.
Um′brage ous [um-brā′jus, um-brā′-je-us], a.
Umbrella [um-brel′la], n.
Umbriferous [um-brif′ẽr-us], a.
Umbrina [um-brī′nȧ], n.
Umpirage [um′pi-raj], n.
Umpire [um′pīr], n. v.
Unanimity [û-na-nim′i-ti], n.
Unanimous [û-nan′i-mus], a.
Una voce [û′na vō′ce], Lat.
Uncial [un′shal], a. n.
Unciform [un′si-form], a.
Uncinate [un′si-nāt], a.
Uncle [ung′kl], n.
Uncouth [un-kōōth′], a.
Unction [ungk′shun], n.
Unctuous [ungkt′û-us], a.
Underneath [un-dẽr-nēth′], ad. prep.
Undine [un-dēn′], n.
Undulation [un-dū-lā′shun], n.
Unguent [ung′gwent], n.
Unguiculate [ung-gwik′û-lat], a.
Unguis [ung′gwis], n.
Ungular [un′gu-lȧ], n.
Ungulata [un-gu-lā′tȧ], n. pl.
Unheard [un-hẽrd′], a.

Unicorn [û′ni-korn], n.
U′niform ity [û-ni-form′i-tĭ], n
Un′ion ism [ûn′yun-izm], n.
Unique [û-nēk′], a.
Unison [û′ni-son], a. n.
Unisonous [û-nis′ō-nus], a.
U′nit arian [û-ni-tā′ri-an], a. n.
Unit′ed ly [û-nīt′ed-li], ad.
Uniter [û-nīt′ẽr], n.
Univer′sal ist [û-ni-vẽr′sal-ist], n.
University [û-ni-vẽr′si-ti], n.
Univocal [û-niv′o-kal], a. n. [a
Unscathed [un-skatht′, un-skā́thḍ′]
Upas [û′pas], n.
Upbraid [up-brād′], v.
Upheaval [up-hēv′al], n.
Uphol′ster er [up-hōl′stẽr-ẽr], n.
Uranic [û-ran′ik], a.
Uranite [û′ran-īt], n.
Uranium [u-rā′ni-um], n.
Uranolite [û′ran-o-līt], n.
Uranoscopy [û-ran-os′ko-pi], n.
Uranous [û′ra-nus], a.
Uranus [û′ra-nus], n.
Urao [û′ra-ō], n.
Urbane [ẽr-bān′], a.
Urbanity [ẽr-ban′i-ti], n.
Urceolus [ẽr-sē′ō-lus], n.
Urchin [ẽr′chin], n.
Urea [û′re-a], n.
Uredo [û-rē′dō], n.
Ureide [û′re-id], n.
Ureter [û′rē-tẽr], n.
Urethra [û-rē′thra], n.
Urinæ [u-rī′nē], n. pl.
Urinal [û′ri-nal], n.
Urine [û′rin], n.
Usage [û′zaj], n.
Use ful [ûs′fool], a.
U′sual ly [û′zhû-al-li], a
Usufruct [û′zu-frukt],
Usurious [û-zhû′ri-us]
Usurp′ ation [û-
Usurper [û-zẽrp′
Usury [û′zhû-re]

Utensil [û-ten′sil], n.
Uterine [û′tėr-ĭn, û′tėr-ĭn], a.
Utilitarian [û-til-i-tā′ri-an], a. n.
Utility [û-til′i-ti], n.
Utopia [û-tō′pi-à], n.
Utricle [û′tri-kl]. n.

Utricular [û-trik′u-lar], a.
Ut′ter ance [ut′tėr-ans], n.
Uvula [û′vu-là], n.
Uxorial [ug-zō′ri-al], a.
Uxoricide [ug-zor′i-sĭd], n.
Uxorious [ug-zō′ri-us], a.

V.

Vacancy [vā′kan-si], n.
Vacation [vă-kā′shŭn], n.
Vaccinator [vak-si-nāt′ėr], n.
Vaccine [vak′sin, vak′sĭn], n.
Vacillation [vas-il-lā′shŭn], n.
Vacuity [va-kû′i-ti], n.
Vacuum [vak′û-um], n.
Vag′abond ism [vag′a-bond-izm], n.
Vagarious [va-gā′ri-us], a.
Vagary [va-gā′ri], n.
Vagina [va-jī′na], n. Vaginæ, pl.
Vaginal [vaj′i-nal], a.
Vaginula [va-jin′u-là], n.
Vagrancy [vā′gran-si], n.
Vague ly [vāg′li], ad.
Vain ly [vān′li], ad.
Valedictory [val-ē-dik′to-ri], a. n.
Valenciennes [vä′lan-si′en′], n.
Valentine [val′en-tin], n.
Valerian [va-lē′ri-an], n.
Valet [val′et, va′lā′], n. v.
Valet de chambre [và′lā′de-shoñ′-
  br], Fr. [Orthoëpist.]
Valetudinarian [val-e-tû-di-nā′ri-an],
  a. n.
Val′iant ly [val′yant-li], ad.
Val′id ity [va-lid′i-ti], n.
Valise [va-lēs′], n.
Valkyr, Valkyria [väl′kir, väl-ki′-
  ri-a], n.
Valley [val′li], n. Valleys, pl.
Val′or ous [val′or-us], a.
Valuable [val′û-a-bl], a.
Valuator [val′û-āt-ėr], a. n.
Value [val′û], n. v.
Valvular [val′vû-lėr], a.
Van′dal ism [van′dal-izm], n.
Vandyke [van-dīk′], a. n.
Vane [vān], n. A weather-cock.
Vanilla [va-nil′la], n.
Vanity [van′i-ti], n.
Van′quish er [vang′kwish-ėr], n.
Vapid [vap′id], a.
Va′por ous [vā′por-us], a.
Vaquero [vä-kā′rō], n.

Venous [vē'nus], a.
Ventilator [ven'ti-lāt-ēr], n.
Ventricle [ven'tri-kl], n.
Ventriloquism [ven-tril'ō-kwizm], n.
Venturous [vent'yoor-us, vent'yēr-us], a.
Venue [ven'ū], n.
Veracious [ve-rā'shus], a.
Veracity [ve-ras'i-ti], n.
Veranda [ve-ran'dā], n.
Ver'bal ist [vēr'bal-ist], n.
Verbē'na ceæ [vēr-be-nā'sē-ē], n. pl.
Verbose [vēr-bōs'], a.
Verbosity [vēr-bos'i-ti], n.
Verdancy [vēr'dan-si], n.
Verdict [vēr'dikt], n.
Verdigris [vēr'di-grēs], n. v.
Verdure [vērd'yoor, vērd'yēr], n.
Verdurous [vērd'yoor-us, vērd'yēr-us], a.
Verification [ver-i-fi-kā'shun], n.
Verisimilar [ver-i-sim'i-lēr], a.
Vermicelli [vēr-ni-chel'li], n.
Vermicular [vēr-mik'ū-lēr], a.
Vermilion [vēr-mil'yun], n. v.
Vermin [vēr'min], n. sing. and pl.
Vernacular [vēr-nak'ū-lēr], a. n.
Vernal [vēr'nal], a.
Versatile [vēr'sa-til], a.
Versifier [vēr'si-fi-ēr], n.
Version [vēr'shun], n. [pl.
Vertebra [vēr'te-brà], n. Vertebræ,
Ver'tical ly [vēr'ti-kal-li], ad.
Verticillate [vēr-tis'il-lāt], a.
Vertigo [vēr'ti-go], n.
Vervain [vēr'vān], n.
Vesicatory [ves'i-ka-to-ri], a. n.
Vesicle [ves'i-kl], n.
Vesicular [ve-sik'ū-lēr], a.
Vessel [ves'el], n.
Vestal [ves'tal], n.
Vestibule [ves'ti-būl], n.
Vesture [vest'yoor, vest'yēr], n. v.
Veteran [vet'e-ran], a. n.
Veterinary [vet'e-ri-na-ri], a.
Vex atious [vek-sā'shus], a.
Vibration [vi-brā'shun], n.
Vibratory [vi'bra-to-ri], a.
Vicar [vik'ēr], n.
Vicarious [vi-kā'ri-us], a.
Vice [vīs], n.
Vicegerent [vīs-jē'rent], a.
Viceroy [vīs'roi], n.
Vicinage [vis'in-āj], n.
Vicinal [vis'i-nal], a.
Vicinity [vi-sin'i-ti], n.

Vicious [vish'us], a.
Vicissitude [vi-sis'i-tūd], n.
Vic'tim ize [vik'tim-īz], v.
Victorious [vik-tō'ri-us], a.
Vic'tor y [vik'to-ri], n.
Victuals [vit'tlz], n. pl.
Vict'ual er [vit'l-ēr], n.
View er [vū'ēr], n.
Vi'gil ance [vij'i-lans], n.
Vignette [vin-yet'], n.
Vi'gor ous [vig'or-us], a.
Village [vil'lāj], a.
Villain [vil'lin], n.
Villanous [vil'la-nus], a.
Villany [vil'la-ni], n.
Villose [vil-lōs'], a.
Villous [vil'lus], a.
Vimen [vi'men], n.
Vimineous [vi-min'e-us], a.
Vinaceous [vi-nā'shus], a.
Vinaigrette [vin-ā-gret'], n.
Vincible [vin'si-bl], a.
Vinculum [vin'ku-lum], n. Vincula, [pl.
Vindicator [vin'di-kāt-ēr], n.
Vindicatory [vin'di-ka-to-ri], a.
Vinegar [vin'e-gēr], n.
Vineyard [vin'yard], n.
Viola [vi'o-lā], n.
Violable [vi'o-la-bl], a.
Violaceous [vi-o-lā'shus], a.
Violator [vi'ō-lāt-ēr], n.
Violence [vi'o-lens], n.
Violin [vi-ō-lin'], n.
Violoncello [vē-ō-lon-chel'lō, ve-ō-lon-sel'lō], n.
Virago [vi-rā'gō], n. Viragoes, pl.
Virent [vi'rent], a.
Vireoninæ [vi-re-o-ni'nē], n. pl.
Vir'gin ity [vēr-jin'i-ti], n.
Virile [vi'ril, vir'il], a.
Virility [vi-ril'i-ti], n.
Vir'tual ly [vēr'tū-al-li, vert'y li, vert'yu-al-li], ad.
Virtue [vērt'ū], n.
Virtuoso [vērt'ū-ō-sō], n. Vir'
Virtuous [vērt'ū-us], a.
Virulence [vēr'ū-lens], n.
Visage [viz'āj], n.
Vis-à-vis [viz'ā'vē], ad. n.
Viscera [vis'se-rà], n. pl.
Viscid [vis'sid], a.
Viscount [vi'kownt], n.
Viscous [vis'kus], a.
Viscus [vis'kus], n.
Visibility [viz'i-bil'
Vis'ion ary [vizh'

Vis'it ation [viz-i-tā'shun], n.
Visitor [viz'i-tor], n.
Visor [viz'ėr], n.
Visual [vizh'ū-al], a.
Vi'tal ity [vī-tal'i-ti], n.
Vitellus [vi-tel'lus], n.
Vitiate [vish'i-āt], v.
Vitreous [vit're-us], a.
Vitrina [vi-trī'nā], n.
Vitriol [vit'ri-ul], n.
Vituperator [vi-tū'pe-rāt'ėr], n.
Vivace [ve-vā'cha], It.
Vivacious [vi-vā'shus], a.
Vivacity [vi-vas'i-ti, vi-vas'i-ti], n.
Viva voce [vī'vā vō'se], Lat.
Vivid [viv'id], a.
Vivify [viv'i-fī], v.
Vix'en ish [vik'sen-ish], a.
Vizier [viz'yer], n.
Vocable [vō'ka-bl], n.
Vocabulary [vō-kab'ū-la-ri], n.
Vocalist [vō'kal-ist], n.
Vocation [vō-kā'shun], n.
Vocative [vok'a-tiv], a. n.
Vociferous [vo-sif'ėr-us], a.
Vocule [vō'kūl, vok'ūl], n.
Voglite [vog'līt], n.
Vogue [vōg], n.
Voice [vois], n. v.
Void [void], a. n.
Volante [vō-län'tā], n.

Volatile [vol'a-til], a.
Volcano [vol-kā'nō], n.   Volcanoes, pl.
Vole [vōl], n. v.
Volition [vō-lish'un], n.
Volley [vol'li], n.
Voltaite [vol'ta-it], n.
Vollameter [vol-lam'e-tėr], n.
Voltigeur [vol-ti-zhėr'], n.
Volubility [vol-ū-bil'i-ti], n.
Volume [vol'ūm, vol'yum], n.
Voluminous [vo-lū'mi-nus], a.
Voluntary [vol'un-ta-ri], a.
Volunteer [vol-un-tėr'], n. v.
Voluptuous [vo-lupt'ū-us], a.
Volute [vo-lūt'], n.
Vomit [vom'it], n. v.
Voracious [vō-rā'shus], a.
Voracity [vō-ras'i-ti], n.
Voraulite [vor'a-līt], n.
Vortex [vor'tex], n.
Vortical [vor'ti-kl], a.
Vortiginous [vor-tij'i-nus], a.
Votary [vō'ta-ri], n.
Vouch er [vowch'ėr], n.
Voyage [voi'ej], n. v.
Vul'gar ity [vul-gar'i-ti], n.
Vulnerable [vul'nėr-a-bl], a.
Vulpine [vul'pin], n.
Vulture [vult'yōōr, vult'yėr], n.   [a.
Vulturine [vult'yōōr-in, vult'yėr-in],

W.

Waft [wȧft], v.
Wag gery [wag'ėr-i], n.   [er.
Wagner [väg'ner], German compos-
Wag'on ette [wag-on-et'], n.
Waif [wāf], n.
Wail [wāl], n. v.   To moan.
Wainscot [wān'skot], n. v.
Waist coat [wāst'kōt], n.
Wait er [wāt'ėr], n.
Waive [wāv], n.   To relinquish.
Wale [wāl], n.   A ridge. v. To mark
  with wales.
Walk [wȧk], n. v.
Wallet [wol'let], n.
Walnut [wȧl'nut], n.
Walrus [wol'rus], n.
Waltz [wȧlts], n. v.
Wampum [wom'pum], n.
Wan [won], a.
Wan'der er [won'dėr-ėr], n.

Wane [wȧn], n. v.   To decrease.
Wanton [won'ton], a. n. v.
Warble [wor'bl], n. v.
Ware [wȧr], n.   Merchandise.
Wariness [wȧ'ri-nes], n.
Warmth [wȧrmth], n.
War'rant ee [wor-ran-tē'], n.
Warranty [wor'ran-ti], n.
Warrior [wȧr'yėr], n.
Wary [wȧ'ri], a.
Wasp ish [wosp'ish], a.
Wassail [wos'sil], a. n. v.
Waste [wȧst], a. n. v.   To destroy;
  to squander.
Watch er [wach'ėr], n.
Water [wȧ'tėr], n. v.   [manner.
Weak ly [wēk'li], ad.   In a weak
Wealth iness [welth'i-nes], a.
Wean [wēn], v.
Weapon [wep'un], n.

Whirl igig [whér'li-gig], n.
Whisk er [whis'kér], n.
Whisky, Whiskey [whis'ki], n.
Whis'per er [whis'pér-ér], n.
Whist [whist], a. n. inter.
Whistle [whis'l], n. v.
White [whit], a.
Whither [whiŧʜ'ér], ad.
Whitsuntide [whit'sun-tïd], n.
Whittle [whit'l], n. v.
Whiz [whiz], n. v.
Whole sale [hōl'sāl], a. n.
Whoop [hōōp], n. v.
Whore dom [hōr'dum], n.
Whorl [whorl], n. A botanic term.
Whortle-berry [whur'tl-be-ri], n.
Whose [hōōz], pron.
Wicked [wik'ed], a. n.
Widgeon [wij'on], n.
Wid'ow er [wid'ō-ér], n.
Wield [wēld], v.
Wife [wïf], n. **Wives,** pl.
Wig gery [wig'ér-i], n.
Wigwam [wig'wom], n.
Wilderness [wil'dér-nes], n.
Wil'ful ly [wil'fool-li], ad.
Wil'low y [wil'lō-i], a.
Wile [wïl], a.

Wondrous [wun'drus], a. ad.
Wont [wunt], a. n. v.
Won't [wônt], v. Contraction of *will not*.
Woodcock [wŏŏd'kok], n.
Woo er [wŏŏ'ėr], n.
Wool len [wŏŏl'n], a. n.
Work [wėrk], n. v.
World ly [wėrld'li], a.
Worm y [wėrm'i], n.
Worse [wėrs], a. ad.
Wor'ship er [wėr'ship-ėr], n.
Worsted [wŏŏrs'ted, wŏŏrs'ted], a. n.
Worth [wėrth], a. n.
Worthily [wėr*th*i-li], ad.
Wound [wŏŏnd], n. An injury. v. To injure. [*Wownd* is antiquated, but is given as an allowable pronunciation by both Worcester and Webster.]
Wound [wownd], p.p. of *Wind*.
Wrack [rak], n.
Wraith [rāth], n.
Wrangle [rang'gl], n. v.
Wrap per [rap'ėr], n. A covering.

Wrasse [ras], n.
Wrath ful [rāth'fŏŏl], a.
Wreak [rēk], v. [pl.
Wreath [rēth], n. Wreaths [rē*th*z],
Wreathe [rē*th*], v.
Wreck er [rek'ėr], n.
Wrench [rensh], n. v.
Wrestle [res'l], n. v.
Wretch ed [rech'ed], a.
Wriggle [rig'l], n. v.
Wright [rit], n. An artificer. [See *Right*, *Rite*, and *Write*.]
Wring [ring], v. To twist or turn with violence : to wrest.
Wrinkle [ring'kl], n. v.
Wrist band [rist'band], n.
Write [rit], v. To trace with pen or pencil.
Writhe [ri*th*], v.
Written [rit'n], a. p.
Wrong [rong], a. ad. n. v.
Wroth [rāth], a.
Wrought [rąt], p.
Wry [rī], a. Twisted.
Wych-hazel [wich'hā-zl], n.

X.

Xanthate [zan'thāt], Im. [zan'that],
Xantheine [zan'the-in], n. [Web. n.
Xanthin [zan'thin], n.
Xantho-carpous [zan-tho-kär'pus],a.
Xanthopous [zan'tho-pus], a. [n.
Xantho-rhamnine [zan-tho-ram'nin],
Xanthosis [zan-thō'sis], n.
Xanthous [zan'thus], a.
Xanthoxylum [zan-thok'si-lum], n.
Xebec [ze'bek], n.
Xenogenesis [zen-o-jen'e-sis], n.
Xeroderma [zē-ro-dėr'ma], n.

Xerophagy [zē-rof'a-ji], n.
Xiphias [zir'i-as], n.
Xiphoid [zif'oid], a.
Xipho-phyllous [zif-o-fil'lus], a.
Xylene, Xylole [zī'lēn, zī'lōl], n.
Xylite [zī'līt], n.
Xylography [zī-log'ra-fi], n.
Xyloidine [zī-loi'din], n.
Xylophagan [zī-lof'a-gan], n.
Xylophili [zī-lof'i-li], n. pl.
Xylotile [zī'lo-til], n.
Xyster [zis'tėr], n.

Y.

Yacht [yot], n. v.
Yak [yak], n
Yam [yam], n.
Yankee-doodle [yang'ke-dŏŏ'dl], n.
Yapock [yā'pok], n.
Yard [yärd], n. v.
Yarn [yärn], n.
Yarrow [yar'ō], n.

Yaup, Yawp [yąp], n.
Yawl [yąl], n. v.
Yawn [yąn], n. v.
Yclept, Ycleped [i-klept'], v.
Yea [yā], ad.
Year [yėr], n.
Yearn [yėrn], v.
Yeast [yēst], n.

wŏŏl ; ūse, us ; ù, Fr. ; g, get ; j, jar ; ñ, Fr. ton: ch, chain ; *th*, then ; th, th

Z.

Zaffre [zaf'fer], n.
Zamia [zā'mi-a], n.
Zeal [zēl], n.
Zealot [zel'ot], n.
Zealous [zel'us], a.
Zebra [zē'bra], n.
Zechariah [zek-a-rī'a], n.
Zechstein [zek'stin], n.
Zenana [ze-nä'na], n.
Zenith [zē'nith], n.
Zeolite [zē'o-līt], n.
Zephaniah [zef-a-nī'a], n.
Zephyr [zef'er], n.

Zero [zīe], n.
Zigzag [zig'zag], a. v.
Zinc [zingk], n. v.
Zinnia [zin'i-a], n.
Zither [zith'er], n.
Zodiac [zō'di-ak], n.
Zodiacal [zo-dī'ak-al],
Zoology [zō-ol'o-ji],
Zoophyte [zō'o-fīt], n.
Zoopsychology [zō-o-sī-
Zoolite [zo-ol'ik], n.
Zouave [zōō-äv'],

āle, add, beâr, ärm, àsk, fạll; mē, met, thêre, hèr; pīne, pin; ōld, wŏŏl; ūse, us; û, Fr.; g, get; j, jar; ñ, Fr. ton; ch, chain; th, ther

MEASURES.

———◆———

A **Measure** is a unit fixed by law or custom as a standard in estimating quantity. The unit may be used in measuring value, extension, time, weight, or any other quantity.

MONEY.

Money is the commodity adopted to serve as the measure of value of all other commodities.

Coin is metal stamped with a die to give it a legal, fixed value, for the purpose of circulating as money. Coins consist of gold, silver, copper, and nickel.

UNITED STATES MONEY.

The currency of the United States is decimal currency, and is sometimes called *Federal Money*.

TABLE.

10 mills (m.)	make	1 cent (ct).
10 cents	"	1 dime (d.).
10 dimes	"	1 dollar ($).
10 dollars	"	1 eagle.

The dollar and the cent only are usually used in naming quantities; dimes and cents being named as cents, eagles and dollars as dollars. The mill is not coined.

The *gold coins* are the double-eagle, eagle, half-eagle, quarter-eagle, three-dollar, and one-dollar pieces.

The *silver coins* are the dollar, half-dollar, quarter-dollar, twenty-cent, and ten-cent pieces.

The *nickel coins* are the five-cent and three-cent pieces.

The *bronze coin* is the one-cent piece.

The trade dollar is designed solely for purposes of commerce.

Government Standard. — By Act of Congress, Jan. 18, 1837, all gold and silver coins must consist of 9 parts (.900) pure metal, and 1 part (.100) alloy. The alloy for gold must consist of equal parts of silver and copper, and the alloy for silver of pure copper.

The nickel coins are 75 parts copper and 25 parts nickel.

CANADA MONEY.

The currency of the Dominion of Canada is decimal, and the denominations are the same as those of the United States Money. The currency was made uniform July 1, 1871.

The *gold coins* used are the British sovereign and half-sovereign; worth $4.86½ and $2.43½, respectively.

The *silver coins* are the fifty-cent, twenty-five-cent, ten-cent, and five-cent pieces. The twenty-cent piece is no longer made.

The *bronze coin* is the cent.

Farthings are generally expressed as fractions of a penny.

The old *f,* the original abbreviation for shillings, was formerly written between shillings and pence, and d , the abbreviation for pence, was omitted. Thus, 2 s 6 d. was written 2/6. A straight line is now used in place of the *f,* and shillings are written on the left of it and pence on the right. Thus, 2/6, 10/3, etc

The *gold coins* are the sovereign (= £1) and half-sovereign (= 10 s.).

The *silver coins* are the crown, half-crown, florin, shilling, six-penny, four-penny, and three-penny pieces.

The *copper* and *bronze coins* are the penny, half-penny, and farthing.

The guinea (= 21 s.) and the half-guinea (= 10 s. 6 d. sterling) are old gold coins, and are no longer coined.

The pound is worth $4.86⅔.

The shilling is worth $0.24⅓.

FRENCH MONEY.

The currency of France is decimal. The franc is the unit, and is worth 19.3 cents.

TABLE.

10 millimes (m.)	make	1 centime (c.)
10 centimes	"	1 decime (d.)
10 decimes	"	1 franc (fr.)

EQUIVALENT TABLE.

fr.		d.		c.		m.
1	=	10	=	100	=	1000
		1	=	10	=	100
				1	=	10

The *gold coins* are the forty-franc, twenty-franc, ten-franc, and pieces.

The *silver coins* are the five-franc, two-franc, and one-franc the fifty-centime and twenty-centime pieces.

The *bronze coins* are the ten-centime, five-centime, two-cen' centime pieces.

GERMAN MONEY.

100 pfennige (Pf.) make 1 mark (RM.)

The mark (or reichsmark) is worth 23.8 cents.

MEASURES OF EXTENSION.

Extension has three dimensions—length, breadth, and thickness.
A **Line** has only one dimension—length.
A **Surface** has two dimensions—length and breadth.
A **Solid** has three dimensions—length, breadth, and thickness.

LONG OR LINEAR MEASURE.

Long Measure is used in measuring distances. The unit of linear measure is usually the yard, or the foot.

TABLE.

12	inches (in.) . . .	make	1 foot . . .	(ft.).
3	feet.	"	1 yard . .	(yd.).
5½ yards, or		"	1 rod . . .	(rd.).
16½ feet				
40	rods	"	1 furlong .	(fur.).
8	furlongs	"	1 mile . .	(mi.)

EQUIVALENT TABLE.

mi.		rd.		yd.		ft.		in.
1	=	320	=	1760	=	5280	=	63360
		1	=	5½	=	16½	=	198
				1	=	3	=	36
						1	=	12

The following are also used :—

3 barleycorns make 1 inch, used by shoemakers.
4 inches . . " 1 hand, {used in measuring the height of horses directly over the fore feet.
9 inches . . " 1 span.
3 feet . . . " 1 pace.
6 feet . . . " 1 fathom, used in measuring depths at sea.

For the purpose of measuring cloth the yard is divided into halves fourths, eighths, and sixteenths.

SURVEYORS' LINEAR MEASURE.

A **Gunter's Chain**, used by land surveyors, is 4 rods or 66 feet long consists of 100 links.

TABLE.

7.92	inches (in.)	make	1 link	(l.).
25	links	"	1 rod	(rd.).
4 rods, or		"	1 chain	(ch.).
66 feet				
80	chains	"	1 mile	(mi.).

EQUIVALENT TABLE.

mi.		ch.		rd.		l.		in.
1	=	80	=	320	=	8000	=	63360
		1	=	4	=	100	=	792
				1	=	25	=	198
						1	=	7.92

The denomination *rods* is seldom used in chain measure, being taken in chains and links.

SQUARE MEASURE.

A **Square** is a figure having four equal sides and four right
Area is the space or surface included within any given
of a square, of a field, of a board, etc.

Square Measure is used in computing areas; as of land, boards, painting, plastering, paving, etc.

TABLE.

144	square inches (sq. in.) make	1 square foot (sq. ft.).
9	" feet. . . . "	1 " yard (sq. yd.).
30¼	" yards . . . "	1 " rod (sq. rd.).
160	" rods . . . "	1 acre . . (A.).
640	acres . . . . . . "	1 square mile (sq. mi.).

EQUIVALENT TABLE.

sq. mi.	A.	sq. rd.	sq. yd.	sq. ft.	sq. in.
1 =	640 =	102400 =	3097600 =	27878400 =	4014489600
	1 =	160 =	4840 =	43560 =	6272640
		1 =	30¼ =	272¼ =	39204
			1 =	9 =	1296
				1 =	144

Workmen estimate as follows :—
Glazing and stone-cutting, by the square foot.
Painting, plastering, paving, ceiling, and paper-hanging, by the square yard.
Flooring, partitioning, roofing, slating, and tiling, by the square of 100 square feet.

SURVEYORS' SQUARE MEASURE.

This measure is used by surveyors in computing the area or contents of land.

TABLE.

625	square links (sq. l.) . . . make	1 pole . . . (P.).
16	poles . . . . "	1 square chain (sq. ch.).
10	square chains . . . . . "	1 acre . . . (A.).
640	acres . . . . "	1 square mile (sq. mi.).
36	square miles (6 miles square) "	1 township . (Tp.).

EQUIVALENT TABLE.

Tp.	sq. mi.	A.	sq. ch.	P.	sq. l.
1 =	36 =	23040 =	230400 =	3686400 =	2304000000
	1 =	640 =	6400 =	102400 =	64000000
		1 =	10 =	160 =	100000
			1 =	16 =	10000
				1 =	625

A square mile of land is also called a section.
Canal and railroad engineers commonly use an engineers' chain, w consists of 100 links, each 1 foot long.
The contents of land are commonly estimated in square miles, acres hundredths; the denomination *rood* is rapidly going into disuse.

CUBIC MEASURE.

A **Cube** is a body having six equal square sides or faces.
The cubic or solid contents of a body are found by multiplying ' breadth, and thickness together.
Cubic Measure, also called solid measure, is used in compu *tents of timber, wood, stone, etc.*

TABLE.

1728	cubic inches (cu. in.) . . make	1 cubic foot . (
27	" feet . . . . . "	1 cubic yard . (
16	" " . . . . . . "	1 cord foot . .
8 cord	" or} . . . . . "	1 cord of wood
128 cubic	"	

A cubic yard of earth is called a load.

A pile of wood 8 feet long, 4 feet wide, and 4 feet high, contains 1 cord ; and a cord foot is 1 foot in length of such a pile.

A perch of stone or of masonry is 16½ feet long, 1½ feet wide, and 1 foot high, and contains 24¾ cubic feet.

MEASURES OF CAPACITY.

Capacity signifies extent of space.

Measures of Capacity are all cubic measures, but solidity and capacity are referred to different units, as will be seen by comparing the tables.

Measures of capacity are subdivided into two classes, measures of liquids and measures of dry substances.

LIQUID OR WINE MEASURE.

Liquid Measure is used in measuring liquors, molasses, water, etc. The unit is the gallon.

TABLE.

4	gills (gi.)	make 1 pint . .	(pt.).
2	pints	" 1 quart .	(qt.).
4	quarts	" 1 gallon .	(gal.).
31½	gallons	" 1 barrel .	(bbl.).
2	barrels, or }	" 1 hogshead	(hhd.).
63	gallons }		

EQUIVALENT TABLE.

hhd.		bbl.		gal.		qt.		pt.		gi.
1	=	2	=	63	=	252	=	504	=	2016
		1	=	31½	=	126	=	252	=	1008
				1	=	4	=	8	=	32
						1	=	2	=	8
								1	=	4

The following denominations are also in use : —

42 gallons	. . . .	make 1 tierce.	
2 hogsheads, or } 126 gallons }	. . . .	" 1 pipe or butt.	
2 pipes, or } 4 hogsheads }	. . . .	" 1 tun.	

The denominations *barrel* and *hogshead* are used in estimating the capacity of cisterns, reservoirs, vats, etc. In Massachusetts the barrel is estimated at 32 gallons. The tierce, hogshead, pipe, butt, and tun are also the names of casks, and do not express any fixed or definite measures. They are usually gauged, and have their capacities in gallons marked on them.

BEER MEASURE.

Beer Measure is a species of liquid measure used in measuring beer, ale, and milk. The unit is the gallon.

TABLE.

2	pints (pt.)	make 1 quart .	(qt.).
4	quarts	" 1 gallon .	(gal.).
36	gallons	" 1 barrel .	(bbl.).
1½	barrels, or }	" 1 hogshead	(hhd.).
54	gallons }		

EQUIVALENT TABLE.

hhd.		bbl.		gal.		qt.		pt.
1	=	1½	=	54	=	216	=	432
		1	=	36	=	144	=	288
				1	=	4	=	8
						1	=	2

This measure is not a standard, and is rapidly falling into disuse.

bu.	pk.	qt.	pt.
I	= 4	= 32	= 64
	I	= 8	= 16
		I	= 2

WEIGHTS.

eight is the measure of the quantity of matter a body contains, (
i by the force of gravity. Weighing consists in comparing the
some conventional standard. Three scales of weight are used i
:d States; namely, Troy, Avoirdupois, and Apothecaries'.

TROY WEIGHT.

oy Weight is sometimes called goldsmith's weight. It is us
ing gold, silver, and jewels; in philosophical experiments, and g
there great accuracy is required. The unit is the pound.

TABLE.

24 grains (gr.) . .	make 1 pennyweight (pwt.) or (dwt.)
20 pennyweights .	" 1 ounce . (oz.).
12 ounces	" 1 pound . (lb.).

EQUIVALENT TABLE.

lb.	oz.	pwt.	gr.
I	= 12	= 240	= 5760
	I	= 20	= 480
		I	= 24

AVOIRDUPOIS WEIGHT.

roirdupois Weight is used for all ordinary purposes. The unit i
L

The weight of the bushel of certain grains and roots has been fixed by statute in many of the States ; and these weights must govern in buying and selling, unless specific agreements be made.

TABLE OF AVOIRDUPOIS POUNDS IN A BUSHEL.

As prescribed by statute in the several States named.

Commodities.	California.	Connecticut.	Delaware.	Illinois.	Indiana.	Iowa.	Kentucky.	Louisiana.	Maine.†	Massachusetts.	Michigan.	Minnesota.	Missouri.	N. Hampshire.	New Jersey.	New York.	Ohio.	Oregon.	Pennsylvania.	Rhode Island.	Vermont.	Washington T.	Wisconsin.
Barley........	50			48	48	48	**48**	32		46	48	48	48		48	48	48	46	47		46	45	48
Beans.........			60	60	60	60	**60**				60				62								
Blue Grass Seed				14	14	14	**14**					14											
Buckwheat.....	40	45		46	50	52	**52**			46	42	42	52		50	48		42	48		46	42	42
Castor Beans...				46	46	46	..						46										
Clover Seed....				60	60	60	**60**				60	60		64	60	60	60				60	60	
Dried Apples...				24	25	24	..				28	28	24					28				28	28
Dried Peaches..				33	33	33	..				28	28	33					28				28	28
Flax Seed......				56	56	56	**56**						56		55	55	56						56
Hair				8			..		11														
Hemp Seed....				44	44	44	**44**						44										
Indian Corn....	52	56	56	52	50	56	**56**	56		56	56	56	52		56	58	56	52	56		56	56	56
Ind. Corn in ear				70	68	68	..																
Ind. Corn Meal				48	50		**50**		50	50									50				
Mineral Coal *				80	70		..						80										
Oats..........	32	28		32	32	35	**33½**	32	30	30	32	32	35	30	30	32	32	34	32		32	36	32
Onions........				57	48	57	**57**			52			57						50		50		
Peas							..								60								
Potatoes		60		60	60	60	**60**		60				60	60	60	60		60			60	60	60
Rye...........	54	56		54	56	56	**56**	32		56	56	56	56		56	56	56	56	56		56	56	56
Rye Meal.....							..		50	50									50				
Salt †........				50	50		**50**						50			56							
Timothy Seed.				45	45	45	**45**						45		44								46
Wheat	60	56	60	60	60	60	**60**	60		60	60	60	60		60	60	60	60	60		60	60	60
Wheat Bran...				20		20	**20**						20										

The weight of a barrel of flour is 7 quarters of old or long ton weight.

The weight of a bushel of Indian corn and rye, as adopted by most of the States, and of a bushel of salt is 2 quarters ; and of a barrel of salt 10 quarters, or ⅛ of a long ton.

The following denominations are also in use :—

56 pounds make	1 firkin of butter.		
100 "	"	1	quintal of dried salt fish.
100 "	"	1	cask of raisins.
196 "	"	1	barrel of flour.
200 "	"	1	" beef, pork, or fish.
280 "	"	1	" salt at the N. Y. State Salt Works.

* In Kentucky, 80 lbs. of bituminous coal or 70 lbs. of cannel coal make 1 bushel.
† In Pennsylvania, 80 lbs. of coarse, 70 lbs. of ground, or 62 lbs. of fine salt make 1 bushel. In Illinois, 50 lbs. of common, or 56 lbs. of fine salt make 1 bushel.
‡ In Maine, 64 lbs. of ruta baga turnips or beets make 1 bushel.

12 ounces . . . . . . " 1 pound (lb.) or (℔).

EQUIVALENT TABLE

lb.	oz.	dr.	sc.	gr.
1 =	12 =	96 =	288 =	5760
	1 =	8 =	24 =	480
		1 =	3 =	60
			1 =	20

APOTHECARIES' FLUID MEASURE.

e measures for fluids, as adopted by apothecaries in the United St
used in compounding medicines, are given in the following table:

TABLE.

60 minims (♏) . . . make 1 fluid drachm (f ʒ).
8 fluid drachms . . " 1 fluid ounce (f ℥).
16 fluid ounces . . . " 1 pint . . (O.).
8 pints . . . . . . " 1 gallon . . (Cong.).

EQUIVALENT TABLE.

Cong.	O.	f ℥	f ʒ	♏
1 =	8 =	128 =	2048 =	61440
	1 =	16 =	128 =	7680
		1 =	8 =	480
			1 =	60

DIAMOND WEIGHT.

mond Weight is used in weighing precious stones

EQUIVALENT TABLE.

yr.	mo.	wk.	da.		h.		min.		sec.
1 =	12	=	{ 365	=	8760	=	525600	=	31536000
			{ 366	=	8784	=	527040	=	31622400
		1 =	7	=	168	=	10080	=	604800
			1	=	24	=	1440	=	86400
					1	=	60	=	3600
							1	=	60

In most business transactions 30 days are called 1 month. The *civil day* begins and ends at 12 o'clock, midnight. The *astronomical day*, used by astronomers in dating events, begins and ends at 12 o'clock, noon. The civil year is composed of civil days.

BISSEXTILE OR LEAP YEAR.

The period of time required by the sun to pass from one vernal equinox to another, called the vernal or tropical year, is 365 da. 5 h. 48 min. 49.7 sec. This is the true year, and it exceeds the common year by 5 h. 48 min. 46.4 sec.
If 365 days be reckoned as 1 year, the time lost in the calendar will be,

In 1 year, 5 h. 48 min. 46.4 sec. ; in 4 years, 23 h. 15+ min.

The time thus lost in 4 years will lack only 44 min. about of 1 entire day. Hence, if every fourth year be reckoned as leap year, the time *gained* in the calendar will be,

In 4 years, 44 min. about ; in 100 years (= 25 × 4 yr.) 18 h. 37 min. about.

The time thus gained in 100 years will lack only 5 h. 22 min. 50 sec. of 1 day. Hence, if every fourth year be reckoned as leap year, the centennial years excepted, the time *lost* in the calendar will be,

In 100 years, 5 h. 22 min. ; in 400 years, 21 h. 31 min.

The time thus lost in 400 years lacks only 2 h. 29 min. of 1 day. Hence, if every fourth year be reckoned as leap year, 3 of every 4 centennial years excepted, the time *gained* in the calendar will be,

In 400 years, 2 h. 28 min. about ; in 4000 years, 24 h. about.

The following rules will, therefore, render the calendar correct to within 1 day, for a period of 4000 years : —

I. Every year that is exactly divisible by 4 is a leap year, centennial years excepted.
II. Every centennial year that is exactly divisible by 400 is a leap year.

Julius Cæsar, the Roman Emperor, decreed that the year should consist of 365 days 6 hours ; that the 6 hours should be disregarded for 3 successive years, and an entire day be added to every fourth year. This day was inserted in the calendar between the 24th and 25th days of February, and is called the *intercalary* day. As the Romans counted the days backward from the first day of the following month, the 24th of February was called by them *sexto calendas Martii* (the sixth before the calends of March). The intercalary day which followed this was called *bis-sexto calendas Martii*. hence the name *bissextile*.
In 1582 the error in the calendar as established by Julius Cæsar had increased to 10 days. To correct this error, Pope Gregory decreed that 10 entire days should be stricken from the calendar, and that the day following the 3d day of October, 1582, should be the 14th.
The year as established by Julius Cæsar is sometimes called the *Julian year*, and the period of time in which it was in force, namely, from 46 years B. C. to 1582, is called the *Julian Period*.

The year as established by Pope Gregory is called the *Gregorian year*, and the calendar now used is the *Gregorian Calendar.*

Most Catholic countries adopted the Gregorian Calendar soon after it was established. Great Britain, however, continued to use the Julian Calendar until 1752. 'At this time the civil year was 11 days behind the solar year. To correct this error, the British Government decreed that 11 days should be stricken from the calendar, and that the day following the 2d day of September, 1752, should be the 14th.

Time before the adoption of the Gregorian Calendar is called *Old Style* (O. S.), and since, *New Style* (N. S.). In Old Style the year commenced March 25, and in New Style it commences January 1.

Russia still reckons time by Old Style, or the Julian Calendar; hence their dates are now 12 days behind ours.

MEASURE OF ANGLES.

Circular Measure is used principally in surveying, navigation, astronomy, and geography. Every circle is divisible into the same number of equal parts; as quarters, called *quadrants;* twelfths, called *signs;* 360ths, called *degrees;* etc. The unit is the degree.

TABLE.

60 seconds (")	make	1 minute (').
60 minutes	"	1 degree (°).
30 degrees	"	1 sign . (S.).
12 signs, or } 360 degrees }	"	1 circle (C.).

EQUIVALENT TABLE.

C.	S.	°	'	"
1 =	12 =	360 =	21600 =	1296000
	1 =	30 =	1800 =	108000
		1 =	60 =	3600
			1 =	60

Minutes of the earth's circumference are called geographic or nautical miles. The denomination *signs* is confined exclusively to astronomy. A degree has no fixed linear extent. When applied to any circle it is always 1-360th part of the circumference; but strictly speaking it is not any part of a circle. 90° make a quadrant or right-angle. 60° make a sextant or ⅙ of a circle.

MISCELLANEOUS.

IN COMPUTATION.			OF PAPER.		
12 units . .	make	1 dozen.	24 sheets . .	make	1 q
12 dozen . .	"	1 gross.	20 quires . .	"	1
12 gross . .	"	1 great gross.			
20 units . .	"	1 score.			

OF BOOKS.

The terms *folio, quarto, octavo, duodecimo,* etc., indicate the leaves into which a sheet of paper is folded.

A sheet folded in	2 leaves	is called	a folio.
"	"	4 " "	a quarto, or
"	"	8 "	an octavo, or
"	"	12 " "	a 12mo.
"	"	16 " "	a 16mo.
"	"	18 " "	an 18mo.
"	"	24 " "	a 24mo.
"	"	32 " "	a 32mo.

FRENCH STANDARDS.

ıe French standard linear unit is the *mètre*.
he French standard unit of area is the *are*, which is a unit 10 metres
re, and contains 100 square metres.
'he French standard unit of solidity and capacity is the *litre*, which is
cube of the tenth part of the metre.

STANDARD OF WEIGHT.

The French Standard unit of weight is the *gramme*, which is determined
follows :— The weight in vacuum of a cubic decimetre or litre of distilled
ıter, at its maximum density, was called a *kilogramme*, and the thousandth
ırt of this was called a *gramme*, and was declared to be the unit of weight.

NOMENCLATURE OF THE TABLES.

The tables are on a decimal scale. The names of the multiples being
'ormed by employing the prefixes *deka* (ten), *hecto* (hundred), *kilo* (thousand),
and *myria* (ten thousand), taken from the Greek numerals ; and the names
of the divisors by employing the prefixes *deci* (tenth), *centi* (hundredth), *mili*
(thousandth), from the Latin numerals.

FRENCH LINEAR MEASURE.
TABLE.

10 millimetres	make	1 centimetre.
10 centimetres	"	1 decimetre.
10 decimetres	"	1 metre.
10 metres	"	1 decametre.
10 decametres	"	1 hectometre.
10 hectometres	"	1 kilometre.
10 kilometres	"	1 myriametre.

The metre is equal to 39.3685 inches, the standard rod of brass on which
the former is measured being at 32° Fahrenheit, at 62°.

FRENCH SQUARE MEASURE.
TABLE.

100 square metres or centiáres (10 metres square) make 1 are.
100 ares (10 ares square) . . . . " 1 hectare.

FRENCH LIQUID AND DRY MEASURE.
TABLE.

10 decilitres	make	1 litre.
10 litres	"	1 decalitre.
10 decalitres	"	1 hectolitre.
10 hectolitres	"	1 kilolitre.

A litre is equal to 61.53294 cubic inches, or 1.06552 quarts of a U. S. liquid
gallon.

Æt. (ætatis). — Aged
Al. or Ala. — Alabama
A. M. or M. A. (Artium Magister). —Master of Arts.
A. M. — Before mid-day.
A. M. (Anno Mundi). — In the year of the world.
Anon. — Anònymous.
App. — Appendix.
Ark. — Arkansas.
Arr. —Arrived.
A. R. A. — Associate of the Royal Academy.
A. R. S. A. — Associate of the Royal Scottish Academy.
A. R. S. S. (Antiquariorum regis societatis socius). — Fellow of the Royal Society of Antiquaries.
A. S. — Anglo Saxon.
Asst. — Assistant.
A U. C. (Anno urbis conditæ or Anno ab urbe condita). — In the year of or from the building of the city (of Rome).
Avoir. — Avoirdupois.

B. A. —Bachelor of Arts.
Bart. or Bt. — Baronet.
B. C. — Before Christ.
Bp. — Bishop.

C. — Centigrade.
C., Ct., or Cent. — A hundred.
C. or Cap. — Chapter.
C. A. — Chartered Accountant.
Cal. — California.
Cam. or Camb. — Cambridge.

Col
Coll. — College.
Com. — Commander ; co. committee.
Conn or Ct. — Connecticut.
Cor. Mem.—Corresponding Member.
Cor. Sec.— Corresponding Secretary.
Cos. — Cosine.
Crim. Con. — Criminal conversation, or adultery.
C. P S. — Keeper of the Privy Seal.
Cr. — Credit ; creditor.
Ct. — Connecticut.
Cur. or curt. — Current ; this month.
Cwt. — A hundred weight.

D. (denarius). — A penny or pence ; 500
D. D. — Doctor of Divinity.
Deg. — Degree.
Del. — Delaware.
Del. (deliniavit). — "He drew it," - meaning the drawer or painter.
Dep. — Deputy.
D. G. (Dei gratia). — By the grac God.
Do. (ditto). — The same.
Doz. — Dozen.
Dr. — Debtor ; doctor ;
D. V. (Deo volente). — (
dwt. — A pennyweight

E. —East.
Eccl. — Ecclesiast
Ed. — Editor ; ed
Edin. — Edinbur
E. E. — Errors ex

E. G. (exempli gratia). — For example.

E. long. — East longitude.

Emp. — Emperor ; Empress.

E.N.E. — East-northeast.

Eng. — England.

Engr. — Engineer.

E.S.E. — East-southeast.

Esq. or Esqr. — Esquire.

Etc. or &c. — And so forth.

Et seq. — And the following.

Ex. — Example ; exception.

Exec. — Executor.

Fahr. — Fahrenheit.

F. A. S. — Fellow of the Society of Arts.

Fcp. — Foolscap.

Fec. — He did it.

Flor. or Fla. — Florida.

F. M. — Field Marshal.

Fo. or fol. — Folio.

F. P. — Fire-plug.

Fr. — France or French.

F. R. A. S. — Fellow of the Royal Astronomical Society.

F. R. C. S. — Fellow of the Royal College of Surgeons.

F. R. G. S. — Fellow of the Royal Geographical Society.

F. R. H. S. — Fellow of the Royal Horticultural Society.

F. R. S. — Fellow of the Royal Society.

F. S. A. — Fellow of the Society of Antiquaries, or Arts.

Ft. — Foot or feet.

F. Z. S. — Fellow of the Zoölogical Society.

Ga. — Georgia.

Gael. — Gaelic.

Gall. — Gallon.

G. B. — Great Britain.

G. C. B. — Grand Cross of the Bath.

Gen. — General.

Gent. — Gentlemen.

Geo. — Georgia.

Gov. — Governor.

G. P. O. — General Post Office.

Gr. — Grains or gross.

Gtt. (guttæ). — Drops.

H. B. C. — Hudson's Bay Company.

Hf.-bd. — Half-bound.

H. J. S. (hic jacet sepultus). — Here lies buried.

H. M. — His or Her Majesty.

H. M. S. — His or Her Majesty's Ship or Service.

Hon. — Honorable.

H. R. — House of Representatives.

H. R. E. — Holy Roman Empire.

H. R. I. P. — Here rests in peace

H. R. H. — His or Her Royal Highness.

H. S. H. — His or Her Serene Highness.

Ind. — Indiana.

Ib. (ibid). — In the same place.

Id. — The same.

i. e. — That is.

I. H. S. (Jesus Hominum Salvator ; properly the initial letters of the name Jesus, in Greek). — Jesus the Saviour of Men.

Ill. — Illinois.

Imp. — Imperial.

Incog. (incognito). — Unknown.

In loc. (in loco). — In its place.

Inst. — Instant ; the present month.

Int. — Interest.

Io. — Iowa.

I. O. O. F. — Independent Order of Odd Fellows.

I. O. U. — I owe you.

I. Q. (idem quod). — The same as.

Jn., Jr., or Jun. — Junior.

Kan. or Ks. — Kansas.

K. B. — Knight of the Bath ; King's Bench.

K. C. B. — Knight Commander of the Bath.

Ken. or Ky. — Kentucky.

K. G. — Knight of the Garter.

K. G. C. B. — Knight of the Grand Cross of the Bath.

K. G. F. — Knight of the Golden Fleece.

Knt. — Knight.

L. or l. — A pound sterling.

La. — Louisiana.

Lat. — Latitude ; Latin.

Lb. (libra). — A pound weight.

l. c. (loco citato). — In the place quoted ; lower case.

Lib. (liber). — A book.

Lieut. — Lieutenant.

Lit. — Literally.

LL. D. — Doctor of Laws.

Lon. or long. — Longitude.

Loq. (loquitur). — Speaks.

L. S. (locus sigilli). — Place of the Seal

L. S. D. (libræ, solidi, denarii). — Pounds, shillings, and pence.

notice.

N. C — North Carolina ; New church.
N.E. — Northeast.
Neb. — Nebraska.
Nem con (nemine contradicente) — No one contradicting
N. F. — Newfoundland.
N. H. — New Hampshire.
N. J. — New Jersey.
N.N.E. — North-northeast.
N N.W. — North-northwest.
No. (numero). — Number
Non seq. (non sequitur) — It does not follow.
Nos. — Numbers.
N.S. — New Style ; Nova Scotia
N T. — New Testament.
N.W. — Northwest.
N. Y. — New York.

Ob. (obiit). — Died.
Obs. — Obsolete.
O. M. — Old Measurement.
O.S. — Old Style.
O. T. — Old Testament.
Oxon (Oxonia). — Oxford.
Oz. — Ounce.

P.; pp. — Page ; pages.
Pa. or Penn. — Pennsylvania.
Par. — Paragraph.
Pd. — Paid.

qr — Quarter ; quire.
qrs — Quarters ; quires.
q s. (quantum sufficit). — Enough
qt — Quart.
q. v. (quod vide). — Which see.

R. (Rex ; Regina). — King ; Queen
Rev — Reverend.
R. I — Rhode Island.
R. I. P. (requiescat in pace). — M: he *or* she rest in peace.
R. M. — Royal Mail ; Royal Marine
R. N. — Royal Navy.
Rt. — Right.
R. V. — Rifle Volunteers.

S. — South.
Sc. or Scil (scilicet). — To wi namely.
Sc. (sculpsit). — He *or* she engrave it.
S. C. — South Carolina.
S. E. — Southeast.
Sec. — Secretary.
Sep. or Sept. — Septuagint.
Seq. (sequentes or sequentia. following.
Serg. or Sergt. — Sergeant.
Sol. Gen. — Solicitor-Gener
S. P. C. K — Society for Christian Knowledge.

S. P. Q. R. (Senatus Populusque Romanus). — The Senate and people of Rome.
SS. — Steamship.
S.S.E. — South-southeast.
S.S.W. — South-southwest.
St. — Saint.
S. T. P. (Sacræ Theologiæ Professor). — Professor of Theology.
Supp. — Supplement.
S.W. — Southwest.
Syn. — Synonymous.

Tenn. — Tennessee.

U. C. — Upper Canada.
Ult. (ultimo). — Last.
Univ. — University.
U. P. — United Presbyterian.
U. S. — United States.
U. T. — Utah Territory.

V. — Numeral for five.
V. (versus). — Against.
V. (vide). — See.
Va. — Virginia.

V. C. — Vice-Chancellor.
Ven. — Venerable
Ver. — Vermont.
Visc. — Viscount.
Viz. — Namely ; to wit.
V. R. — Victoria Regina.
V. S. — Veterinary surgeon.
Vul. — Vulgate.

W. — West.
W. C. — West Centre.
W.I — West Indies.
Wis. — Wisconsin.
W.N.W. — West-northwest.
W.S.W. — West-southwest.

X. — Numeral for ten.
X or Xt. — Christ.
Xm., Xmas., or Xms. — Christmas.
Xn. or Xtian. — Christian.

Yd. — Yard.

&. — And.
&c. — And so forth.

LIST OF WORDS, PHRA*SES*, ETC.,

FROM THE LATIN, FRENCH, AND OTHER LANGUAGE

WITH TRANSLATIONS.

[L., Latin; Fr., French; It., Italian; Sp., Spanish; Gr., Greek; Ger., German.]

------◆------

A bas. Down! down with! [Fr.]
Ab extra. From without. [L.]
Ab initio. From the beginning. [L.]
A bon droit. Justly; according to reason. [Fr.]
A bon marché. Cheap. [Fr.]
Ab origine. From the beginning. [L.]
Ab ovo. From the beginning (*lit.* from the egg). [L.]
Ab ovo usque ad mala. From the beginning to the end (*lit.* from the
  to the apples). [L.]
Abrégé. Abridgment. [Fr.]

à l'abri. Under shelter. [Fr.]

à la dérobée. By stealth. [Fr.]

à la mode. According to the fashion [Fr.]

Alea est jacta. The die is cast; the step is taken. [L.

Al fresco In the open air [It.]

Alias. Otherwise. [L.]

à l'improviste. Unawares. [Fr.]

Alma mater. A benign mother. [L.]

à l'outrance. To the uttermost. [Fr.]

Alter idem. Another exactly similar. [L.]

Alter ipse amicus. A friend is a second self. [L.]

A main armée. By force of arms. [Fr.]

Amende honorable. Satisfactory apology; reparation.

A mensâ et thoro. From bed and board; divorced.

à merveille. To a wonder. [Fr.]

Amor patriæ. The love of our country. [L.]

Amour propre. Vanity; self-love. [Fr.]

Anglicè. In English. [L.]

Anguis in herbâ A snake in the grass. [L.]

Anno Domini. In the year of our Lord. [L.]

Anno mundi. In the year of the world. [L.]

Annus mirabilis. The year of wonders. [L.]

Ante meridiem. Before mid-day. [L.]

Aperçu. A sketch. [Fr.]

à perte de vue. Beyond the range of vision. [Fr.]

à point. To a point exactly. [Fr.]

A posse ad esse. From possibility to actuality. [L.]

A posteriori. From the effect to the cause; by induc

A priori. From the cause to the effect; by deduction

à propos. To the point; seasonably; in due time. [

Au courant. Perfectly acquainted with. [Fr.]
Audi alteram partem. Hear the other party; hear both sides. [L.]
Au fait. Expert; skilful. [Fr.]
Aufklärung. Illuminism. [Ger.]
Au fond. To the bottom. [Fr.]
Au pis aller. At the worst. [Fr.]
Au reste. For the rest. [Fr.]
Au revoir. Farewell till we meet again. [Fr.]
Auri sacra fames. The accursed appetite or thirst for gold. [L.]
Aut Cæsar, aut nullus. Either Cæsar or no one. [L.]
Aut vincere aut mori. Either to conquer or die. [L.]
Aux armes. To arms. [Fr.]
Avant propos. Prefatory matter. [Fr.]
A verbis ad verbera. From words to blows. [L.]
A vinculo matrimonii. From the bond or tie of marriage. [L.]
A votre santé. To your health. [Fr.]

Bas bleu. A blue stocking. [Fr.]
Beau monde. The fashionable world. [Fr.]
Beaux esprits. Men of wit. [Fr.]
Bel esprit. A person of genius; a brilliant mind. [Fr.]
Ben trovato. Well invented. [It.]
Bête noir. An eye-sore; a bugbear (*lit.* a black beast). [Fr.]
Billet doux. A love letter. [Fr.]
Bis dat qui cito dat. He gives twice who gives quickly. [L.]
Bonâ fide. In good faith; in reality. [L.]   [Fr.]
Bon chien chasse de race. — Children have the qualities of their parents.
Bon gré, mal gré. Whether willing or not. [Fr.]
Bonhomie. Good nature. [Fr.]
Bon jour. Good day. [Fr.]
Bonne. A nurse. [Fr.]
Bonne bouche. A delicate morsel. [Fr.]
Bon soir. Good evening. [Fr.]
Bon ton. The height of fashion. [Fr.]
Bon vivant. A good liver. [Fr.]
Breveté. Patented. [Fr.]
Brevi manu. Off hand; summarily (*lit.* with a short hand). [L.]
Brevis esse laboro, obscurus fio. When laboring to be concise, I become
  obscure. [L.]
Brutum fulmen. A harmless thunderbolt. [L.]

Cacoëthes scribendi. An itch for scribbling. [L.]
Cacoëthes loquendi. An itch for talking. [L.]
Campus Martius. A place of military exercise (*lit.* field of Mars). [L.]
Canaille. The rabble. [Fr.]
Cap-à-pie. From head to foot. [Fr.]
Capias. A writ to authorize the seizure of a defendant's person. [L.] Law.
Caput mortuum. The worthless remains. [L.]
Carpe diem. Make a good use of the present. [L.]
Casus belli. A cause for war. [L.]
Cave canem. Beware of the dog. [L.]
Cavendo tutus. Safe by caution. [L.] Motto.
Ce n'est que le premier pas qui coûte. It is only the first step that is
  difficult (*lit.* costs). [Fr.]
Certiorari. To order the record from an inferior to a superior court. [L.]
  Law.
C'est une autre chose. That's another matter. [Fr.]
Ceteris paribus. Other things being equal. [L.]
Chacun à son goût. Every one to his taste. [Fr.]

Chargé d'affaires. A subordinate diplomatist. [Fr.]
Chef de cuisine. A head cook. [Fr.]
Chef-d'œuvre. A masterpiece. [Fr.]
Chemin de fer. The iron way ; the railway. [Fr.]
Chevalier d'industrie. One who lives by persevering fraud (*lit.* a knight of industry). [Fr.]
Ci-devant. Former. [Fr.]
Ci-gît. Here lies. [Fr.]
Circulus in probando. Begging the question (*lit.* a circle in the proof). [L.]
Claqueur. One hired to applaud. [Fr.]
Clarior e tenebris. The brighter from the obscurity. [L.]
Clarum et venerabile nomen. An illustrious and honored name. [L.]
Cogito, ergo sum. I think, therefore I am. [L.]
Comme il faut. As it should be. [Fr.]
Commune bonum. A common good. [L.]
Communi consensu. By common consent. [L.]
Compagnon de voyage. A fellow-traveller. [Fr.]
Compos mentis. Of sane mind. [L.]
Compte rendu. A report ; an account. [Fr.]
Con amore. With love ; earnestly. [It.]
Concio ad clerum. An address to the clergy. [L.]
Concours. A competition. [Fr.]
Confrère. A brother monk or associate. [Fr.]
Congé d'élire. A leave to elect. [Fr.]
Consilio et animis. By counsel and courage. [L.]
Contra bonos mores. Against good morals. [L.]
Contraria contrariis curantur. Contraries are cured by contraries. [L.]
Contre-temps. A mischance. [Fr.]
Cordon bleu. A skilful cook (*lit.* a blue ribbon). [Fr.]
Corps diplomatique. The diplomatic body. [Fr.]
Corpus delicti. The body of the offence. [L.] Law.
Couleur de rose. A flattering representation. [Fr.]
Coup d'essai. First attempt. [Fr.]
Coup de soleil. Sun-stroke. [Fr.]
Coup d'état. A sudden stroke of policy. [Fr.]
Coup de théâtre. Theatrical effect. [Fr.]
Coup de grace. The finishing stroke. [Fr.]
Coup de main. A bold effort. [Fr.]
Coup-d'œil. A rapid glance of the eye. [Fr.]
Courage sans peur. Courage without fear. [Fr.]
Coûte que coûte. Let it cost what it may. [Fr.]
Cui bono ? To what good. [L.]
Cuique suum. His own to every one. [L.]
Cul de sac. A street or lane that has no outlet. [Fr.]
Cum grano salis. With a grain of salt (*i. e.* with some allowance). [L.]
Cum privilegio. With privilege. [L.]
Currente calamo. With a running pen. [L.]
Custos rotulorum. The keeper of the rolls. [L.]

Da capo. From the beginning. [It.]
De bonne grace. With good grace ; willingly. [Fr.]
Deceptio visus. Optical illusion. [L.]
De die in diem. From day to day. [L.]
De facto. In point of fact. [L.]
Dégagé. Free and unrestrained. [Fr.]
De gustibus non disputandum. There is no disputing about tastes.
Dei gratia. By the grace of God. [L.]
Dejeûner à la fourchette. A meat breakfast. [Fr.]
De jure. By right. [L.]

Delectando pariterque monendo. By imparting at once pleasure and instruction. [L.]

Delenda est Carthago. Carthage must be destroyed. [L.]

De mortuis nil nisi bonum. Let nothing be said of the dead but what favorable. [L.]

De nihilo nihil fit. From nothing nothing is produced. [L.]

De novo. Anew. [L.]

Deo gratias. Thanks to God. [L.]

Deo ignoto. To the unknown God. [L.]

Deo juvante. With God's help. [L.]

Deo volente. With God's will. [L.]

De profundis. Out of the depths. [L.]

Dernier ressort. A last resource. [Fr.]

Desideratum. A thing desired, but regretfully wanting. [L.]

Detour. A circuitous march. [Fr.]

De trop. Too much. [Fr.]

Dies non. A day when there is no court. [L.]

Dieu et mon droit. God and my right. [Fr.]

Die Wacht am Rhein. "The watch on the Rhine." [Ger.] A German national song.

Dii penates. Household gods. [L.]

Disjecta membra. Scattered remains. [L.]

Distingué. Distinguished; eminent. [Fr.]

Distrait. Absent in mind. [Fr.]

Divide et impera. Divide and govern. [L.]

Docendo discimus. We learn by teaching. [L.]

Dolce far niente. Sweet idleness. [It.]

Dominus providebit. The Lord will provide. [L.]

Domus et placens uxor. Thy house and pleasing wife. [L.]

Double entendre. A double meaning. [Fr.]

Double entente. Double signification. [Fr.]

Dramatis personæ. Characters represented. [L.]

Droit des gens. The law of nations. [Fr.]

Dulce domum. Sweet home. [L.]

Dulce est desipere in loco. It is pleasant to jest at the proper time. [L.]

Dulce et decorum est pro patria mori. It is sweet and glorious to die for one's country. [L.]

Dum spiro, spero. While I breathe, I hope. [L.] Motto.

Dum vivimus, vivamus. Let us live while we live. [L.]

Durante vita. During life. [L.]

E contra. On the other hand. [L.]

Ecce homo! Behold the man! [L.]

E contrario. On the contrary. [L.]

Edition de luxe. A splendid and expensive edition of a book. [Fr.]

Editio princeps. The original edition. [L.]

Ego et rex meus. I and my king. [L.]

Eloignement. Estrangement. [Fr.]

Emeritus. One retired from active official duties. [L.]

Empressement. Ardor. [Fr.]

En ami. As a friend. [Fr.]

En attendant. In the meantime. [Fr.]

En famille. In a domestic state. [Fr.]

Enfans de famille. Children of the family. [Fr.]

Enfans perdus. The forlorn hope (*lit.* lost children). [Fr.]

Enfant gâté. A spoiled child. [Fr.]

Enfant trouvé. A foundling. [Fr.]

En foule. In a crowd. [Fr.]

En grand tenue. In full dress. [Fr.]

En masse. In a body. [Fr.]

En passant. By the way. [Fr.]

En rapport. In relation ; in connection. [Fr.]

En règle. According to rules. [Fr.]

En route. On the way. [Fr.]

En suite. In company. [Fr.]

En tourage. Surroundings. [Fr.]

Entre nous. Between ourselves. [Fr.]

En vérité. In truth. [Fr.]

Errare humanum est. It is human to err. [L.]

Espérance en Dieu. Hope in God. [Fr.]

Esprit de corps. Spirit of brotherhood or a corps.

Esse quam videri. To be rather than to seem.

Est modus in rebus. There is a mean in everything.

Esto perpetua. Let it be perpetual. [L.]

Et hoc genus omne. And everything of this kind.

Et tu, Brute. And you, Brutus. [L.]

Ex abrupto. Without preparation. [L.]

Ex æquo. By right. [L.]

Ex animo. From the soul ; heartily. [L.]

Ex cathedrâ. From the chair ; with authority.

Excelsior. Still higher. [L.]

Exceptio probat regulam. The exception proves.

Ex concesso. Admittedly. [L.]

Ex curia. Out of court. [L.]

Ex delicto. From the crime. [L.]

Exempli gratia. By way of example. [L.]

Ex mero motu. From one's own free will.

Ex nihilo nihil fit. Nothing produces nothing. [L.]

Ex officio. By virtue of his office. [L.]

Ex parte. On one part or side. [L.]

Ex pede Herculem. We judge of the size of the foot. [L.]

Experimentum crucis. A decisive experiment of the.

Experto crede. Believe one who has had experience.

Ex post facto. After the event. [L.]

Ex professo. Like one who knows. [L.]

Extra muros. Beyond the walls. [L.]

Ex ungue leonem. The lion may be known by all by.

Ex uno disce omnes. From one judge of all.

Faber suæ fortunæ. The maker of his own fortune.

Fach. Department. [Ger.]

Facile princeps. The admitted chief ; with ease.

Facilis est descensus Averni. The descent to hell road is an easy one. [L.]

Fac simile. An engraved resemblance of a man's like). [L.]

Factotum. A man of all work (lit. do everything).

Fainéant. Do-nothing. [Fr.]

Fait accompli. A thing already done. [Fr.]

Fasti et nefasti dies. Lucky and unlucky days.

Fata obstant. The fates oppose it. [L.]

Faux pas. A false step. [Fr.]

Fecit. He did it. [L.]

Felo de se. A suicide. [L.] Law.

Femme de chambre. A chambermaid. [Fr.]

Festina lente. Hasten slowly. [L.]

Fête champêtre. A rural feast. [Fr.]

Fidei defensor Defender of t...

Fides Punica. Punic faith; treachery. ...

Fidus Achates. The faithful Achates , a trusty frie...

Filius nullius The son of nobody. [L]

Filius terræ. A son of the earth ; one low born. [L.]

Fille de chambre. A chambermaid. [Fr.]

Fille de joie. A woman of pleasure. [Fr.]

Finis coronat opus. The end crowns the work. [L.]

Flagrante bello. During the war. [L.]

Flagrante delicto. In the very act. [L.]

Fortiter et recte. Courageously and honorably. [L.] Motto

Fortiter in re. With firmness in action. [L.]

Fortuna favet fortibus. Fortune favors the brave. [L.]

Fortuna multis dat nimium, nulli satis. To many fortu
much, to none enough. [L.]

Fortuna sequatur. Let fortune follow. [L.] Motto.

Frangas, non flectes. You may break, but you will not bend

Fronti nulla fides. There is no trusting to appearances. [I

Fugit irreparabile tempus. Irrecoverable time is flying aw

Fuimus. We have been. [L.] Motto.

Fuit Ilium. Troy was. [L.]

Furor loquendi. A rage for speaking. [L.]

Furor scribendi. A rage for writing. [L]

Gaieté de cœur. Gayety of heart. [Fr.]

Gallicè. In French. [L.]

Garçon. A boy ; a waiter. [Fr.]

Garde à cheval. Mounted guard. [Fr.]

... du corps. A body guard. [Fr.]

... care. [Fr.] Motto.

...ith. [Fr.] Motto.

Hoc genus omne. All persons of that kind. [L.]
Hoc opus, hic labor est. This is a work, this is a toil. [L.]
Homme des affaires. A business man. [Fr.]
Homme d'esprit. A witty man. [Fr.]
Homo unius libri. A man of one book. [L.]
Honi soit qui mal y pense. Evil be to him that evil thinks. [Fr.] Royal motto.
Hors de combat. Out of condition to fight. [Fr.]
Hôtel de ville. A town hall. [Fr.]
Hôtel Dieu. The house of God; the name of a hospital. [Fr.]
Humanum est errare. To err is human. [L.]

Ibidem. In the same place. [L.]
Ich dien. I serve. [Ger.]
Id est. That is. [L.]
Id genus omne. All persons of that description. [L.]
Ignis fatuus. A deceiving light; a "Will-o'-the-wisp." [L.]
Ignotum per ignotius. The unknown by the still more unknown. [L.]
Il n'a ni bouche ni éperon. He has neither wit nor courage (*lit.* he has neither mouth nor spur). [Fr.]
Il penseroso. The pensive man. [It.]
Imperium in imperio. A government within a government. [L.]
Imprimatur. Let it be printed. [L.]
In æternum. Forever. [L.]
In articulo mortis. At the point of death. [L.]
In curia. In the court. [L.]
Index expurgatorius. An expurgated index. [L.]
In esse. In being. [L.]
In extenso. At full length. [L.]
In extremis. At the point of death. [L.]
In formâ pauperis. As a poor man. [L.]
In hoc signo vinces. By this sign thou shalt conquer. [L.]
In loco parentis. In the place of a parent. [L.]
In medias res. Into the midst of things. [L.]
mean. [L.]
memoriam. To the memory of. [L.]
In nubibus. In the clouds. [L.]
In partibus infidelium. In unbelieving countries. [L.]
In præsenti. At present. [L.]
In propriâ personâ. In person. [L.]
In puris naturalibus. Stark naked. [L.]
In re. In the matter of. [L.]
In rerum natura. In the nature of things. [L.]
In secula seculorum. For ages and ages. [L.]
In situ. In its original situation. [L.]
In statu quo. In the state in which it was. [L.]
Inter alia. Among other matters. [L.]
Inter nos. Between ourselves. [L.]
Inter pocula. At one's cups. [L.]
In terrorem. As a warning. [L.]
Intra muros. Within the walls. [L.]
In transitu. In passing. [L.]
In vacuo. In empty space. [L.]
In vino veritas. There is truth in wine (*i. e.* the truth comes out influence). [L.]
Ipse dixit. He himself said it; dogmatic assertion. [L.]
Ipsissima verba. The very words. [L.]
Ipso facto. In the fact itself. [L.]
Ipso jure. By the law itself. [L.]

or brevis est. Anger is a short madness. [L.]
est scripta. Thus the law is written. [L.]

est alea. The die is cast. [L.]
sais quoi. I know not what. [Fr.]
eau. A jet of water. [Fr.]
e main. A practical joke. [Fr.]
le mots. A play on words, or pun. [Fr.]
d'esprit. A witticism. [Fr.]
de théâtre. A stage trick. [Fr.]
divino. By divine law. [L.]
humano. By human law. [L.]
civile. The civil law. [L.]
divinum. Divine law. [L.]
et norma loquendi. The law and rule of language. [L.]
gentium. The law of nations. [L.]
uste milieu. The golden mean. [Fr.]

alendæ Græca. Never. [L.] See *Ad Græcas Kalendas*.

Laborare est orare. To labor is to pray. [L.]
Labore et honore. By labor and honor. [L.]
Labor ipse voluptas. Labor itself is pleasure. [L.] Motto.
Labor omnia vincit. Labor conquers everything. [L.]
La critique est aisée, et l'art est difficile. Criticism is easy, and art is
    difficult. [Fr.]
Laisser faire. To let things alone and take their course. [Fr.]
L'allegro. The merry man. [It.]
La maladie sans maladie. Hypochondria. [Fr.]
Lapsus calami. A slip of the pen. [L.]
Lapsus linguæ. A slip of the tongue. [L.]
Lapsus memoriæ. A slip of the memory. [L.]
Lares et penates. Household gods. [L.]
Laus Deo. Praise to God. [L.]
L'avenir. The future. [Fr.]
Legatus a latere. An extraordinary Papal ambassador. [L.]
Le grand monarque. Louis XIV., the grand monarch. [Fr.]
Le pas. Precedence in place or rank. [Fr.]
Le roi et l'état. The king and the state. [Fr.]
Le roi le veut. The king wills it. [Fr.]
Les affaires font les hommes. Business makes men. [Fr.]
Le savoir faire. The knowing how to act. [Fr.]
Le savoir vivre. The knowing how to live. [Fr.]
Lèse majesté. High treason. [Fr.]
Le tout ensemble. The whole together. [Fr.]
Lettres de cachet. Private sealed letters from the king.
Lex non scripta. The common law. [L.]
Lex scripta. The statute law. [L.]
Lex talionis. The law of retaliation. [L.]
Lex terræ. The law of the land. [L.]
L'incroyable. The incredible. [Fr.]
Lite pendente. During the lawsuit. [L.]
Litera scripta manet. The written letter remains (
ocum tenens. A deputy or substitute. [L.]
lucus a non lucendo lucus. *Lucus*, a grove, from
there being no light in it) ; a fanciful derivation.
us in fabula. The wolf in the fable. [L.]
us naturæ. A monstrosity ; a freak of nature.

Ma foi. My faith. [Fr.]
Magister dixit. The master said so. [L.]
Magna civitas, magna solitudo. A great city is a great desert. [L.]
Magna est veritas, et prævalebit. Truth is powerful, and will ultimately prevail. [L.]
Magni nominis umbra. The shadow of a great name. [L.]
Magnum bonum. A great good. [L.]
Magnum opus. A great work. [L.]
Magnus Apollo. A great oracle. [L.]
Maison de santé. A mad-house. [Fr.]
Maison de ville. A town-house. [Fr.]
Maître d'hôtel. A house-steward. [Fr.]
Maladie du pays. Home-sickness. [Fr.]
Mala fide. In bad faith. [L.]
Mal à propos. Ill-timed. [Fr.]
Mandamus. We order; a law writ. [L.] Law.
Manège. Riding-house; horsemanship. [Fr.]
Manibus pedibusque. With might and main (*lit.* with hands and feet). [L.]
Manu propria. With one's own hand. [L.]
Mariage de convenance. A marriage from considerations of advantage. [Fr.]
Materia medica. Substances used in medicine; therapeutics. [L.]

[Fr.]

e bashfulness. [Fr.]

[L.]
[L.]
[L.]

de. [L.]
nd body. [L.]
rank. [Fr.]

for the stage. [Fr.]

Mont de piété. Pawnshop; originally store   money to lend to poor people without interest. [Fr.]
Morceau. A morsel; a bit. [Fr.]
More suo. After his own manner. [L.]
Mors omnibus communis. Death is common to all. [L.]
Mot de guet. Watchword. [Fr.]
Mots d'usage. Phrases in common use. [Fr.]
Multum in parvo. Much in little. [L.]
Mutatis mutandis. After making the necessary changes. [L.]
Mutato nomine, de te fabula narratur. Change the name, and the story will apply to yourself. [L.]

Naturam expellas furcâ, tamen usque recurret. You may drive out nature by violence (*lit.* with a pitchfork), but she will ever come rushing back again. [L.]
Nec Deus intersit, nisi dignus vindice nodus. Let not a god be introduced, unless the difficulty be worthy of such intervention. [L.]
Necessitas non habet legem. Necessity has no law. [L.]

Nec placida contentus quiete est. Nor is he contented with quiet repose [L.] Motto. [L.]

Nec scire fas est omnia. The gods do not permit us to know everything. [L.]

Né, *m.* ; **Née,** *fem.* Born. [Fr.]

Ne Jupiter quidem omnibus placet. Not even Jupiter pleases everybody.

Nem. con. Abbreviation for *nemine contradicente ;* without opposition. [L.]

Nem. dis. Abbreviation for *nemine dissentiente ;* without opposition. [L.]

Nemo me impune lacessit. No one annoys me with impunity. [L.] Motto of Scotland.

Nemo mortalium omnibus horis sapit. No man is wise at all times. [L.]

Ne plus ultra. What cannot be surpassed; perfection (*lit.* no more beyond). [L.]

Ne sutor ultra crepidam. Let not the shoemaker go beyond his last. [L.]

Nihil ad rem. Nothing to the purpose. [L.]

Nil admirari. To wonder at nothing. [L.]

Nil desperandum. Never despair. [L.]

N'importe. It matters not. [Fr.]

Nisi prius. Unless before ; a judicial writ. [L.]

Noblesse oblige. Rank has its obligations. [Fr.]

Nolens volens. Whether he will or not. [L.]

Noli me tangere. Touch me not. [L.]

Nolle prosequi. To be unwilling to proceed. [L.]

Nom de guerre. An assumed name. [Fr.]

Nom de plume. Assumed name of an author. [Fr.]

Non assumpsit. He did not assume (a legal plea). [L.]

Non compos mentis. Not sound in mind. [L.]

Non est vivere, sed valere vita. Life is not mere existence, but th enjoyment of health. [L.]

Non generant aquilæ columbas. Eagles do not bring forth pigeons. [L. Motto.

Non multa, sed multum. Not many things, but much. [L.]

Non sequitur. It does not follow. [L.]

Non sibi, sed patriæ. Not for himself, but for his country. [L.] Mott

Noscitur ex sociis. He is known by his companions. [L.]

Nota bene. Mark well. [L.]

Nôtre Dame. Our Lady. [Fr.]

Nous avons changé tout cela. We have changed all that. [Fr.]

Nous verrons. We shall see. [Fr.]

Novus homo. A new man ; a man risen from obscurity. [L.]

Nulli secundus. Second to none. [L.]

Nullus dies sine linea. No day without something done. [L.]

Nunc aut nunquam. Now or never. [L.]

Nunquam aliud natura, aliud sapientia dicit. Nature never say thing, and wisdom another. [L.]

Nunquam non paratus. Always ready. [L.] Motto.

Obiit. He or she died. [L.]

Obiter dictum. A thing said by the way. or in passing. [L.]

Obsta principiis. Resist the beginnings. [L.]

Odi profanum vulgus, et arceo. I loathe and repulse the profa

Odium theologicum. Hatred among theologians. [L.]

Œil de bœuf. Bull's eye. [Fr.]

Omne ignotum pro magnifico. Everything unknown is thou magnificent. [L.]

Omne trinum perfectum. There is a threefoldness or trinit perfect. [L.]

Omnia vincit amor. Love conquers all things. [L.]

Omnia vincit labor. Labor conquers all things. [L.]

On dit. They say : a flying rumor. [Fr.]

On ne donne rien si libéralement que ses conseils. Men give nothing so liberally as their advice. [Fr.]
Onus probandi. The weight of proof. [L.]
Ora et labora. Pray and labor. [L.]
Ora pro nobis. Pray for us. [L.]
Ore rotundo. With full round voice. [L.]
Origo mali. The origin of the evil. [L.]
O si sic omnia. O that he had always spoken or acted thus! [L.]
O tempora, O mores! O the times and the manners! [L.]
Otium cum dignitate. Ease with dignity. [L.]
Ouvriers. Artisans. [Fr.]

Pace tua. With your leave. [L.]
Pacta conventa. Terms agreed on. [L.]
Palmam qui meruit ferat. Let him who has won the palm bear it. [L.]
Palma non sine pulvere. The palm is not gained without labor. [L.] Motto.
Par excellence. By way of eminence. [Fr.]
Pari passu. With equal steps or pace. [L.]
Par nobile fratrum. (Ironically) a noble pair of brothers. [L.]
Particeps criminis. An accomplice. [L.]
Passim. Everywhere. [L.]
Passe-partout. A master key. [Fr.]
Pater familias. The father of the family. [L.]
Pater patriæ. The father of his country. [L.]
Patience passe science. Patience surpasses knowledge. [Fr.] Motto.
Patria cara, carior libertas. My country is dear, but liberty is dearer. [L.] Motto.
Pauca, sed bona. Few, but good. [L.]
Pax in bello. Peace in war. [L.] Motto.
Pax vobiscum. Peace be with you. [L.]
Peccavi. I have done wrong. [L.]
Pede poena claudo. Punishment follows crime with a slow foot. [L.]
Peine forte et dure. Strong and severe pain. [Fr.]
Pense à bien. Think for the best. [Fr.] Motto.
Per contra. Contrariwise. [L.]
Per diem. By the day. [L.]
Per fas et nefas. Through right and wrong. [L.]
Per mare, per terras. By sea and land. [L.]
Per saltum. By a leap. [L.]
Per se. By itself. [L.]
Perseverando. By perseverance. [L.] Motto.
Petit-maître. A fop. [Fr.]
Peu de gens savent être vieux. Few persons know how to be old. [Fr.]
Pinxit. He painted it. [L.]
Pis aller. The last resource. [Fr.]
Pleno jure. With full authority. [L.]
Poco à poco. Little by little. [It.]
Poëta nascitur, non fit. Nature, not study, forms the poet. [L.]
Point d'appui. Point of support; a rallying point. [Fr.]
Pondere, non numero. By weight, not by number. [L.]
Pons asinorum. The asses' bridge. [L.]
Posse comitatûs. The civil force of the country. [L.]
Possunt quia posse videntur. They are able because they think they are so. [L.]
Poste restante. To remain until called for. [Fr.]
Post-mortem. After death. [L.]
Postulata. Things required. [L.]
Pour passer le temps. To pass the time. [Fr.]

Pour prendre congé. To take leave. [Fr.]
Præmonitus, præmunitus. Forewarned, forearmed. [L.]
Prendre la lune avec les dents. To aim at impossibilities (*lit.* to seize moon with the teeth). [Fr.]
Prêt d'accomplir. Ready to perform. [Fr.] Motto.
Preux chevalier. A brave knight. [Fr.]
Primâ facie. On the first view, or appearance. [L.]
Primum mobile. The main spring; the first impulse. [L.]
Primus inter pares. First among his equals or peers. [L.]
Pro aris et focis. For our altars and our hearths. [L.]
Probatum est. It has been proved. [L.]
Pro bono publico. For the public good. [L.]
Probum non pœnitet. Honesty repents not. [L.] Motto.
Procès-verbal. A written statement. [Fr.]
Pro Deo et ecclesia. For God and the Church. [L.]
Pro et con. For and against. [L.]
Pro hac vice. For this time. [L.]
Projet de loi. A legislative bill. [Fr.]
Pro patria. For our country [L.]
Pro rata. In proportion. [L.]
Pro salute animæ. For the health of the soul. [L.]
Pro tanto. As far as it goes. [L.]
Pro tempore. For the time being. [L.]
Punica fides. Carthaginian faith; treachery. [L.]

Quæ fuerunt vitia, mores sunt. What were vices once are now
Quanti est sapere. How valuable is wisdom. [L.]
Quantum. How much. [L.]
Quantum libet. As much as you please. [L.]
Quantum sufficit. As much as is sufficient. [L.]
Quid novi? What news? [L.]
Quid nunc? What now? a newsmonger. [L.]
Quid prodest? What is the use? [L.]
Quid pro quo. One thing for another. [L.]
Quid rides? Why do you laugh? [L.]
Qui vive? Who goes there? [Fr.]
Quoad hoc. To this extent. [L.]
Quo animo? With what purpose or intention? [L.]
Quod erat demonstrandum. Which was to be proved. [L.]
Quod erat faciendum. Which was to be done. [L.]
Quod scripsi, scripsi. What I have written, I have written. [L.]
Quod vide. Which see. [L.]
Quondam. Former. [L.]
Quos Deus vult perdere, prius dementat. Those whom God ?
  to destroy, he first deprives of their senses. [L.]
Quot homines, tot sententiæ. So many men, so many opinior
Quo warranto? By what warrant? [L.] A legal writ.

Raison d'état. A reason of state. [Fr.]

Rentes. Funds bearing interest; stocks. [Fr.]
Rente viagère. An annuity [Fr.]
Rentier. One who enjoys an income. [Fr.]
Requiescat in pace. May he rest in peace. [L.]
Res angusta domi. Narrow circumstances at home. [L.]
Res gestæ. Exploits. [L.]
Res judicata. A case already decided. [L.]
Respublica. The commonwealth. [L.]
Resurgam. I shall rise again. [L.]
Revenons à nos moutons. Let us return to our subject. [Fr.]
Rien n'est beau que le vrai. Nothing so lovely as truth. [Fr.]
Ruse contre ruse. Diamond cut diamond. [Fr.]
Ruse de guerre. A stratagem. [Fr.]
Rus in urbe. The country in town. [L.]
Rusticus expectat dum defluat amnis. The rustic waits till the ri
flow by. [L.]

Sal atticum. Wit (*lit.* Attic salt) [L.]
Salus populi suprema est lex. The supreme law is the welfare of
people. [L.]
Sanctum sanctorum. The holy of holies. [L.]
Sang froid. Indifference; apathy. [Fr.]
Sans cérémonie.}
Sans façon.} Without ceremony. [Fr.]
Sans changer. Without changing. [Fr.] Motto.
Sans Dieu rien. Nothing without God. [Fr.] Motto.
Sans peur et sans reproche. Without fear and without **reproach.** [Fr
Sans souci. Without care; free and easy. [Fr.]
Sartor resartus. The tailor patched. [L.]
Satis superque. Enough and more. [L.]
Satis verborum. Enough of words. [L.]
Sauve qui peut. Save himself who can. [Fr.]
Savoir faire. Tact. [Fr.]
Savoir vivre. Good manners. [Fr.]
Secundum artem. According to rule. [L.]
Semper fidelis. Always faithful. [L.] Motto.
Semper idem. Always the same. [L.]
Semper paratus. Always ready. [L.] **Motto.**
Se non è vero, è ben trovato. If not true, **it is well invented.** [It.]
Seriatim. In a series. [L.]
Servabo fidem. I will keep faith. [L.] **Motto.**
Sic passim. So everywhere. [L.]
Sic transit gloria mundi. Thus passes away the glory of the world. [
Sic vos non vobis. Thus you do not labor for yourselves. [L.]
Similia similibus curantur. Like things are cured by like. [L.]
Si monumentum quaris, circumspice. If you seek his monument, l
around. [L.]
Sine die. Without a day being appointed. [L.]
Sine quâ non. An indispensable condition. [L.]
Si sit prudentia. If there be but prudence. [L.] Motto.
Siste, viator. Stop, traveller. [L.]
Si vis pacem, para bellum. If you wish peace, prepare **for war.** [L.]
Soi-disant. Self-styled. [Fr.]
Sola nobilitas virtus. Virtue alone is true nobility. [L.] Motto.
Sotto voce. In an undertone. [It.]
Spectemur agendo. Let us be tried by our actions. [L.] Motto.
Spero meliora. I hope for better times. [L.] Motto.
Spes mea in Deo. My hope is in God. [L.] Motto.
Spirituel. Intellectual; witty. [Fr.]

Spolia opima. The richest of the spoil. [L.]

Stans pede in uno. While standing on one leg (*i. e.* easily executed). [L.]

Status quo. The state in which the thing is; as things were before. [L.]

Status quo ante bellum. The state in which both parties were before the war. [L.]

Stet. Let it stand. [L.]

Sua cuique voluptas. Every man has his own pleasures. [L.]

Suaviter in modo, fortiter in re. Gentle in the manner, but vigorous in the deed. [L.]

Sub judice. Under consideration. [L.]

Sub pœna. Under a penalty. [L.]

Sub rosa. Under the rose; privately. [L.]

Sub silentio. In silence. [L.]

Sufficit. It is enough. [L.]

Sui generis. Of its own kind. [L.]

Suivez raison. Follow reason. [Fr.] Motto.

Summum bonum. The chief good. [L.]

Suo Marte. By his own exertion. [L.]

Sursum corda. Keep up your heart. [L.]

Suum cuique. Let every man have his own. [L.]

Tableau vivant. A scene in which statues or pictures are represented by living persons. [Fr.]

Table d'hôte. A common table for guests. [Fr.]

Tabula rasa. A smooth or blank tablet. [L.]

Tâche sans tâche. A work without stain. [Fr.]

Tam Marte quam Minervâ. As much by his courage as genius. [L.]

Tantæ molis erat. It was such a task. [L.]

Tant mieux. So much the better. [Fr.]

Tant pis. So much the worse. [Fr.]

Tel maître, tel valet. Like master, like man. [Fr.]

Tempus edax rerum. Time that devours all things. [L.]

Tempus fugit, et nunquam revertitur. Time flies, and never returns. [L.]

Tempus omnia revelat. Time discloses all things. [L.]

Teres et rotundus. Smooth and round. [L.]

Terminus a quo. The starting-point. [L.]

Terræ filius. A son of the earth. [L.]

Terra incognita. An unknown country. [L.]

Tête-à-tête. Face to face; a private conversation. [Fr.]

Tiens ta foy. Preserve thy faith. [Old Fr.] Motto.

Tiers état. The third estate; the commons. [Fr.]

Tirer le diable par la queue. To pull the devil by the tail; to take the bull by the horns. [Fr.]

Toga virilis. The gown of manhood. [L.]

Tot homines, tot sententiæ. So many men, so many opinions. [L.]

Totidem verbis. In so many words. [L.]

Toties quoties. As often as. [L.]

Toto cœlo. By the whole heavens; as wide as the poles asunder. [L.]

Tour de force. A feat of strength or skill. [Fr.]

Tourner casaque. To turn one's coat; to change sides. [Fr.]

Tout-à-fait. Quite. [Fr.]

Tout bien ou rien. The whole or nothing. [Fr.] Motto.

Troja fuit. Troy was. [L.]

Tu ne cede malis. Yield not to misfortune. [L.]

Tu quoque! You too! [L.]

Ubique. Everywhere. [L.]

Ubi supra. Where above mentioned. [L.]

Ultima ratio regum. The last reasoning of kings (*i. e.* arms). [L.]

Ultimus Romanorum. The last of the Romans. [L.]
Ultra vires. Beyond the powers or rights possessed. [L.]
Unâ voce. With one voice; unanimously. [L.]
Unum et idem. One and the same. [L.]
Urbi et orbi. For the Rome (*lit.* the city) and the world. [L.]
Usque ad nauseam. To utter disgust. [L.]
Utile dulci. The useful with the agreeable.
Ut infra. As below. [L.]
Ut supra. As above stated. [L.]

Vade in pace. Go in peace. [L.]
Vade mecum. Go with me; a constant companion. [L.]
Vade retro. Avaunt. [L.]
Væ victis! Woe to the vanquished! [L.]
Vanitas vanitatum. Vanity of vanities. [L.]
Variorum notæ. Notes of various authors. [L.]
Veni, vidi, vici. I came, I saw, I conquered. [L.]
Ventis secundis. With favoring winds. [L.]
Ventre affamé n'a point d'oreilles. A hungry belly has no ears. [Fr.]
Verbatim et literatim. Word for word, and letter for letter. [L.]
Verba volant, scripta manent. Words fly, writings remain. [L.]
Verbum dat sapienti. A word is enough to a wise man. [L.]
Vérité sans peur. Truth without fear. [Fr.] Motto.
Vestigia nulla retrorsum. There are no traces, or steps, backward· [L.] Motto.
Via media. A middle course. [L.]
Vice. In place of. [L.]
Vice versâ. The terms being exchanged. [L.]
Vi et armis. By main force (*lit.* by force and arms). [L.]
Vincit amor patriæ. The love of our country prevails. [L.]
Vincit veritas. Truth conquers. [L.] Motto.
Virtute et fide. By virtue and faith. [L.] Motto.
Virtuti nihil obstat et armis. Nothing can resist valor and arms. [L.] Motto.
Virtuti non armis fido. I trust to virtue and not to arms. [L.] Motto·
Virtutis amor. The love of virtue. [L.] Motto.
Vis-à-vis. Opposite; face to face. [Fr.]
Vis inertiæ. Inert property of matter. [L.]
Vivâ voce. By or with the living voice. [L.]
Vive la bagatelle. Success to trifling. [Fr.]
Vive la république. Long live the republic. [Fr.]
Vive le roi. Long live the king. [Fr.]
Voilá une autre chose. That 's quite another matter. [Fr.]
Volo non valeo. I am willing but unable. [L.] Motto.
Vox et præterea nihil. A voice and nothing more. [L.]
Vox populi, vox Dei. The voice of the people is the voice of God. [L.]

Zonam predidit. He has lost his purse. [L.]
Zonam solvere. To unloose the virgin zone.

KEY TO PRONUNCIATION

OF

SEVERAL MODERN LANGUAGES.

———◆———

THE four European languages most frequently met are French, Ger Italian, and Spanish ; and therefore we give the rules which apply to t only, premising that the Dutch, Swedish, and Danish very much rese the German in pronunciation and otherwise, as the Portuguese doe Spanish.

FRENCH WORDS.

The vowel **a**, in French, has two distinct sounds : the first long, foun *pas*, as in the English word *far ;* the second short, found in *bal*, as in The circumflex *â*, however, has a sound broader than *a* in *pas*, being i mediate between that in *far* and that in *fall*.

e has three sounds : the first short and acute, like *e* in *met*, as *été ;* second open and more prolonged, like *a* in *hale*, as *tête ;* and the t obscure, like *e* in *battery*, as *retour*.

i is distinguished by two sounds : the first found in *il*, nearly as in English word *fig ;* the second in *exil*, like *ie* in *field*.

o has three sounds : the first in *trône*, sounded nearly as in *robe ;* second in *parole*, sounded as in *rob ;* the third in *corps*, sounded as in *l*

u, which has no precise equivalent in English, takes nearly the v sound of *ue* in *flue ;* although with the nasal *n*, as in *un*, it takes the sc of *ung*.

y is similar to the French *i*.

ai is like *è* or *a*.

au is like *o*.

ei is like *è*.

eu is similar to the sound of *u* in *tub*, only more prolonged, and ne resembles *u* in *fur*.

ie is like *ee* in English, or *i*.

oi usually sounds like *wä ;* e. g. *moi* is pronounced *mwä* or *mwäh*.

ou sounds like *oo* in English.

b, c, d, f, k, p, t, v, and **z** sound the same as in English.

g before *a, o*, and *u* is hard, as in the English word *gap ;* before *y* it is soft, having the sound of *zh*, or of *s* in *pleasure*.

gu sounds like **g** hard; thus *gué*, *guide*, are pronoun...

h is never pronounced in French so forcibly as orthoëpists say that **h** has no sound in French.

j sounds like soft **g** in French, or **sh** in English.

l has usually the same sound as in English; but wh... preceded by *i*, or when *ll* follows *i*, in any situation, it u... called its liquid sound. This may be said to answer near... *lli* in *million*, the sound of *l* in such cases being blend... (consonant); e. g. *papillon* is pronounced *pä'-peel'-yôn'*; *t... teel-yé*, etc.

m and **n**, when followed by a vowel or when double, have ... as in English; but when at the end of a word, not immediat... another word beginning with a vowel, or when followed by ... nant in the middle of a word, they have what is termed the... which resembles that of *ng*, as in *long*, *pang*, etc., but is ... Thus, *m* and *n* are nasal in such words as *comparer*, *contente*... natural sound in such as *commune*, *connu*.

q or **qu** in French generally sounds like *k*; e. g. *quel* is pro... *qui*, *kee*; etc.

r is like the English *r*, but is trilled more strongly, espe... precedes another consonant, or stands at the end of a word... *punir*; in similar cases the English *r* itself is but very slightly...

s, when single and between two vowels, sounds like *z*; in ot... the same as in English.

x generally has the same sound as it has in English, but... sounded like *s*; e. g. in *six*, pronounced *sees*, and *Brux...* pronounced *bru-sell'*; and occasionally like *s*, as in *dixième*,...

ch is like *sh* in English; *th* is like *t*.

gn (the same as in the Italian) has a sound which blends t... (consonant), or, in other words, is equivalent to the sound of... Thus *Avignon* is pronounced *ä'-veen'-yong.*

The vowel *e* at the end of a word, when not marked wi... invariably mute, e. g. in *parle*, *contente.*

The French consonants, when occurring at the end of a ... erally not pronounced, unless they are immediately followed ... ginning with a vowel: as in *content*, *Bordeaux*, *dents.* If... are followed by a mute *e*, or any other vowel, they must al... lated, e. g. *contente*, *dente*, etc.

It may be observed that the French language has no ac... in which we employ this term. The marks called accents... over the different vowels, serve only to indicate the pa... these letters. Thus the accent over the *e* in some ... vowel has its first French sound, and at the same time di... *parle*, another form of the same verb, in which it serve... flex imparts to the vowels over which it is placed a ... sound than ordinary; e. g. in *hâte*, *tempête*, etc.

GERMAN WORDS.

a, in German, usually sounds as in the English word *far*, though it sor times approximates the *a* in *fat*.

e, when long, sounds like *a* in *fate ;* when short, like *e* in *met ;* frequer however, it has an obscure sound, like *e* in *battery.*

i, long, sounds like *i* in *marine,* or *ee* in English ; *i,* short, sounds lik in *pit.*

o, long, is like that in *no ; o,* short, like that in *on.*

u, long, is like *oo* in *cuckoo ; u,* short, is like *oo* in *good.*

y sounds like the German *i.*

ae, or **ä**, is similar to the German *e,* or to the English *a* in *fate.*

oe, or **ö**, nearly resembles the *eu* in French, but has no parallel sound English ; the sound in our language nearest to it is that of *e* in *her,* or a *fur ;* the German poets often rhyme it with *e* (*ä* or *ě*).

ue, or **ü**, is like the French *u.*

au is equivalent to the English *ou* in *our.*

äu and **eu** resemble in sound the English *oi,* as in *oil.*

ei and **ey** have the sound of *i* in *mine.*

ai is similar to the preceding, but somewhat broader.

ui sounds like $\overline{oo}$-*e.*

ie is equivalent to *ee* in English.

The consonants **f, k, l, m, n, p, q, t,** and **x,** are pronounced as in Eng **b** and **d,** at the beginning of a word, have the same sound as in Eng at the end of a word, *b* is pronounced like *p,* and *d* like *t.*

c, before *a, o,* and *u,* sounds like *k ;* before *e, i,* and *y,* like *ts.*

ch has a sound unknown in our language, and which, consequentt be learned from an oral instructor only. It somewhat resembles that *h,* with a strong aspiration ; after *a, o,* and *u,* it is guttural : for ex in the word *ack.* When it follows *e, i, ä, ö, ü, äu,* or *eu,* it seem sounded more in the palate, as in *ich.*

g, at the beginning of a word, sounds as in the English word *g* other situations it should be pronounced like the German *ch.* I German dialects, however, it is sounded in all cases nearly like *g* English.

h is pronounced only when it begins a word.

g and **h,** occurring after a vowel, lengthen its sound ; e. g. in *T. Flöh,* etc. When **g** and **h** occur in the middle of a compound · have the same sound as when they are initial.

j has the sound of the English *y* (consonant).

q is used only before *u,* and sounds as in the English word *q*

r is pronounced like *rr* in the English word *terror,* but som strongly.

s, at the beginning of a word, or between two vowels, i cases it is sharp, as in *this.* **ss** is always sharp·

sch sounds like the English *sh ;* **ss,** like *ss.*

th is pronounced like *t.*

v sounds like *f* in English, except when between two vowels ; it is then usually pronounced like our *v*.

w resembles our *v ;* but in pronouncing it the upper teeth should not be allowed to touch the lower lip, as is done in uttering the English *v.*

z and tz sound like *ts.*

ITALIAN WORDS.

a, in Italian, is like the English *a* in *far*, though its sound varies somewhat in different situations.

e has two sounds : first close, as *a* in *fate ;* second open, like *e* in *met.*

i is like *e* in *me,* or *i* in *fig.*

o has two sounds : first close, as in *note ;* second open, similar to *o* in *not,* but rather broader.

u is like *oo* in English.

ai and au, in Italian, are *proper* diphthongs. Accordingly *Cairo* is to be pronounced *ki'-ro,* and *Ausa, ou'-să,* etc.

The consonants b, d, f, l, m, n, p, q, s, t, and v are similar to the English.

k, w, x, and y are not used by the Italians, except in spelling foreign words.

c and cc, before *a, o,* and *u,* are sounded like *k ;* before *e, i,* and *y,* like *ch* or *tsh.*

As c, when immediately before *a, o,* or *u,* is never pronounced like *ch,* in order to express this sound in such cases, the vowel *i* is inserted ; thus, *cia, cio, ciu,* are pronounced *chă, cho, choo.*

ch is employed to express the sound of *k* before *e* and *i.*

g, before *a, o,* and *u,* is hard, as in the English word *get ;* before *e, i,* and *y,* it sounds like the English *j ; gia, gio, giu* are pronounced *jă, jo, joo.*

gh is used to express the sound of hard *g* before *e* and *i.*

gli has the sound of the liquid *l* (ll), or of *li* in *million ;* thus *Boglio* is pronounced *bolĕ'-yo.*

gn has the same sound as in French ; or, in other words, is like the Spanish *n ;* e. g. *Bologna* is pronounced *bo-lonĕ'-yă.*

h is never sounded in Italian.

j at the beginning of a syllable is like the English *y* (consonant) ; at the end of a word it is equivalent to *ii* (Italian).

r resembles the French, but is trilled somewhat more strongly.

sc, before *e* and *i,* is like the English *sh ;* e. g. *Scio* is pronounced *shee'-o.*

z has commonly the sound of *dz* in English ; *zz* is pronounced like *ts.*

SPANISH WORDS.

The Spanish a sounds as in the English word *far ;* e like *a* in *ale :* i like *e* in *mete ;* o as in English ; u like *oo* ; and y like Spanish *i.*

ai and ay are like long *i* in English. au sounds like *ou* in our. ei or ey are pronounced *ă'-ĕ.*

The consonants f, l (single), m, n, p, s, t, and v are pronounced as in English.

b at the beginning of a word sounds as in English; but between two vowels, its sound resembles that of *v*, with this is pronounced with the upper teeth placed against the unde sound of the Spanish *b* is formed by bringing the lips loosel contact. This sound seems to be between that of *v* and the

c, before *a, o,* and *u,* is pronounced as in English; befor the sound of *th* in the word *thin.* In the Catalan dialect it is English.

ch has the same sound as in English, except in the dialec where it is pronounced like *k.*

d, at the beginning of a word, is sounded very nearly as is pronounced with the tip of the tongue against the upper pronouncing the English *d* the tongue is made to touch mouth.

g, before *e* and *i,* and **j** before every vowel, are pronounce guttural *h,* similar to the German *ch* in *ach.*

g, before *a, o,* and *u,* is hard, as in English.

gua and **guo** sound somewhat like *gwä, gwo,* but the *g* i is scarcely perceived; so that in these cases the sound of *g* proximate very nearly that of the English *w.* **gu,** before *e* a sounded like *g* hard; thus, *Guiana* is pronounced *ghe-än'-ä.*

h, in Spanish, is never pronounced, except in words begin and then very slightly.

ll (now sometimes written *l*) has a sound which combines (consonant), and is similar to the liquid *l* in French; e. g. *v* pronounced *veel'-yä ; Llerena, lyä-rä'-nä.*

n, in a similar manner, unites the sounds of *n* and *y,* a French; thus, *peña* is pronounced *pan'-yä.*

q, in Spanish, is always followed by *u.* **qu,** before *a* an as in English; or, in other words, equivalent to *kw ;* before *e* nounced like *k,* unless the *u* be marked with a diæresis, in like *kw.*

r is similar to the French, but is trilled more strongly.

t is to be pronounced by putting the tip of the tongue ag teeth.

x is usually sounded like the Spanish *j,* which letter, ac present mode of spelling, has been generally substituted for it of the old spelling, *Ximenes, Xucar,* etc., we now see *Jis* etc.

RULES FOR SPELLING.

MONOSYLLABLES ending in *f, l,* or *s,* immediately preceded by a single vowel, double the final consonant; as, *mass, bill, staff,* etc., with the following exceptions· as, *clef, gas, has, his, if, is, of, pus, this, thus, us, was, yes.*

Monosyllables not ending in *f, l,* or *s* do not double the final consonant; as, *man, rod,* etc. Exceptions: *add, burr, butt, buzz, ebb, egg, err, fizz, fuzz, in, odd.*

The final *e* of a primitive word is rejected before a suffix beginning with a vowel; as, *have, having.* Exceptions: Words ending in *ce* or *ge* retain the *e* before *able* or *ous;* as, *trace, traceable; outrage, outrageous.* The *e* is also retained in verbs ending in *ee* and *oe;* as, *see, seeing; shoe, shoeing.* *Singe, swinge,* and *tinge* retain *e* followed by *ing;* as, *singe, singeing.*

The final consonant of a monosyllable, and accented final syllable, if preceded by a single vowel, is doubled before a suffix beginning with a vowel; as, *run, runner.* Exceptions: When the derivative does not retain the accent of the root, the final consonant is not always doubled; as, *refer, reference. x, s,* and *k* are never doubled. Words derived from *gas* (except *gassing* and *gassy*) have only one *s;* as, *gas, gases.*

The final *y* of a primitive word, when preceded by a consonant, is changed into *i* before a suffix which does not commence with *i;* as, *glory, glorious.* Exceptions: *y* is retained in words derived from *dry* and *sky;* as, *shy, shyly.*

Words ending with a double letter preserve it double in their derivatives, unless the suffix begins with the same letter; as *skill, skillful.*

PUNCTUATION MARKS,

. Period.
? Interrogation.
! Exclamation.
: Colon.
; Semicolon.
, Comma.
— Dash.
( ) Parenthesis.
[ ] Brackets, *or* crotchets.
' Apostrophe.
. Hyphen.
´ Acute accent.
` Grave accent.
ˆ Circumflex accent.
~ Circumflex, *or* tilde.
¯ The long, *or* macron.
˘ The short, *or* breve.

.. Diæresis.
^ Caret.
" " Quotation mark
} Brace.
• • • Ellipsis.
.... Ellipsis ; also !
—— Ellipsis.
• Asterisk.
† Dagger, *or* ol
‡ Double dagg
§ Section.
‖ Parallels.
¶ Paragraph.
☞ Index.
•.• *or* •*• Aste

..... : —

A MEMOIR OF ADONIS AND PENELOPE.

BY A TRUTHFUL BIOGRAPHER.

An Exercise in Pronunciation.

ADONIS was a grimy tatterdemalion, amenable to no one. He was mischievous and subtle, the ally of other juvenile gamins in all street altercations. His parents lived in such a maelstrom of bestial vice and squalor a bourgeois under whose surveillance he came prophesied that he would end his life on the gallows as a fit chastisement. Adonis came to feel the contumely of his position, and breaking away from his comrades and his dog, a mangy, canine mongrel, he began a maritime career. His herculean strength, equable temper, acumen, fidelity, probity, heroism, and latent genius soon raised him to the rank of mate. The ship anchored in a bayou of Siam, and before the crew was acclimated a plague broke out, and Adonis was the only Caucasian who escaped death. He took peremptory command of the ship and reinforced the crew with Malays, then set sail for New York. There he sold the ship and its contents, — a cargo of almonds, anchovies, spermaceti, cement, caoutchouc, and cayenne pepper. This put his finances in good condition. He invested in the mercantile trade and soon demonstrated his incomparable ability as a financier, and gained precedence and prestige as a man of wealth. Chagrin at his humble birth made him a misanthrope and forbade all pretence to gallantry, and led him to isolate himself from society ; though he would have been received with éclat by scheming papas and mammas. He was inveigled into making his début at a dinner given in honor of distinguished literati. His vis-à-vis at the table was a comely matron. Next her sat a lovely piece of femineity, whose cognomen was Penelope. Adonis was a connoisseur of beauty, and he thought her more beautiful than any houri of the harem he had seen in the East. Her figure was lithesome, her pedal extremities tiny and pretty, her naïveté of manner charming. On inquiry he learned that she was an accomplished pianist, and equally skilful in treading the pedals of the organ ; in the terpsichorean art she was marvellous ; and her culinary skill was unsurpassed, especially in the making of truffles. Adonis was weary of celibacy, and showed himself an aspirant for her favor. He threw down the gauntlet to other combatants and heeded not their jocund badinage. The fine contour of his face, his supple, stalwart form, his suavity and courteousness pleas Penelope, and she showed by her receptivity that his attentions were

onerous. As a prelude indicative of his intentions, Adonis laid at
of his inamorata lozenges, bananas and apricots. He brought a b
hydrangea, creamy white like her skin ; a spray of gladiolus which vi
the carmine of her lips ; and bouquets from the florist, composed o
lias, cyclamen, clematis, wistaria, weigelia, and oxalis. The roman
tinued in tête-à-têtes under the azure sky, against which gleamed the
borealis. An aureola seemed to surround her as he played to her u
flageolet or violoncello. He called her his patron saint, his good
and implored her to become his fiancé. She replied, " Aye, I will 1
for aye."

The clangor of wedding-bells was heard as they approached the
neal altar, where the diocesan bishop awaited them. Adonis was at
a suit of jean ; Penelope in a white décolleté robe over a mauve sa
moral. Her coiffure was adorned with jasmines ; her only ornamen
rare onyx brooch of Byzantine make.

Coupon-bonds, a piano-forte, candelabrum, chiffonnier, bureau,
and other furniture were bestowed as wedding gifts.

After the nuptial vows were taken, Adonis, who was a nomad by
proposed an extended tour. A favorite laundress was engaged as ma
the trio sailed for the Arctic sea, where the Esquimau darts among
bergs in his kayak. The cold soon drove· them eastward to the Bo
where days of leisure were spent in listening to the sonorous soug
waves, and in watching the caiques that filled the water. They tr
the arid deserts of Africa on the backs of docile dromedaries until the
weary of the chicanery and hypocrisy of Arab sheiks and the garr
guides. The glaciers of Switzerland lured them northward, and the
ered lichens and Alpine flowers through the livelong day. They
Venice, and floated in fairy gondolas past campanile, church, and
Attracted by the beautiful façade of St. Mark's, they entered the
and were struck by its acoustic properties as they listened to the cl
of the Kyrie Eleison. A priest began an extempore address with
mence of an exhorter. He warned the people against the dangero
of the Protestants ; he claimed that they were worse than the 1
medieval ages or the vagaries of legendary mythology. In his
he showed implacable hatred of the national principle of the A
chise ; and he continued in a tirade against the sacrilegious, ir
of Americans in their churches, and declared that a prec
established and a placard posted forbidding their entra
drove them to Rome, where, in the Coliseum, they witn
West Show." There was a joust between a knight dre
cuirass, with a falchion in his hand, and an Indian cacique

air of bravado on a bicycle. Aeronauts ascended in balloons; conjurers, dressed as Chinese mandarins, performed strange feats; a wonderful pageant with weird scenic effect was displayed in pantomime, and simultaneously was heard a strange orchestral accompaniment from a calliope.

The glamour investing Rome waned; and they began to complain of the cuisine of the Italian table d'hôte. The water seemed poisoned by the faucet through which it flowed; they grew weary of mayonnaise dressing and farina dessert, and longed for a taste of pumpkin pie.

Penelope became enervated, and her flaccid muscles and fetid breath showed exhaustion. It was soon apparent that her invalidism was no forgery, and Adonis removed her at once to Paris, having a presentiment of danger. They could not agree upon a doctor. Penelope wanted a homœopathist, and urged that in the past this treatment had carried her safely through tonsillitis, asthma, bronchitis, and diphtheria. But Adonis was deaf to her entreaties, and called an allopathist, who said that her respiratory apparatus was defective, that she was suffering from hysteria, and was threatened with cerebral meningitis. He ordered an unguent from the pharmaceutist, composed of an alkali salt, iodine, oleomargarine, benzine, quinine, and nicotine. He administered strychnine, morphine, and cocaine until a comatose state was produced, from which poor Penelope never rallied. Adonis refused the condolence of friends, and was in a lamentable condition. With a prescience of approaching death, he took his will from its envelope and added a codicil, revoking all former bequests and leaving his entire fortune of more than five million ducats to the city of Rome, on condition that the ashes of himself and wife should repose in the Pantheon.

Intent upon suicide he rushed from the house, and encountered a band of communists, singing the Marseillaise and crying, "Down with the guillotine!" "Down with all who will not join us!" They tried to force Adonis into their ranks. He resisted them, and in the mêlée was shot in the abdomen with a carbine, his jugular vein was severed by a poniard, and his assailants were killed by the explosion of a dynamite bomb.

According to a request found in the will, the bodies of Adonis and Penelope were wrapped in the same cerement and taken to the crematorium at Milan. Their ashes were placed in an urn and conveyed to Rome, where they found sepulture in the Pantheon.

Abdomen, ab-dō′men, *not* ab′do-men.
Acacia, a-kā′shi-a, *not* a-ka′shi-a.
Acclimate, ak-klī′māt, *not* ak′kli-māt.
Accompaniment, ak-kum′pa-ni-ment, *not* ak-kumpt′ni-ment.
Accomplish, ak-kom′plish, *not* ak-kum′plish.
Acoustic, a-kow′stik, *not* a-kōō′stik.
Acumen, a-kū′men, *not* ak′u-men.
Address, ad-dres′, *not* ad′dres.
Adonis, a-dō′nis, *not* a-don′is.
Aeronaut, ā′ér-ō-nąt, *not* a-er′ō-nąt.
Albumen, al-bū′men, *not* al′bu-men.
Alkali, al′ka-li, *preferred to* al′ka-lī.
Allopathist, al-lop′a-thist, *not* al′lo-path-ist.
Ally, al-lī′, *not* al′lī *nor* al′li.
Almond, ä′mund, *not* al′mund.
Alpine, al′pin *or* al′pin.
Altercation, al-tér-kā′shun, *not* al-...
... al′tér-nāt.

Azure, ā′zhur *or* azh′o
Badinage, bä′dĕ′nazh′,
Balloon, bal-lōōn′, *not*
Balmoral, bal-mor′al, *n*
Banana, ba-nä′na *or* ba-nan′a.
Bayou, bī′ōō, *not* bī′ō
Benzine, ben′zin, *not* l
Bestial, best′yal, *not* l
Bicycle, bī′si-kl, *not* l
Biographer, bī-og′ra-ra-fér.
Bomb, bum, *not* bom
Bosporus, bos′pō-rus
Bouquet, bōō′kā′ *or* kā′.
Bourgeois [a citizen] bur-jois′.
Bourgeois [type], bōōrzh′wą′.
Bravado, bra-vä′d
Bronchitis, brong kĕ′tis.

Cayenne, kā-en′, *not* kī′en.
Celibacy, sel′i-ba-si, *not* se-lib′a-si.
Cement [noun], sem′ent, *not* se-ment′; [verb], se-ment′.
Cerebral, sĕr′ĕ-bral, *not* se-rē′bral.
Cerement, sēr′ment, *not* ser′e-ment.
Chagrin, sha-grēn′ *or* sha-grin′. [The weight of dictionary authority is in favor of the first pronunciation, common usage of the second.]
Chamelion, ka-mē′lē-on, *not* ka-mel′i-on.
Chant, chảnt, *not* chant.
Chastisement, chas′tiz-ment, *not* chas-tiz′ment.
Chicanery, shi-kān′ér-i, *not* chi-kan′ér-i.
Chiffonnier, shif-fon-ēr′ [Eng. pro.]; she′fon′nyä′ [Fr. pro.]. Chiffonniere (shif′fon′ne′är′) is the fem. form of the word, meaning a rag-picker, and is sometimes incorrectly used for the piece of furniture.
Chinese, chi-nēz′, *not* chi-nēs′.
Clangor, klang′gēr, *not* klang′ēr.
Clematis, klem′a-tis, *not* klem-ā′tis.
Cocaine, kō′ka-in, *not* kō′kēn.
Codicil, kod′i-sil, *not* kō′di-sil.
Cognomen, kog-nō′men, *not* kog′no-men.
Coiffure, koif′fūr, *no′* kof′fūr.
Coliseum, Colosseum, kol-i-sē′um, *not* ko-los′sē-um.
Comatose, kō′ma-tōs, *not* kom′a-tōs.
Combatant, kum′ba-tant *or* kom′ba-tant.
Comely, kum′li, *not* kōm′li.
Communist, kom′mūn-ist, *not* kom-mū′nist.
Comparable, kom′pa-ra-bl, *not* kom-par′a-bl.
Comrade, kom′rād *or* kum′rād, *not* kom′rad.
Condolence, kon-dōl′ens, *not* kon′dol-ens.
Conjurer, kun′jēr-ēr, *not* kon-jū′rēr.
Connoisseur, kon′is′sūr′ *or* kon′is′sēr′.
Contents, kon-tents′ *or* kon′tents.
Contour, kon-tōōr′, *not* kon′tōōr.
Contumely, kon′tu-me-li *or* kon′tu-mē-li, *not* kon-tūm′e-li.
Coupon, kōō′pon′, *not* kū′pon. [A indicates the sound of the French nasal vowel, formed by the combination of a *vowel* and *n* or *m*. To

acquire this sound the organs of speech should be kept in *the same position* as when uttering the simple vowel that is to be nasalized; the back part of the tongue being raised enough to close the passage between the mouth and the nose.]
Courteousness, kēr′te-us-nes *or* kōrt′-yus-nes.
Crematorium, krem-a-tō′ri-um, *not* krē-ma-tō′ri-um.
Cuirass, kwē′ras′, *not* kū-ras′.
Cuisine, kwē′zēn′, *not* kū-zen′.
Culinary, kū′lin-a-ri, *not* kul′in-a-ri.
Cyclamen, sik′la-men, *not* sī′kla-men.
Deaf, def, *not* dēf.
Début, dā′bū′, *not* dā-bōō′. [See note under *Début*, p. 30.]
Décolleté, dā′kol′le′tä′, *not* dek-o-let′.
Deficit, def′i-sit, *not* de-fis′it.
Demonstrate, de-mon′strāt, *not* dem′on-strāt.
Depot, de-pō′ *or* dē′pō.
Desert [noun], dez′ért; [verb], de-zért′.
Dessert, dez-zért′, *not* dez′ért.
Diocesan, di-os′e-san, *not* di-ok′e-san.
Diphtheria, dip-thē′ri-a *or* dif-thē′ri-a.
Divan, di-van′, *not* dī′van.
Docile, dos′il, *not* dō′sil.
Dromedary, drum′e-da-ri, *not* drom′e-da-ri.
Ducat, duk′at, *not* dū′kat.
Dynamite, din′am-it, *not* dī′nam-it. [Webster alone gives dī′nam-it.]
Éclat, ā′klä′, *not* ē-klä′.
Enervate, e-nĕrv′āt, *not* en′ĕr-vāt.
Envelope, en′ve-lōp *or* än′ve-lōp, *not* en-vel′up.
Epoch, ep′ok, *not* ē′pok.
Equable, ē′kwa-bl, *not* ek′wa-bl.
Esquimau, es′ki-mō, *not* es′ki-maw.
Example, egz-am′pl, *not* eks-am′pl.
Exhaustion, egz-hạst′yun, *not* eks-ạst′yun.
Exhorter, egz-hort′ér, *not* eks-ort′ér.
Exhortation, eks-hor-tā′shun, *not* egz-or-tā′shun.
Exquisite, eks′kwi-zit, *not* eks-kwiz′it.
Extempore, eks-tem′po-re, *not* eks-tem′pōr.
Façade, fa-säd′ *or* fa-säd′.
Fairy, fâr′i, *not* fā′ri.
Falchion, fạl′chun, *not* fal′shun.

Florist, no____.
Forbade, for-bad', ___ ____.
Forgery, fōrj'e-ri, *not* fōr'jě-ri.
Fortune, for'tūn *or* fort'yōōn.
Franchise, fran'chiz, *not* fran'chiz.
Furniture, fėr'ni-tūr, *not* fer'ni-chōōr.
Gallantry, gal'lant-ri, *not* gal-lant'ri.
Gallows, gal'lus, *not* gal'lōz
Gamin, ga'man', *not* gam'in. [See note under *Coupon*.]
Garrulity, ga-rōōl'i-ti, *not* ga-rul'i-ti.
Gasometer, gaz-om'et-ėr, *not* gas-o-mē'tėr.
Gauntlet, gänt'let, *not* gạnt'let.
Genius [talent], jēn'yus, *not* jē'ni-us.
Genius [a spirit], jē'ni-us, *not* jēn'yus.
Genuflection, jē-nu-flek'shun, *not* jen-ū-flek'shun.
Glacier, glas'i-ėr, *not* glā'zhėr.
Gladiolus, glad-ī'o-lus, *not* glad-i-ō'lus.
Glamour, glă'mėr *or* glä'mōōr, *not* glam'mėr.
Gondola, gon'dō-là, *not* gon-dō'là.
Granary, gran'a-ri, *not* grā'na-ri.
Grimace, gri-mās', *not* grim'ās.
Grimy, grī'mi, *not* grim'mi.
Guillotine, gil-lo-tēn' *not* gil'lo-tin.
Harem, hā'rem, *not* har'em.
Hearth, härth, *not* hėrth.
Height, hīt, *not* hījhth.
Herculean, hėr-kū'le-an, *not* hėr-ku-lē'an.
Heroism, her'ō-izm, *not* hē'ro-izm.
Homage, hom'āj, *not* om'āj.
Homœopathist, hō-mē-op'a-thist, *not* hō-mē-ō-path'ist.
Houri, how'ri, *not* hōō'ri.
Hydrangea, hī-dran'je-a, *not* hī-drān'je-a.
Hymeneal, hī-me-nē'al, *not* hī-mē'ni-al.

Ingenious, _____.
Ingenuous, in-jen'ū___
Inquiry, in-kwī'ri,
Integral, in'te-gral
Invalid [adjective lėd, *commonly* in
Inveigle, in-vē'gl, _
Iodine, ī'od-in, *not*
Irrefragable, ir-re re-fraj'a-bl.
Isolate, iz'o-lāt, _____
Italian, i-tal'yan, _
Jasmine, jăz'min, _
Jean, jān, *not* jēn.
Jocose, jōk-ōs', _____
Jocund, jok'und, _
Joust, just, *not* jo___
Jugular, jū'gu-lar, _
Juvenile, jū've-nil,
Kayak (kī'yck?) b_____ nunciation ; [kä'___ Web. and Im.
Kyrie eleison, kī'_____ cording to Englis_
Lamentable, lam'_____ men'ta-bl.
Latent, lā'tent, *no*_
Laundress, lăn'dre_
Legend, lē'jend *or*
Legendary, lej'enc_____ a-ri.
Leisure, lē'zhur, _
Lenient, lē'ni-ent,
Lichen, lī'ken, *no*_
Literati, lit-ėr-ā'_____
Lithsome, lith's_____
Livelong, l_____
Lozenges, l_____
Maelstrom _____
Malay, mä_____

mma, ma-mä', *not* mäm'a.

ndamus, man-dä'mus, *not* man'-a-mus.

ndarin, man-da-rēn', *not* man'da-in.

angry, măn'ji, *not* man'ji.

arltime, mar'i-tim, *not* mar'i-tīm.

arseillaise, mär'säl'yäz', *not* mar-sel-lēz'.

latin, mat'in, *not* mä'tin.

latricide, mat'ri-sīd, *not* mä'tri-sīd.

latron, mä'tron, *not* mat'ron.

Mauve, mōv, *not* mav.

Mayonnaise, mà'on'āz', *not* mī-on-āz'.

Medieval, med-i-ē'val, *not* mē-di-ē'-val.

Mêlée, mā'lā', *not* me-lē'.

Memoir, mem'wor *or* mĕm'wor.

Meningitis, men-in-ji'tis, *not* men-in-jē'tis.

Mercantile, mér'kan-til, *not* mér-kan-tēl'.

Milan, mil'an, *preferred to* mi-lan'.

Misanthrope, mis'an-thrŏp, *not* mis-an'thrŏp.

Mischievous, mis'chiv-us, *not* mis-chēv'us.

Misconstrue, mis-kon'strōō, *not* mis-kon-strōō'.

Monad, mon'ad, *not* mō'nad.

Mongrel, mung'grel, *not* mon'grel.

Morphine, mor'fin, *not* mor'fēn.

Mythology, mith-ol'ō-ji, *not* mī-thol'-ō-ji.

Naïveté, nä'ēv'tā', *not* näv'ta.

National, na'shun-al, *not* nä'shun-al.

Nature, nā'tūr [Im. and Stormonth], nāt'yoor [Web.], nāt'yèr [Wor.].

Nicotine, nik'ō-tin, *not* nik'ō-tēn.

Nomad, nom'ad, *not* nō'mad.

Nuptial, nup'shal, *not* nup'chal.

Octavo, ok-tā'vō, *not* ok-tä'vō.

Oleomargarine, o-le-o-mär'ga-rin, *not* ō-le-o-mär'ja-rēn.

Onerous, on'ér-us, *not* ō'nèr-us.

Onyx, ō'niks, *not* on'iks.

Orchestral, or'kes-tral, *not* or-kes'tral.

Ordeal, or'dē-al, *not* or-dē'al.

Oxalis, oks'a-lis, *not* oks-al'is.

Oyer, ō'yèr, *not* oi'èr.

Pageant, paj'ent, *not* pā'jent.

Palace, pal'as, *not* pal'ās.

Pantheon, pan-thē'on [Eng. pro.]; pan'the-on [Classical pro.]

Pantomime, pan'to-mim, *not* pan'-to-mēm.

Papa, pa-pä', *not* pä'ŗä.

Parent, pâr'ent, *not* par'ent *nor* pä'rent.

Patent, pat'ent. [There is good authority also for *pā'tent*.]

Patriotism, pä'tri-ot-izm, *not* pat'ri-ot-izm.

Patron, pä'tron, *not* pat'ron.

Pedal [adjective], pē'dal ; [noun], ped'al.

Penelope, pe-nel'ō-pe, *not* pen'e-lōp.

Peremptory, per'emp-to-ri, *not* pér-em'to-ri.

Pharmaceutist, fär-ma-sū'tist, *not* fär-ma-kū'tist.

Pharmacopœia, fär-ma-ko-pē'ya, *not* far-ma-kōp'i-a.

Pianist, pi-än'ist, *not* pē'an-ist.

Piano-forte, pē-ä'nō-fōr'tā, *not* pē-ä'nō-fōrt.

Placard, pla-kärd' *or* plak'ärd.

Plague, plāg, *not* pleg.

Poniard, pon'yard, *not* poin'yard.

Precedence, pre-sēd'ens, *not* pre'sē-dens.

Precedent [noun], pres'e-dent, *not* pre-sē'dent.

Prelude [noun], prel'ūd *or* prē'lūd ; [verb], pre-lūd'.

Prescience, prē'shi-ens, *not* pre'shens.

Presentiment [previous conception], pre-sen'ti-ment, *not* pre-zent'ment.

Prestige, pres'tij [Eng. pro.] ; prās'-tēzh' [Fr. pro.].

Pretence, pre-tens', *not* prē'tens.

Pretty, prit'ti, *not* pret'ti.

Pristine, pris'tin, *not* pris'tīn.

Probity, prob'i-ti, *not* prō'bi-ti.

Prologue, prol'og *or* prō'log.

Pronunciation, prō-nun-she-ā'shun, *not* pro-nun-si-ā'shun.

Protestant, prot'es-tant, *not* prō'tes-tant.

Pumpkin, pump'kin, *not* pun'kin.

Quinine, kwi-nīn' *or* kwī'nīn, *not* kē-nēn'.

Receptivity, res-ep-tiv'i-ti, *not* rē-sep-tiv'i-ti.

Recess, re-ses', *not* rē'ses.

Respiratory, re-spir'a-to-ri, *not* res'pi-ra-to-ri.

Romance, rō-mans' *not* rō'mans.

Sacrilegious, sak-ri-lē'jus, *not* sak-ri-lij'us.

Scenic, sen′ik, *not* sē′nik.
Sepulture, sep′ul-tūr, *not* se-pul′tūr.
Sheik, shĕk, *not* shek.
Siam, sī-ain′, *not* sī′am.
Simultaneous, sĭ-mul-tā′ne-us, *not* sim-ul-tā′ne-us.
Sonorous, so-nō′rus, *not* son′or-us.
Sough, suf, *not* sow.
Spermaceti, sper-ma-sē′ti, *not* sper-ma-set′i.
Squalor, skwä′lor, *not* skwol′ĕr.
Stalwart, stạl′wĕrt, *not* stäl′wĕrt.
Strategic, stra-tej′ik, *not* stra-tēj′-ik.
Strychnine, strik′nin *or* strik′nin.
Suavity, swav′i-ti, *not* swạv′i-ti.
Subtile, sub′til, *not* sut′l.
Subtle, sut′l, *not* sub′til.
Supple, sup′l, *not* sōō′pl.
Surveillance, sėr-vāl′yans, *not* sėr′va-làns.
Table d'hôte, tä′bl′dōt′.
Tatterdemalion, tat-tėr-de-mal′yun, *no′* tat-tėr-de-mäl′yun.
Tenet, ten′et, *not* tē′net.
Terpsichorean, tėrp-si-ko-rē′an, *not* tėrp-si-kŏr′e-an.

Tête-à-tête, tät′ä′tät′.
Tiny, tī′ni, *not* tin′i.
Tirade, ti-rād′, *not* tī′rād.
Tonsilitis, ton-sil-ī′tis, *not* ton-sil-lē′tis.
Tour, tōor, *not* towr.
Trio, trī′ō *or* trē′ō. [All authoritie give *trī′ō* the preference, but Web The Im., and Stormonth give *trē′* as an allowable pronunciation.]
Truculence, trōō′kŭ-lens, *not* truk′ū-lens.
Truffle, trōō′fl, *not* truf′fl.
Truth, trōōth, *not* trōōtk.
Unguent, ung′gwent, *not* un′jent.
Vagary, va-gā′ri, *not* vā′ga-ri.
Vehemence, vē′he-mens, *not* ve-hē′-mens.
Violoncello, vē-ô-lon-chel′lo *or* vē-ô-lon-sel′lô, *not* vi-ô-lon-sel′lô.
Vis-à-vis, viz′ä′vē′, *not* vis′a-vis.
Visor, viz′ėr, *not* vī′zėr.
Weigelia, wi-gē′li-ä, *not* wi-jē′li-ä. [The name is derived from *Weigel*, a German naturalist.]
Weird, wērd, *not* wē′ėrd.
Wistaria, wis-tä′ri-à, *not* wis-tē′ri-à.

- - - - - -

Murdered English.

Brown, Jones & Co., Furriers, beg to announce t! they will make up gowns, capes, etc., for ladies out their own skin.

An inscription painted on a board adorns a fence Kent; "Notis: if any man's or woman's cow gets i these here oats, his or her tail will be cut off as 1 *case may be.*"

Publications of The Burrows Brothers Co.,
23, 25, 27 Euclid Ave., Cleveland, O.

AVERY'S ANCESTRAL TABLETS.

In Stout Manilla Portfolio. Price. FIFTY cents. A collection of diagrams so arranged that any number of generations of the ancestors of any person may be recorded in a simple and connected form. Additional sheets may be had separately at FIVE cents each ; or FIFTY cents a dozen, postage paid.

INDEXED MAP OF OHIO.

The Best! The Cheapest! The Latest!

Price, TEN cents. At the date of publication this is the most complete, the most accurate, the latest, and the cheapest map of Ohio in existence.

INDEXED MAP OF CLEVELAND.

Price, TEN cents. Over fifteen thousand copies have been sold in the last two years of this map. This is a greater number than has been sold of any previous map, or maps, in the last ten years. This fact alone speaks for its excellence, and the price is below any thought of criticism.

THE GAME OF SOLO-SIXTY.

BY JUNIUS.

Price, TWENTY-FIVE cents. Edited from Traditional Sources. Bound in white vellum paper, with a remarkably odd and neat cover design in five colors. *One of the most attractive souvenirs or dainty gifts of the year.* Please send for a sample copy. One dealer has had one thousand copies, and many others very liberal quantities.

RUSK'S MODEL SELECTIONS.

Six numbers, paper, each FIFTEEN cents. No. 1 contains a chapter on the principles of Elocution, embracing the subject of Elementary Sounds, Pitch, Volume, Quality, Movement, Accent, Emphasis, Articulation, Gesture, etc. No. 4 is devoted to selections for the young. Nos. 5 and 6 are just out, and have many fresh and attractive pieces. Lithographed covers, about 150 pages, 12mo, in each number.

INDEXED MAP OF NEW YORK.

The Best! The Cheapest! The Latest!

Price, TEN cents. At the date of publication this is the most complete, most accurate, the latest, and the cheapest map of New York in existence.

' THE MORGAN

ONE-PIECE ADJUSTABLE BOOK COVE

Patented May 15, 1888.

This is the only perfect One-Piece Adjustable Book Cove made, and it is destined to work a revolution in book coveri Adjustable Covers.

THE LATEST!   THE BEST!!

Made in the most workmanlike manner from very l manilla ; warranted extra tough.

Size A, for Books from 6 to 8 inches tall .   . $2.50
Size B, for Books from 8 to 10 inches tall   . 3.0
Size C, for Books from 10 to 13 inches (Geog-
    raphies) 5.0

Samples mailed without charge to Dealers and Liberal discounts to dealers.

CPSIA information can be obtained
at www.ICGtesting.com
Printed in the USA
BVHW04*0159230818
525056BV00011BB/659/P